Person-Centred Experiential Counselling
for
Depression

Sara Miller McCune founded SAGE Publishing in 1965 to support the dissemination of usable knowledge and educate a global community. SAGE publishes more than 1000 journals and over 800 new books each year, spanning a wide range of subject areas. Our growing selection of library products includes archives, data, case studies and video. SAGE remains majority owned by our founder and after her lifetime will become owned by a charitable trust that secures the company's continued independence.

Los Angeles | London | New Delhi | Singapore | Washington DC | Melbourne

Person-Centred Experiential Counselling *for* Depression

2nd Edition

DAVID MURPHY

bacp
British Association for
Counselling & Psychotherapy

Los Angeles | London | New Delhi
Singapore | Washington DC | Boston

Los Angeles | London | New Delhi
Singapore | Washington DC | Melbourne

SAGE Publications Ltd
1 Oliver's Yard
55 City Road
London EC1Y 1SP

SAGE Publications Inc.
2455 Teller Road
Thousand Oaks, California 91320

SAGE Publications India Pvt Ltd
B 1/I 1 Mohan Cooperative Industrial Area
Mathura Road
New Delhi 110 044

SAGE Publications Asia-Pacific Pte Ltd
3 Church Street
#10-04 Samsung Hub
Singapore 049483

Editor: Susannah Trefgarne
Assistant editor: Talulah Hall
Production editor: Rachel Burrows
Copyeditor: Solveig Gardner Servian
Proofreader: Brian McDowell
Indexer: Gary Kirby
Marketing manager: Samantha Glorioso
Cover design: Sheila Tong
Typeset by: C&M Digitals (P) Ltd, Chennai, India
Printed in the UK

Library of Congress Control Number: 2018967072

British Library Cataloguing in Publication data

A catalogue record for this book is available from
the British Library.

ISBN 978-1-5264-4680-0
ISBN 978-1-5264-4681-7 (pbk)

At SAGE we take sustainability seriously. Most of our products are printed in the UK using responsibly sourced
papers and boards. When we print overseas we ensure sustainable papers are used as measured by the PREPS
grading system. We undertake an annual audit to monitor our sustainability.

Contents

List of Figures and Tables

Figures

Tables

About the Author

David Murphy, PhD, is a Chartered Psychologist, Full Member of the Division of Counselling Psychology and Associate Fellow of the British Psychological Society. He is currently Associate Professor at The University of Nottingham, England and is Course Director for the Master of Arts Degree in Person-Centred Experiential Counselling and Psychotherapy.

David's edited books include the official British Psychological Society–Wiley published *Counselling Psychology: A Textbook for Study and Practice* (2017). He is co-editor of *Relational Depth: New Perspective and Developments* (2012, with Rosanne Knox, Sue Wiggins and Mick Cooper), published by Palgrave MacMillan, and co-editor of *Trauma and the Therapeutic Relationship* (2013, with Stephen Joseph) published by Palgrave MacMillan. He has over 60 published journal papers and book chapters in the field of counselling and psychotherapy research and education. He is currently editor of the journal *Person-Centered & Experiential Psychotherapies*, an international journal for the World Association for Person-Centred and Experiential Psychotherapies and Counselling.

Acknowledgements

There are many people that helped with the production of this book. First, I would like to thank Pete Sanders and Andy Hill for their work in producing the first edition; thank you for asking me to take on the role of writing the second edition and for giving your permission to use the text from the first edition. This was a significant, and personally meaningful, demonstration of trust; I hope that I haven't let you down. Thank you, Professor Michael Barkham of University of Sheffield, for your support throughout the process. Thank you to Peter Pearce for your encouragement and honesty when you had to step back from the process of co-authoring. Thanks to Susannah Trefgarne and her team from SAGE for supporting me and steering us all through some of the more challenging times in the process. My colleague, at the University of Nottingham, and close friend, Professor Stephen Joseph, who has been my sounding board for fresh ideas and new thinking; you were restorer of my confidence when it was wavering, thank you. Very special thanks to my friends and colleagues Kate Hayes and Emma Tickle: you have supported me through the writing of this text, I drew from your extensive experience to help create the dialogues that feature so prominently in this second edition; thank you for your commitment to the development of person-centred experiential therapy. Finally, and most importantly, thank you to Lisa, Ellie, Megan, and Joseph for being you.

List of Abbreviations

BAPCA   British Association for the Person-Centred Approach

BDI   Beck Depression Inventory

CBT   cognitive behavioural therapy

CCT   client-centred therapy

CES-D   Centre for Epidemiologic Studies – Depression

CfD   Counselling for Depression

CPD   continuing professional development

DSM   *Diagnostic and Statistical Manual of Mental Disorders*

EBP   evidence-based practice

EFT   emotion-focused therapy

ES   effect size

FIT   feedback-informed treatment

GAD   generalised anxiety disorder

GDG   Guideline Development Group

GP   General Practitioner

HEPs   humanistic-experiential psychotherapies

IAPT   Improving Access to Psychological Therapies

MAOIs   monoamine oxidase inhibitors

MDD   major depressive disorder

NHS   National Health Service

NICE   National Institute for Health and Care Excellence

NMDS   National Minimum Data Set

OVP   organismic valuing process

PBE   practice-based evidence

PCE   person-centred experiential

PCE-CfD   PCE-counselling for depression

PCEPS   Person-Centred and Experiential Psychotherapy Scale

PCT   person-centred therapy

PHQ   Patient Health Questionnaire

RCT   randomised control trial

RI   real–ideal

RO   real–ought

SSRIs   selective serotonin reuptake inhibitors

TCAs   tricyclic antidepressants

UPR   unconditional positive regard

UPSR   unconditional positive self-regard scale

1

Introduction

The problem of psychological distress and human suffering is a significant one. Many people are struggling with the demands of a modern society and the fast evolving culture. As society becomes more unequal between rich and poor, as homelessness continues to rise in all parts of the developed world, and as education systems place increasingly unrealistic expectations on children and young people, it is hardly surprising that more and more people report feeling depressed. This book is about person-centred experiential (PCE) counselling and can be used as a guidebook for helping you to understand your work with clients who are depressed. It is not intended or advised to be used as a manual or instruction book. PCE therapy is a creative and emergent process and the intention of this book is to offer a description of this process using theory to understand working with clients who present as depressed. It is hoped that for many experienced therapists the contents of this description will be familiar and, for others, something they might at least recognise.

In the sections below the PCE approach will be set in context. This includes outlining the development of the PCE-Counselling for Depression (PCE-CfD) approach. As many readers will know, humanistic psychology, on which the person-centred approach was founded, grew out of a field of psychological enquiry based on psychologists' interests in the positive aspects of human functioning just as much as the pathological. In this sense, humanistic psychology is located within a growth paradigm and was particularly interested in the heights of human potentiality. This approach offered an alternative to the deficit-based medical model paradigm that was and remains dominant in modern society. PCE-CfD offers a way of challenging the current dominant medical model that provides the prevailing backdrop to mental health care systems. This chapter will introduce some of the key ideas and thinking that will help to begin the task of presenting the alternative to a medical model approach to working with depression. To do this, we need to understand depression from within the growth paradigm, set out the theory of this therapy and demonstrate how it is different from other approaches. To do this, the sections that follow will begin to articulate another way of thinking about depression to the deficit model, and each subsequent chapter in the book will further elucidate a way of working with clients in a way that does not pathologise their experiences. Whether you are a trainee on a PCE-CfD course, any other kind of counsellor looking for a way out of medical model thinking, or someone feeling depressed who wants to understand a different way of getting out of the distress you experience, then I hope that you will find something in this book that will support you.

Positioning PCE-CfD

The development of PCE-CfD marks a significant step in the PCE approach being recognised by the National Health Service (NHS) and the initiative used to roll out the large-scale provision of talking therapy at the primary care level known as Improving Access to Psychological Therapies (IAPT). This book, and more broadly the approach, owe credit to the many years of work by the founders, scholars, practitioners and clients who have all contributed to what Sanders (2011) has referred to as the 'tribes' of person-centred and experiential counselling. Some readers will have already noticed that the approach being referred to here, 'PCE', is presented as a unified term and approach to therapy[1].

---

[1]In the first edition of this book (Sanders & Hill, 2014), the approach was identified using an 'and' that was sitting between the 'person-centred' and 'experiential'. For many this caused confusion by indicating an integrative approach. It is understandable that this 'and' was used to distinguish between what some see as two separate approaches; namely, the 'person-centred' and the 'experiential'. Placing the 'and' in between these two terms reflected the many years of debate within the person-centred tradition and what for some represents an irreconcilable difference with the experiential dimension. It is also fair to say that the use of the 'and' also reflected the range of studies from which the competences used to formulate a manual were being drawn, and that the therapeutic approach had to be situated within the context of an evidence-based practice.

Since the first edition of this book the context has changed and using this new term enables PCE to be acknowledged as a distinct therapy that is not integrative, but a unique and emerging expression of the PCE paradigm. Baker (2012) has suggested that PCE as a therapy evolved from Carl Rogers' work in the late 1950s as his theories became enhanced by Gendlin's (1962) interests in the importance of 'experiencing'. Baker (2012) used the term 'experiential person-centred' to describe a specific tribe within the person-centred approach, and prior to this Lietaer (1984) was writing about the experiential nature of person-centred therapy (PCT). Indeed, Lietaer has stated that it came as an almost seismic shock to him when he learned that the classical school were not conceptualising client-centred as an experiential therapy.

In this book, whilst recognising and drawing on debates and discussion in the past (Bozarth, 1998; Kirschenbaum, 2012), the term PCE (Murphy, 2017) is used as the most contemporaneous way to define the approach. The addition of the term CfD can then simply be recognised as an indication that our focus here is on the context of working with clients who are experiencing depression. This will typically, but not exclusively, be relevant when discussing therapeutic work undertaken with clients in a healthcare setting. PCE-CfD is not therefore an integration of disparate approaches (such as the integration of person-centred therapy and emotion-focused therapy competences put forward in the CfD manual). PCE therapy can be defined as a contemporary evolution of a radical paradigm for therapy. It is a bold step to take, but the task of this book is to present PCE therapy as it applies to a specific phenomenon: depression.

Background to PCE-CfD

Given that PCE therapy is part of a long-established and evolving paradigm of therapeutic practice, how did the need for adding a specific focus of depression arise? Could we not simply refer to the approach as 'PCE therapy'? Let's take each of these issues in turn. PCE-CfD, as outlined in this book, is an approach to therapy that is by and large available and practised in NHS psychological therapies services. In recent years this has been provided under the IAPT programme. IAPT was rolled out after successful lobbying in the period following publication of *The Depression Report* (CEPMHPG, 2006) that saw the implementation of National Institute for Health and Care Excellence (NICE) guidelines for common mental health problems such as anxiety and depression. Whilst the implementation of IAPT has put psychological therapies in the NHS 'on the map', as Sanders and Hill (2014) noted, this has been delivered through a top-down, centralised agenda that caused significant harm to the grassroots development of a pluralistic array of psychological therapies in primary care general practitioner (GP) surgeries. A major consequence of this was that cognitive-behavioural therapy, with its vast quantity of randomised control trial (RCT) evidence supporting its effectiveness, became the frontline therapy and most other approaches were swiftly relegated to the margins.

Sanders and Hill (2014) have suggested that part of the fall-out following the introduction of IAPT was the spread of the therapeutic competences agenda.

The process of developing therapist competences for humanistic therapies was led by Professor Tony Roth in conjunction with academics including Professors Mick Cooper, Robert Elliott and Germain Lietaer. They were accompanied by Janet Tolan from the British Association for the Person-Centred Approach (BAPCA) and other staff from the British Association for Counselling and Psychotherapy (BACP). As Sanders and Hill (2014) noted, this was the genesis of the development of therapeutic competences specifically for working with depression. The challenge for those involved in bringing a more specific description of a person-centred counselling approach to depression which drew from the wide range of humanistic competences was significant. Their task was to bring to bear a description of PCE therapy that could be deemed effective for depression and linked to RCTs. This was a challenging task as PCE therapy had never used diagnostic criteria as a basis for describing its practice. The humanistic competences per se were considered too broad to serve as a description for practice for individual therapists that would also be acceptable to NICE requirements for evidenced-based practice. Hence, a selection of published RCT studies was identified that included person-centred and emotion-focused therapy (EFT) to provide sufficient evidence for a specification of the wider humanistic competences to focus on the application to depression. These trials are reviewed later in Chapter 8 but, importantly, what emerged from this process was the identification of a competency framework that formed the basis for PCE therapy when working with depression. A trainers' and practitioners' manual was produced that provided a detailed description of the approach, highlighting how it might be practised in the NHS and IAPT setting. This had to be presented as a manual which identified key skills and competences. The framework was accepted by NICE and described within the IAPT programme as follows:

> Counselling for depression is a manualised form of psychological therapy as recommended by NICE (NICE, 2009) for the treatment of depression. It is based on a person-centred, experiential model and is particularly appropriate for people with persistent sub-threshold depressive symptoms or mild to moderate depression. Clinical trials have shown this type of counselling to be effective when 6–10 sessions are offered. However, it is recognised that in more complex cases which show benefit in the initial sessions, further improvement may be observed with additional sessions up to the maximum number suggested for other NICE recommended therapies such as CBT: that is, 20 sessions. (BACP, 2010)

This statement marked a major step for PCE therapy as it was formally recognised by NICE, implemented as part of IAPT, and positioned as a legitimate alternative to cognitive behavioural therapy (CBT) for the range of severity of distress in primary care services.

The position then was this: the therapy is identified and recognised as suitable for working with clients who present with depression. However, the PCE approach, at least in the UK, had a strong investment in being an alternative to a medical model approach. How can these differences be reconciled?

Reading the above is likely to stir a mixture of feelings. It certainly does when writing. For those of us rooted in the PCE therapy approach for many years it is difficult to reconcile the tension between the radical theoretical position of the person-centred approach and its newly developed link with the IAPT project, the latter of course denoting an association with the medical model. An immediate cost of the link with IAPT is the identification of PCE therapy for a specific diagnostic category. Why not simply call it PCE 'counselling' and drop the 'for depression'? In the ideal situation this would indeed be preferable. However, in the current situation there is still the legacy of the development of IAPT and its links to NICE. These agendas demand that any therapy that is offered must be evidenced as effective. If therapists want to work in these settings, then it seems these are the rules that currently govern the field. This is not to say that these authorities and the rules shouldn't be questioned and challenged, they should and must. However, for PCE-CfD to be available to the public in a national model of health provision, there is undeniably a compromise. But are there also opportunities, and can PCE-CfD use this position as an opportunity to work on the system and bring changes to it?

Setting out a positive psychology for depression

In this book it is intended to show how the PCE-CfD approach presents a positive psychology and growth model for working with clients who experience depression. For some practitioners within the PCE approach, the very idea of developing a descriptive account of PCE therapy for a specific diagnostic category is something of an anathema. Indeed, there's no doubt that the PCE approach has little in common with the medical model dominating current mental health systems. Developing PCE-CfD that focuses only on those symptoms associated with depression would be an act of collusion with the medical model paradigm. Not only this, but to do so would be to over-simplify a complex dimension of human function. It would be to reduce the person as a whole to a set of symptoms and deficiencies and neglect a wide range of human capabilities. In contrast to other approaches recommended by NICE, the PCE approach is unique in the growth metaphor of human development.

As a growth paradigm approach, it is rooted in a positive psychology that was originally proposed by the humanistic psychologists interested in not only the alleviation of distress but also the heights of human potential (Joseph, 2015). The term 'positive psychology' has become known as an unhelpful concept but humanistic therapies cannot alter the fact that they were developed from positive psychology. Instead, we should reclaim this term and demonstrate the true meaning of the growth paradigm. This is a unique feature of the PCE approach to therapy and one that must not be lost or appropriated by the medical model. The growth paradigm and the PCE approach brings with it radical consequences for individuals who participate in the therapy. Clients receiving PCE-CfD are met by a therapist who does not reduce them to a set of symptoms but considers their experiencing as part of an integrated whole. The person is understood in their social context and is thought to be striving for growth. Depression, in this sense, is an expression of thwarted actualisation processes. The person is considered not as deficient but to be making the best of what resources are currently available.

Throughout, this book will show how it is possible to present a set of descriptive competences for working with clients within PCE-CfD, whilst retaining the connection to the growth paradigm from which the approach originates. To do this, it is necessary to examine the concept of depression. The stance taken is to conceptualise the phenomenology of depression as a set of experiences that exist at one end of a bi-polar construct. Doing this turns the phenomena of depression into a continuous variable, with another set of experiences (best associated with being fully functioning) positioned at the opposite end on the continuum. Researchers who have already proposed that depression is a continuous variable include Joseph (2007) and Joseph and Wood (2010).

In recent years, there has been a shift within the literature surrounding the construct of depression. Interestingly, this shift has been driven by those with strong allegiances with the underlying philosophy of PCE therapy and the growth paradigm but operating within the counselling and clinical psychology fields. This recent shift has meant the focus within psychology (and psychiatry to some extent) moved towards a rejection of the use of diagnosis and disorder (Johnstone et al., 2018). Instead, mental health professionals are searching for alternative approaches to conceptualising and understanding psychological distress. 'Wellbeing' has become an important feature in shaping mental health services (Department of Health, 2009), although the use of this term has become associated with the deconstruction of long-term and deep therapy provided within the public sector and replaced with 'light touch' approaches that fail to appreciate the significance of people's distress. This is unfortunate, as the word 'wellbeing' and the concept of psychological wellbeing are grounded in the philosophical approach termed 'eudaimonia'; this refers to the tradition of becoming deeply engaged with the difficulties of life and of personal growth. Additionally, the concept is part and parcel of the PCE approach and since inception PCE therapists have claimed this concept and understood its true meaning. The use of the term 'wellbeing' as a corporate tool, pacifying and subjugating workers, is indeed pernicious and detracts from the ideas that underpin the growth model of psychological functioning. PCE therapists have a model of wellbeing that is defined in the terms of a fully functioning person and this notion needs to be maintained and remain a central feature of the approach.

For PCE therapy, the idea of full functioning logically, positions depression at one end of a continuum and is not a new way of understanding psychological distress. Nevertheless, there is a danger that in recent years some PCE therapists might have lost sight of the fact that they, and the approach, are situated within a growth model (Joseph, 2007). This inevitably requires a broader vision that can accommodate a more complex and sophisticated understanding of human functioning. Positioning depression at one end of a bi-polar continuum was recently empirically supported (Wood, Taylor, & Joseph, 2010; Siddaway, Wood & Taylor, 2017). Joseph (2007) suggested that the Centre for Epidemiologic Studies - Depression (CES-D) scale, a well-known and widely used measure of depression in research and policy studies, measures both symptoms of depression and phenomena associated with wellbeing. For example, the scale contains items such as 'I felt sad' and 'I felt happy' with the aim to measure depression. However, as Joseph (2007) argues, if a respondent scores zero overall on the test, they must have given the lowest score possible ('rarely or none of the time') when endorsing all negatively worded items (e.g. 'I feel sad'), and the highest score possible ('most or all of the time') when endorsing all positively worded items (e.g. 'I felt happy'). What this example shows is that a score of zero overall on the scale means that the respondent must have indicated far more than an absence of depression. They have instead also indicated positive wellbeing by affirming all the positively valenced items such as 'I felt happy'.

A study by Siddaway, Wood and Taylor (2017) confirmed that the CES-D scale does indeed measure a depression/wellbeing continuum. Moreover, using a large sample of adolescents they also showed that as wellbeing increases depression decreases and, importantly, so do levels of a range of distressing symptoms that are associated with other problems (such as anxiety, aggression and substance misuse). What this study shows is how important it is within mental health practice to focus on all aspects of the client's functioning and to not get hooked on the idea that eliminating symptoms is the only indicator of psychological growth. That is, we will be able to help clients more when we do not focus exclusively on what might be considered as the symptoms of depression. We should be, based on this research, tuned in and aware of other aspects of our client's functioning that might also be indicative of personal growth, even when the client's experiential processing is indicative of distress. Working with all these aspects of the client can be fruitful and meaningful in the client's life.

PCE-CfD and the medical model

In some ways the original CfD project and development of the competences that resulted in having the approach recognised by IAPT was something of a Trojan horse. The approach was metaphorically 'wheeled in' as if it were just another specialised treatment for a medicalised form of psychological distress. There's no doubt that we are now in a position where PCE-CfD, whilst grounded in idiographic rather than nomothetic practices, is seeking to articulate itself with the nomothetic stance of IAPT. What can be done to resolve this conundrum of PCE-CfD existing within an overly prescriptive, diagnostically focused and medicalised mental health system? Pearce (2014) argued for adopting an approach that seeks to bring about change from within. He advocates for working 'within' the systems that operate to provide psychological therapies in the NHS as the most realistic approach for change to happen. This is in contrast to the position proposed by Sanders (2017), who argues for the strategic and principled opposition to the medicalisation of distress and everything that it uses to further advance the medicalisation of human experiencing. This raises whether an approach to therapy, such as PCE-CfD, can be both radical and central at the same time. So, who is right, Pearce (2014) or Sanders (2017) – or can it be both? Can a PCE-CfD therapy that is grounded on a growth model of human experiencing remain true to its roots whilst also being available and situated in the delivery of psychological therapy in a national health model, when that model is endemic in its medicalised stance? Is it possible for humanistic psychology's principles and values to be advanced through an approach that in any way adopts and/or engages in a medical model? Or is this a compromise too far? These questions are too important to avoid and all PCE-CfD practitioners must consider them or else deny the roots on which the approach is premised. Throughout this book these issues will be addressed further. Suffice to say at this point, all PCE-CfD practitioners, supervisors and trainers are cautioned to be clear within themselves about both the positionality of the PCE-CfD approach and its relation to the medical model, the impact of the setting in which it is practised, and the potential impact that a slide towards the medical model might have for practice.

PCE-CfD, evidence, treatment guidelines and access

For any therapy to have the backing of NICE and IAPT, it must be considered an evidence-based practice (EBP). EBPs are those that have been empirically supported through the findings of randomised controlled trials. The process of determining and selection of evidence as to what constitutes acceptable evidence is not neutral or value free. Guidelines are developed based on the findings of research provided that it meets the standards set by the NICE and based on methodologies more suited to medical drug trials. The evidence selected is then reviewed by panels charged with evaluating all the suitable trial evidence for a specific diagnostic category. Problems with this process have been highlighted recently in response to the NICE guideline for depression in adults (NICE, 2009) currently undergoing review. In a recent paper, Barkham, Moller and Pybis (2017) critically examined the process and methods used by NICE for developing the revised guidelines for depression and raised several important concerns regarding the development of 'best available evidence'. Their concerns both challenge the type of evidence and the way that it is currently used, and the questions that the evidence is being used to answer. For example, they suggest that what might be best evidence to answer a question about efficacy might not be the best evidence to answer a question about cost-effectiveness. They suggest that different evidence might be required and this might involve different methodologies. Similarly, the quality and type of evidence that might be used to inform NICE guidelines, they suggest, can be extended to include practice-based evidence (PBE) and qualitative research that might report on the views of people who benefit from using psychological therapies for depression. PBE is gathered not in the context of highly controlled randomised trials but from naturalistic studies where data is gathered as part of routine practice. Interestingly, the kind of PBE that Barkham, Moller and Pybis are referring to is widely available and collected through the National Minimum Data Set (NMDS) required by all IAPT services.

An example is a recent study conducted by Pybis, Saxon, Hill and Barkham (2017) that looked at the outcome data for 33,243 clients accessing therapy across 103 IAPT sites. They compared the effectiveness of CBT and counselling for all clients who scored above the clinical cut-off on the PHQ-9 (patient health questionnaire, a measure of presence of depression symptoms) and found no significant difference in the effectiveness of the two therapies. With such a large sample of PBE gathered as it occurs 'on the ground', it seems questionable for such findings to be deemed unsuitable for consideration. One could reasonably question why NICE guideline development does not include such evidence. That it doesn't raises important issues about the factors, underlying motivations and competing agendas surrounding the field of psychological therapies. It seems clear that the development of guidelines for delivery through IAPT is skewed in favour of a particular form of evidence that lends itself to some therapies more than others. PCE-CfD practitioners will benefit from being conversant with the evidence from both that presented in NICE guidelines *and* that developed through studies such as that carried out by Pybis et al. (2017).

Another factor related to evidence and the development of treatment guidelines is that evidence-based therapies are evaluated upon their merits as discrete therapeutic approaches. An important distinction to make within the literature is in regard to the generic use of the term 'counselling' from forms of counselling that are theoretically and empirically derived and which can be applied in a specific context. This is another important point that Barkham, Moller and Pybis (2017) note concerning the 2009 NICE guideline for depression. They pointed out that evidence used to inform the recommendations in the 2009 guidelines had evaluated studies where the generic term 'counselling' had been used to compare its effects against other studies that had used specific and theoretically informed types of counselling such as person-centred therapy (PCT). Barkham et al. (2017: 255) stated that with there being two distinct forms of counselling we must be transparent about the differences. The first is the generic term that might include basic and generic competences that will be common to all forms of counselling. Second, there is a 'model-specific form of counselling, such as person-centred experiential'. Using the generic term of 'counselling' really can only refer to the 'generic' competences as even the 'basic' competences require an understanding of the philosophical and psychological concepts that underpin an approach. Given that there is not a single agreed-upon approach that covers the generic use of the term counselling, it is better to always refer to model-specific forms of therapy and make clear in the guidelines when evidence is being evaluated in regard to either the generic version or a model-specific version.

At the time of writing the issue of evidence and treatment guidelines has reached fever pitch. During 2018, NICE released the draft documents for the revised guidelines for depression in adults. What followed was a furore of responses from across the field of psychological therapies, psychology and psychiatry, all expressing concerns about the methodology NICE had followed.

Much of the concern was centred on the neglect of evidence other than RCTs and meta-analyses of RCTs. Such was the level of dissatisfaction with the proposed guidelines, that NICE were left with no option but to withdraw the draft guidelines and engage in an unprecedented further round of consultation. The arguments between NICE and the various stakeholders within the profession, including the professional bodies representing the wide range of approaches and practitioners continued. The final guidelines will be released in 2019 and it is not yet known whether PCE-CfD will be included. The issue of inclusion in a guideline is, whether one agrees with the practices and principles upon which NICE and IAPT are based, critical for the availability of PCE-CfD to the public where it is free at the point of access.

About this book

A number of sections in this book are virtually unchanged or a lightly edited version of the edition published by Sanders and Hill (2014) who should be acknowledged for their work on the first edition. The changes in the second edition have been made in light of developments in the professional landscape since the first edition was published. The first edition was clearly a landmark in that it was vitally important to convey to the field information about the development of the competences and to establish PCE-CfD as a response to the demand of IAPT. Similarly, for PCE therapy to survive in the IAPT setting, tough decisions had to be made that no doubt shaped the way that PCE therapy is now considered. For example, the focus in the first edition was on showing the process of development of competences necessary to situate the approach within the NHS. However, several years on, now with hundreds of practitioners trained and qualified in PCE-CfD and working in the NHS, a somewhat different story can be communicated. One that is hopefully reflective of the progress that has been made and allows for greater focus and attention to be given to the theory and practice and less on the competency framework and IAPT related issues.

With this in mind, in the next chapter PCE therapy is introduced in more detail. The aim is to show how the PCE approach has developed and evolved over the years. The chapter will show how the approach has emerged from more classical PCT towards a greater focus on the experiential. A change initiated towards the end of Carl Rogers' time in academic research and which incorporates the significant contribution of Eugene Gendlin. In addition to these developments, the approach has also incorporated emotion theory developed within EFT which helps to inform and shape PCE-CfD. The chapter will also provide an overview of several major theoretical concepts that PCE-CfD practitioners need to understand. This includes an introduction to the philosophical underpinnings, the theory of personality and development, the theory of therapy and the therapeutic relationship.

Following this in Chapter 3, attention turns towards the concept of depression and how this can be understood within the PCE-CfD theory. This involves drawing on theory from humanistic psychology in addition to covering theoretical concepts such as self-discrepancy, conditions of worth and the process conception of psychotherapy and experiencing. These concepts are considered through a lens of positive psychology that draws on concepts of wellbeing, demonstrating how PCE-CfD is firmly embedded in a growth paradigm. The key role of emotions and their part in processing experiences will be explored and how problems in emotion processing can lead to frustrations in the actualisation process.

Following this there are four chapters that look in more detail at the practical application of the theory to client presentations and experiences of depression. The sense gained from talking to trainees on PCE-CfD courses and their trainers is that access to examples of the theory-in-practice is what really helped them learn how the approach might work. PCE-CfD, as it is available in the NHS, is designed to be available for 16 to 20 sessions of therapy. This means it is time-limited, although it is common that some services might offer even fewer sessions, maybe six to ten sessions. Through the case examples the intention is to link practice to theory and, where appropriate to highlight examples of the various competences associated with the approach. The use of case examples of PCE-CfD will cover a course of therapy from the beginning, middle and ending phases. To this end, a series of four chapters present the approach across different phases of the therapeutic process by critically and reflectively analysing the process of the therapeutic encounters. Chapter 4 will look at first meetings and Chapter 5 considers the early stage of therapy with a client. Chapter 6 considers the middle phase and Chapter 7 considers the final phase and ending of therapy. In each chapter, alongside exploring a different phase of the therapy, other issues are also explored further. For example, through the case examples opportunities for demonstrating the facilitation of emotion processes are highlighted. The issues of medication and measurement of outcomes are also discussed. Through each of the chapters, key theoretical concepts are brought to life through exploration of key issues. The goal is to offer an account of the approach in an engaging and meaningful way for trainees to relate to and with the hope that they will be able to recognise their own practice as they develop their work along the lines of PCE-CfD.

The remaining two chapters pick up on critical issues for the future. Chapter 8 considers the process of training and supervision, and adds an update to the research in PCE-CfD. An introduction is made to the Person-Centred and Experiential Psychotherapies Scale (PCEPS) and helpful information about training in the use of the scale is provided. There is also a focus on the recent PRaCTICED trial that has been conducted to explore the non-inferiority of PCE-CfD to CBT for depression. In Chapter 9, conclusions are drawn together with a reflection on the process of developing the book as a basis for looking to the future for PCE therapy. This will consider the future of PCE-CfD as a development within the field and look more broadly in the context of NICE, IAPT, the NHS and the recent scoping review of training carried out by three of the major professional bodies.

It is hoped that readers will find the book useful and informative and that it will act as a useful guide for training and preparation for practice with clients who experience depression. Ultimately, the hope is that the book can support therapists so that clients can be encountered wholly, accommodating the full range of their experiencing and offering a counter-cultural therapeutic approach in the context of the IAPT.

2

Person-Centred Experiential Therapy

Chapter overview

- Philosophical underpinnings
  - What is real
  - Ways of knowing

- Theory of personality
  - A perceptual theory
  - Experiencing as the central construct
  - Human motivation
  - Development of a self-concept and conditions of worth
  - Psychological tension

- Theory of therapy
  - Psychological contact
  - Client incongruence
  - Therapist congruence
  - Unconditional positive regard
  - Empathy
  - Client perception

- Theory of change
  - Stages of change

Person-centred experiential (PCE) therapy is the most recent iteration in the adaptation and evolution of Carl Rogers' (1951) client-centred therapy (CCT). In the years since the client-centred approach was first developed there have been several significant developments in regard to the theoretical evolutions and practical adaptations of CCT. The need to define therapist competences for PCE-CfD within the UK has provided an opportunity to consolidate some of these developments and to demonstrate how these can come together in relation to specifically working with clients' life experiences presented as the phenomenon of depression. The PCE approach is an expression of a constantly evolving form of therapy and PCE-CfD is just one example of this expression. The approach is now practised widely amongst therapists working in the NHS and IAPT services. In the previous edition of this book, the therapy was presented as an amalgamated approach, one drawn primarily from the person-centred approach but combining aspects of EFT (Greenberg, Rice & Elliott, 1993). For some, PCE therapy is a therapeutic approach in its own right (Murphy, 2017), rooted in PCT whilst drawing on the developments in understanding of experiencing proposed by Gendlin (1962) and the emotion theory associated with EFT (Greenberg, Rice & Elliott, 1993). Additionally, it is proposed that PCE therapy is the term given to the approach that picks up from where Rogers left off at the time of the conclusion of the Wisconsin Project. PCE therapy accepts the premise that in the course of Rogers' career there were many developments and evolutions that moved his work continually forward and increasingly towards the experiential aspect of human being (Baker, 2012). This means that there are some key features that help to differentiate and consolidate PCE therapy as an approach. Hart (1970) stated that there have been basically three stages to the development of the person-centred approach. Since then, it could be argued that two further phases have evolved. The fourth was the differentiation in and identification of the Tribes; this was a period of conflict and disharmony within the approach. More recently, it is claimed that we are seeing the emergence of a fifth phase. This is defined by a synergy of the Tribes and a unified PCE paradigm can now be added. This is best identified with the emergence of the PCE approach. Table 2.1 is adapted from Hart (1970) to show all five stages.

In the remainder of this chapter a general overview of the central features of the PCE approach are presented. This will highlight several of the important developments moving the original client-centred approach that have occurred between the 1950s through to the early 2000s. It is the culmination of these developments and the synergy created through the assimilation of the theory of experiencing and the understanding of emotion processing theory that consolidates the emergence of PCE therapy. It is understood that for many experienced person-centred therapists this chapter might repeat well-known points, and yet for others it might represent a challenge to their conceptualisation of PCE therapy. However, as the book is written for those who might not be so familiar with the original theory, the aim is to address as potentially wide an audience as possible, covering many of the basics and showing some of the advances too.

Table 2.1 The five stages of person-centred therapy

	Functions of the therapist	**Personality changes**
Period 1: 1940–1950 Non-directive Psychotherapy	Creation of a permissive, non-interpretive atmosphere; *acceptance* and *clarification*.	Gradual achievement of *insight* into one's self and situation.
Period 2: 1950–1957 Reflective Psychotherapy	*Reflection* of feelings, avoiding threat in relationship.	Development of congruence of self-concept and the phenomenal field.
Period 3: 1957–1990 Experiential Psychotherapy	Wide range of behaviours to express basic attitudes. Focus on the client's experiencing. Expression of the therapist's experiencing.	Growth in the process continuum of inter- and intra-personal living by learning to use direct experiencing.
Period 4: 1990–2010 Tribes	Practice is divided and determined by the Tribe to which one belongs. Could be any of the above but seen as separate to one another.	Similarly, to the practice, changes are conceived of by the Tribe that is being practised.
Period 5: 2010–Present Person-Centred Experiential Synergy	To create relationship attitudes, empathising with full range of client experiencing. Meaning making with client. Therapist draws on experience for supporting process facilitation.	Client more connected to OVP; more emotionally and cognitively flexible and agile. Living more fully and in an existential way.

Source: Hart, 1970

Philosophical underpinnings

Few training courses in counselling or psychotherapy take the time to explore and understand their philosophical underpinnings relevant to the theoretical approach being studied. To begin training in PCE-CfD, it is necessary to appreciate that the major schools within psychotherapy and counselling are each based on a distinct view of human nature. Consequently, to understand PCE-CfD, it is helpful to reflect on the philosophical ideas about the person upon whom the approach is grounded. That is, we need to understand what is the basis of human nature, and how is this put forward by PCE theory. In technical terms, this area of philosophical study is referred to as *ontology*. Ontology is the strand of philosophy that attempts to study what is 'real', or putting it another way, what exists. Regarding human beings, this can be applied to asking what is 'real about human nature'? This is something that most people do often without even realising it. For example, we all have an implicit view of human nature, but we might not have spent time reflecting on this or considered what we think that it might be. Culturally, for example, in the West at least, this is often presented as differences between 'good' and 'evil' people. However, the concepts of good and evil are not really about the very basic nature of human beings and are instead often based on people's interpretations of the meaning of actions.

In addition to understanding something about the ontological assumptions of the approach, it will be helpful if we can also understand and explore the different 'ways of knowing', and how this can be applied to PCE-CfD practice. The field of philosophy that is concerned with studying 'ways of knowing' is referred to as *epistemology*, and this is also important for PCE-CfD therapists to examine. In this section then, we will first consider the ontological assumptions of PCE-CfD and then explore some of the epistemological assumptions. It should be said that many psychotherapists do not concern themselves with the study of ontology. As Craig (2015) points out, this has been a shortcoming on the part of psychotherapy generally, although we might be sympathetic to it. It is not an easy task, so it is easy to appreciate the temptation to avoid such a discussion. Nevertheless, it can also be argued that it is important enough, despite the challenges, to consider the most basic and foundational elements to the approach.

What is real in human nature?

This heading presents us with a really big question with which to begin any attempt to present a general theoretical overview of PCE therapy. However, a useful place to begin exploring the ontological view of PCE therapy might be by trying to describing what *is* a *person*. This can help us get into some of the underlying assumptions of the approach. Such an enquiry will also take us further into understanding the basic nature of human persons that Rogers advocated. Rogers described the nature of a person as being basically trustworthy, and went on to suggest that some of our basic characteristics and potentials are being

> towards development, differentiation, cooperative relationships; whose life tends to move from dependence to independence; whose impulses tend naturally to harmonise into a complex and changing pattern of self-regulation; whose total character is such as to tend to preserve himself and his species, and perhaps to move towards its further evolution. (1957a: 201)

This description points clearly towards a view of the person that is socially constructive and as having a tendency for movement towards harmony and greater complexity. Lietaer (2002) has added to this by suggesting the ontological image of a *person* means to be also both *proactive* and *reactive*, and that we are driven by a tendency toward *actualization*. A person, he suggested, has also a *margin of freedom* and is therefore not completely determined. For Lietaer, therefore, human nature is *pro-social*; expressed through the basic tension between *autonomy* and *belonging*.

Schmid (2013) doesn't entirely agree with Lietaer (2002), for Schmid's explanation of the basic elements of the person has added emphasis to the organismic perspective. Schmid suggested that the term *person*-centred rests on the ontological image of the person as having both a substantial (physical organism) and relational (social) dimension. The substantial refers to the 'independence and uniqueness, freedom and dignity, unity, sovereignty and self-determination, responsibility, human rights' of a person, whereas the relational dimension highlights the importance of 'relationship, dialogue, partnership, connection with the world, interconnectedness and community' (2013: 68). As we shall see in the next chapter, these ontological assumptions become important for our understanding of the phenomenology of depression; that is, as the consequence of thwarted or sub-optimal interaction between the human person as an organism and their socio-environmental factors. Understanding the person in this way means that depression can be understood as a response to the attempt of the organism to fulfil its potential as an organism but that this is thwarted due to environmental factors (e.g. harsh parenting, neglect, loss of status, lack of development opportunities). If the person, at their most basic, really is to be considered in both substantial and relational terms, then we must naturally consider the place of both the physical organism and the social environment in developing our understanding of depression.

Even though many approaches to counselling and psychotherapy do not consider their ontological roots, it is clear that already we can see that PCE therapy is based on the ontological assumptions of human persons as trustworthy, pro-social, being towards differentiation, moving from dependence to independence, with an innate capacity for self-regulation and self-determination and of being towards the development and preservation of the species. However, the actualisation of any or all of these capacities can be thwarted due to the social-environmental conditions.

In consideration of the place of ontology in psychotherapy, Craig (2015) comments that the ontological basis to Rogers' theory deserves significant credit. He said that it represents one of the most serious presentations of an ontological basis to a psychological theory of therapy. In doing so, Craig challenges other therapies, including the existentialists that he was writing for at the time, to replicate Rogers' efforts. Drawing on the work of Tillich (1952), May (1961) and Boss (1988), he calls the need for ontological arguments to be developed as they represent the underpinning to all theories of therapy.

This section has provided a brief but necessary introduction to the ontological underpinning to PCE therapy. You might now ask yourself how well you think that your personal views of human nature match with those outlined above, or whether they will present a difficulty in learning and practising PCE-CfD. For example, do you really trust that human nature is socially constructive or do you believe that some people are just destructive by nature? Do you consider depression to be an entirely biologically based 'illness' or do you see that social-environmental factors might play a significant role in causing distress leading to depression? These are just a couple questions that might help to get you thinking from the PCE-CfD frame.

Ways of knowing

Following this brief introduction to an understanding of human nature within the PCE theory, the next step is to begin thinking about the 'ways of knowing'. It could be argued that there are two main ways of knowing in PCE therapy. The first of these refers to what is called the organismic valuing process (OVP). This process refers to that which Schmid (2013) termed the 'substantial dimension' of the person. The OVP is a person's innate capacity to experience and evaluate internal states and to process this information and to guide them in moving forward. The OVP is an expression of a person's striving toward actualising their potential. This way of knowing refers to the way clients know themselves, their preferences, their choices, their needs and so on. For a person to know themselves in this way they require the basic human capacity to turn inwards, attending to their internal, subjective experiencing.

To know *that* we experience is what makes humans different from other living beings. Introspection, for example, requires people to examine their own internal states. Gendlin (1962) referred to this innate capacity of an OVP as the direct referent. Both Rogers (1951) and Gendlin (1962) proposed that the individual can know *from the inside* through a specific mode of experiencing that acts as the inner datum. It is this datum that can be relied upon for guiding action and orienting the self-direction of the organism. It is this aspect of the person, according to PCE theory, which can be trusted. Rogers said that there is no higher order form of knowing than experiencing.

It is because of this understanding of the person that in PCE-CfD the therapist's stance is not one of pathologising clients but rather to consider that each person is acting in a way that 'they' perceive to be to the best interests for their survival or enhancement. For the PCE-CfD therapist, this means that trust can be placed in people's capacity for self-direction because they are, in the ontologically relational sense proposed by both Lietaer (2002) and Schmid (2013), by nature socially constructive. Being socially constructive should not be confused with the idea that people are 'good' or that the theory cannot account for destructive behaviours or actions. It can, and it does, account for destructive potentials to develop, but that is a separate issue for discussion which will be addressed later. For now, it is sufficient to say that human persons have the capacity to subjectively know themselves through their experiencing of the OVP.

The second way of knowing in PCE therapy is concerned with how the therapist knows the client. This refers to the means by, and the extent to which, the therapist comes to know the internal subjective experiencing of their client. To know the client's experiencing, the PCE therapist must in large part adopt the internal frame of reference of the client (Rogers, 1951). This means seeing the world through the client's experiences. However, as each person is a unique individual, it is not possible for the therapist to have the exact direct experience that the client has for themselves. For this reason, Rogers (1957b) was keen to always state that the therapist knows the client's experiencing 'as if' they were the client. The 'as if' quality to this way of knowing is especially important in PCE-CfD. By coming to know the client, the therapist is aiming to get as close as possible to the client's implicit feeling process. Gendlin (1962) referred to the implicit as the felt meaning of the direct referent (we could also call this the awareness of the OVP) of experience.

Importantly, the implicit is always felt in awareness. Whilst this part of experiencing might not have been given full symbolisation, at least not in terms of having word-symbols to make it explicit, implicit felt meanings are not unconscious and they can be symbolised in a different way through inner sensing, perhaps in the body. In fact, if we follow Gendlin's hypothesis it could be argued that even the idea of the unconscious is contestable, but that is not for discussion here. It is, however, important to know that in PCE therapy, the therapist comes to know the client through the client's interaction process. That is, between their felt meaning and their carrying forward of the implicit meaning. Carrying forward means the interaction between the felt meaning and the symbols used to explicate the felt meaning. Most often this is by way of putting words together to produce a statement that conveys, symbolically, the completed implicit meaning of an experience. One important note here is that explicit, symbolised meanings are quite different from implicit felt meanings. The implicit felt meaning can be unfolded in many directions and is not simply a 'hidden explicit meaning' just waiting to be brought to the surface (the implicit is not like the idea of an unconscious mind that is a reservoir of repressed thoughts, emotions, beliefs etc., that is the kind of knowing more familiar to the psychoanalytic approach). Felt meanings, according to Gendlin (1962), are completed as they are explicated, and the therapist plays a vital part in the process of explicating the client's meanings. Knowing then, in this sense, is a process of interaction between client and therapist that is focused on the client's internal, subjective interactive process of explication that the therapist can access through empathic understanding.

The best way to describe the therapist's way of knowing the client within this process of explicating meaning, and of the client completing the implicit felt meaning, is through the empathic understanding process. That is, therapists know their clients through the effortful development of an empathic understanding for the client's meaning making process. We will look more closely at empathy later in the chapter, but we can say for now that it is considered central to the PCE-CfD therapeutic process. It is far more than a technique as it often is in other therapies. Empathy was to Rogers (1970) an *unappreciated way of being*. For Schmid (2001), empathy is the *art* of comprehension and is the primary epistemological (way of knowing) approach within PCT. Similarly, in both focusing and EFT, approaches from which PCE-CfD draws, the empathic process is crucial to helping the client become aware of their implicit meaning or their inner emotion schemes and conflicts, respectively. The PCE therapist is going to be more helpful to the client when adopting and maintaining this way of knowing. Unlike other therapeutic approaches, the PCE-CfD therapist does not need to formulate a theoretical plan for treating the client and is not so concerned with their own frame of reference. The PCE-CfD therapist does not rely on any prior (theoretical) knowledge for making interpretations, or bidding to raise up hidden explicit meanings. Instead, they are focusing on the client's frame of reference and the client's intended goal for communication as it is rooted in their process of explicating the implicit. That is, the intended goal for communication is the implicit felt meaning; although often the client will report on many things, including external things, the therapist can help the client to become freer and more fluid in their experiencing process by listening and empathising with the implicit felt meaning.

This section has provided some thoughts about the philosophical underpinnings of PCE therapy and linked these to the PCE-CfD approach. It is important for all PCE-CfD therapists to have considered the philosophical foundations of the approach. Understanding one's own views on human nature and the ways of knowing for both client and therapist will help to orientate the PCE-CfD therapist. These philosophical concepts can also be helpful in supporting the PCE-CfD therapist in their practice setting, especially if the practice setting is quite different in the philosophical foundations from which it is operating. Having the language and understanding to engage with other professionals in the practice setting can be empowering for the PCE-CfD therapist.

Theory of personality

The practice of PCE therapy is grounded in the original theory of personality and behaviour (Rogers, 1951) and incorporates the evolution in focus of the central role of *experiencing* (Rogers, 1959, 1961; Gendlin, 1978/2003, 1998) and more contemporaneously the emotion theory developed by Greenberg (1984) and Greenberg and Safran (1989). In this section important aspects of this theory are mapped out providing a descriptive theoretical synthesis with the aim of presenting a clear and concise outline of personality development within PCE theory.

A perceptual theory[1]

Above, several references were made to the client's subjective experience and this was linked to the phenomenology of depression. The terms *experience* and *phenomenology* are an important feature to the theory of personality. First, Rogers (1951) originally based his ideas in the philosophical tradition of phenomenology. Such was the importance of this to the theory that Rogers

---

[1]Some sections of the text for this chapter are edited versions of the first edition and are acknowledged to Sanders and Hill (2014).

presented the client's experience of the perceived world as constituting their reality. He presented this through two propositions:

> Every individual exists in a continually changing world of experience of which he is the center. (1951: 483)

> The organism reacts to the field as it is experienced and perceived. This perceptual field is, for the individual, 'reality'. (1951: 484)

For PCE-CfD practitioners, this means that when the client makes changes to their perceptions and experiencing these will be assumed to indicate changes in the person-as-a-whole. As the client comes to see the world differently, they will also inevitably behave differently. Importantly, in PCE-CfD it is the perception of reality, and the construction of meaning that clients attribute to experiences, that the therapist is trying to comprehend. As pointed out already above, therapists comprehend the client's reality through the way of knowing which is known as empathic understanding.

Experiencing as the central construct

In the later stages in Rogers' (1961) development of his theory he focused attention more on the role of experiencing and found in this a rich new vein for advancing his theory. In working with very distressed clients at the Mendota State Hospital whilst at Wisconsin University, he and Gendlin began to identify the way that clients made use of their experiencing as a core internal process from which they could understand how people process events, memories, thoughts and feelings. From this they learnt how the changes in the processing of these experiences marked the movement towards constructive personality change.

As an organismic theory, the place of experiencing is central to understanding how the body has a role in processing experiences. We are embodied, and therefore when we say we are distressed (or depressed), this inevitably also means that this is experienced physically. If you might think that this suggests that depression will later be positioned as a 'brain disease', I can state categorically that it won't: physiological changes occur because we become psychologically distressed first, and not the other way around. As we will see later, the sources for psychological distress can be understood as largely social, but it is important to stress the order of events. To help understand the embodied nature of psychological distress, Rogers explained what he meant by this when he said:

> I mostly want to call attention to this part we just played [where the client says] 'I'm just a pleading little boy' and here again he used kinaesthetic means. In trying to get at what he was feeling he put his hands in supplication ... Here it seems to me that he's really *experiencing* himself as pleading ... in the immediate moment. (Rogers, 1958, cited in Kirschenbaum, 2007: 288)

PCE theory of experiencing draws from Gendlin's theoretical advances in this area, and from the EFT theory of emotion processing. It is important for PCE-CfD therapists to become familiar with the idea that experiencing can refer to all self-experiences of the client and these may be in the form of bodily sensations, emotions, memories, thoughts and urges or beliefs. Any of these might be experienced in awareness in a clear and highly differentiated way or they may be unclear, poorly differentiated, fuzzy or imprecise. PCE-CfD therapists must be comfortable and accept the client's unclear and fuzzy feelings just as much as they are able with clear and differentiated ones. As Gendlin (1978/2003) pointed out, it is not necessary for the client to make all experiences clear in order for them to have their meaning explicated. Often it is the effort to work on the explication, the attention and focus to the internal experiencing and felt sense, that can be all that is required for the client to experience changes in their processing style.

Human motivation and the specific role of emotions

The primary source of motivation in persons, according to PCE theory, is the 'actualising tendency' (Rogers, 1951). The actualising tendency is presented as a fundamental need of the organism to 'actualise, maintain and enhance' itself (p. 486) and that all other needs, be they organic or psychological, 'may be described as partial aspects of this one fundamental need' (p. 487–8). An important feature of the actualising tendency as a source of motivation is that it forms part of the ontological understanding of human nature described earlier. There is an absence of self or other destructiveness inherent to the organism's motivational tendency. Even when a person experiences psychological distress and the tension of being pulled in different directions, such as when they are feeling depressed, the actualising tendency theory shows that it is the unified whole of the person that is responding, striving, and moving towards its goal of trying to survive and grow. In this sense we can say that the phenomenon of depression is a specific kind of expression of an actualising tendency that is, for some reason or another, being thwarted from reaching its potential.

Recently, there have been several published studies looking at the actualising tendency concept. For example, Beitel et al., (2013) found strong correlations in a cross-sectional sample of students that showed self-actualisation was correlated with psychological mindedness. In addition, other researchers have linked actualisation to mindfulness (Beitel et al., 2014) and another study suggested that wellbeing in adults over 36 years of age is associated with higher motivation for self-actualisation (Ivtzan et al., 2013). In yet another study, it was shown that following one's intrinsic aspirations – a concept related to actualisation – was associated with personal growth and self-acceptance (Murphy, Demetriou & Joseph, 2015). These studies offer just a small sample to help demonstrate how the actualising tendency concept, whilst difficult to prove through directly measuring it, can be shown to be associated with similar and important developmental and motivational concepts. Providing evidence consistent with the theory of actualisation is a key step in advancing the theory, and research on actualising processes needs to remain a focal point for researchers in the field of PCE human development research.

To help explain how the PCE-CfD model has advanced from the traditional person-centred approach, we can highlight the role of emotion in the theory of actualisation. This will help to further differentiate our understanding of motivation and its links to behaviour. To do this, it will be helpful to begin by looking at Rogers' (1951) proposal about the role of emotions in motivation when he wrote his 19 propositions. Then, it will be necessary to develop this line of inquiry further by showing how assimilating emotion theory enhances the explanatory power of the PCE therapy theory. This can all be done without compromising the fundamental and central tenet of the actualising tendency as the primary motivational source.

In describing the role of emotions in behaviour, Rogers said:

> Emotion accompanies and in general facilitates ... goal-directed behavior, the kind of emotion being related to the seeking versus the consummatory aspects of the behavior, and the intensity of the emotion being related to the perceived significance of the behavior to the maintenance and enhancement of the organism. (1951: 492–3)

Here it is possible to see that the intensity of emotion that is experienced is linked to the actualising tendency and to behaviour; especially behaviour that might be perceived to play a role in the survival or growth of the organism. Similarly, Rogers asserted that there are two classifications of emotions that might be experienced. The first are the anticipatory, excited or even unpleasant emotions, and the second are those feelings that are satisfied, pleasant or calm. Emotions are linked closely to behaviours, and this is an important feature that is discussed more below. In addition, emotions are linked closely to thoughts, and for Rogers there is truly little to separate between a feeling and a thought, and because we know that emotions accompany behaviour we might also add that behaviour and emotions are also equally closely related:

> [The] experiencing of a feeling ... denotes an emotionally tinged experience, together with its personal meaning. Thus it includes the emotion but also the cognitive content of the meaning of that emotion in its experiential context. It thus refers to the unity of emotion and cognition as they are experienced inseparably in the moment. (1959: 198)

So, emotions can contribute to our motivation in three main ways:

- they initiate goal-directed behaviour
- they amplify goal-directed behaviour
- they become associated with goal-directed behaviour and by this association can come to represent goal-directed behaviours.

Importantly and in addition to this, Sanders and Hill (2014) noted that emotion precedes symbolisation and that through the process of symbolisation, infants develop a capacity to fuse emotion and cognition (as in Rogers, 1959). If we bring these points together with the emotion theory presented by Elliott (2012) it is possible to develop a sophisticated understanding of the place of emotion in human functioning and development, and link this with the actualising tendency as the primary source of human motivation.

Elliott (2012) has described that within the internal experiential world we develop emotion schemes. These emotion schemes are available to awareness but only when we engage in active self-reflection. Our emotion schemes act as networks wherein activation of one emotion scheme can lead to the activation of another related scheme and so on. As it is possible to experience emotion without symbolisation, it is therefore quite possible that perceptions become affected by emotion schemes and vice versa. As stated above, there is little to differentiate between emotion and cognition at this level of experiencing. This then positions emotion schemes and conditions of worth as very closely (theoretically) related to one another. In much the same way that emotion schemes are represented as networks, so too are conditions of worth. When originally presented by Standal (1954), he proposed that the developing person has an ever-evolving *complex* of conditions of worth that he termed the 'regard complex'. This is similar to the concept of emotion schemes and provides a synthesis of emotions, cognitions and behaviours showing how they are all inextricably linked and yet can be accounted for within a single theory. As the description unfolds it becomes clearer that there is but a hair's breadth between these aspects of human functioning. And, as we will see below, the synthesis of theories that PCE-CfD draws upon allows us to understand the phenomenological experience of depression – and our whole functioning for that matter – as an interrelated web of experiential processing.

Development and emergence of a self-concept

Within PCE theory, human growth and development is a lifelong, unidirectional process towards the actualisation of potentials. However, whilst the unidirectional nature of actualisation is always growthful, and towards greater differentiation and complexity of the organism, this directional tendency is also non-specific. Hence the reason why the actualising tendency can and will be lived out differently for each person. In this sense, PCE theory offers a non-pathologising way to understanding the diversity of human experiencing, including a wide variety of expressions of distress of which depression might be one. In PCE theory, the experience of psychological distress can include extremely negative self-critical and self-destructive thoughts and feelings. When this is the case, such experiences are to be valued and embraced as expressions of uniqueness and diversity and not so much as the symptoms of a disorder that need to be extinguished.

As noted above, the mature human organism is a unified, complex system of experiencing. However, in early life infants are less differentiated organisms regarding their affective-cognitive processing systems. Rogers (1951) suggested that the early infant first experiences a largely undifferentiated world. One can posit that this experience is of being connected to all things. However, as the infant matures over time, and through repeated interactions with caregivers and their environment, some experiences become identified as distinguishable from others. Some experiences might become known as 'me' and others as 'not me'.

During this early stage of development there is much change happening. Whilst we have noted that human development is a lifelong process, during the initial stages of our lives our intrinsic capacity for processing experiences is developing at a rapid rate (Warner, 2005). More is to be said about processing capacities in the next chapter when looking more closely at depression; for now, it is enough to recognise that these processing capacities are a significant aspect of functioning and are the mechanism that enables the processing of the continual flux of stimulation from both inside the person and outside from the environment. Importantly, as the basic building blocks of the cognitive aspects of the self-concept develop, so too do the emotion schemes, and to this we can now add our processing capacities. These attributes of the person are developed before language emerges. As the natural process of development continues towards further differentiation, this is also the case for the development of our experiential processing capacities. What begins to emerge from this complex system is a more ordered consistent experiencing that becomes identified by the infant as 'I' or 'me' and is the beginning of the formation of a self-concept. The emerging self-concept at this point is immature and vulnerable to influence from the social-environmental conditions, and of course forms only part of the experiential field. However, it is an important part of the experiential field as experiences become identified with it; there is a shift of the locus of experience that is gradually internally located and centred from within the emerging self-concept. What was once an immature OVP is now slowly maturing, but as this occurs the perceived location of this referent is shifted slightly towards the self-concept. As we will see below, this is a crucial step.

Often the idea of the self-concept is misunderstood to represent some form of homogenised self when in fact Rogers (1959) and others since (e.g. Mearns, 1999) have described the self-concept as a process. In this regard, the self-concept is best thought of as a hypothetical construct that we can relate experiences associated with a sense of 'I am ...'. The broader idea of a self-structure is useful for understanding the multiplicity that exists within the human organism and how we might have numerous self-configurations that are each in a constant state of interaction and communication with each other. Here, it is useful to recall the idea of emotion schemes that are all linked together within the broader self-structure but become activated through experiences derived from interaction with the environment (such as in a relationship or social situation) or through internal experiences (such as a memory, perhaps of a particularly difficult or traumatic event that might have been shaming). Some emotion schemes might be more likely to become activated when a specific self-configuration is present in a situation.

Within PCE theory, communication within the self-structure and between its constituent self-configurations and their concomitant conditions of worth and emotion schemes is crucial for development. A trajectory of healthy development will likely be indicated by free and uninhibited communication between the different systems within us, including the accurate symbolisation of thoughts and emotions and crucially the expression of these through behaviours that are felt as consistent. Psychological distress is indicated by communication within the self-structure that is problematic. In the section below, we will outline the ways this system develops such problematic communication across the various subsystems involved in experiential processing.

Conditions of worth

Conditions of worth are a central feature of the PCE theory of personality and functioning. They form a major strand in understanding the way that distress is formulated within the personality theory. This section will consider how and why conditions of worth are formed and once more show how these are linked to emotion processes. As mentioned previously in this chapter, emotion schemes are the main way in which distress is understood in EFT. By linking these to conditions of worth, it is possible to show how emotion theory further differentiates and can add qualitatively to the development of our understanding of distress in the PCE approach.

Conditions of worth are formed at a deep level within the structure of personality (Murphy, 2017). As infants and young children, we are developing a need for positive regard from caregivers. When this is provided unconditionally, with consistency and in a genuinely empathically attuned relationship, then development is likely to be towards health and wellbeing in functioning. However, as any parent or carer will know, experiencing positive regard unconditionally is beyond the capacity of almost all people. This is because everyone has, to some extent, their own conditions of worth. As a result, every child is, to some extent, raised in sub-optimal conditions. For example, when a young child is developing it is quite typical that they will find satisfaction from exploring and playing with their own body. They will explore their genitals and may experience sexual pleasure from doing so. This pleasure will be associated with positive experience and assimilated into their general growth process. The play and exploration are a self-regulated activities. If a caregiver disrupts this self-directed exploration and play in a scolding tone or behaviour, then the child will feel the threat of withdrawal of positive regard. In this instance the caregiver is responding with conditional regard. If the child then also comes to associate the caregiver's values in relation to their experiences as their own, and then acts in accord to the introjected value, then we can say a condition of worth has developed.

A condition of worth will include both cognitive and affective elements. Cognitive elements are thoughts, images or basic meaning units that will form beliefs about situations and the self or others. The affective element includes emotions associated with experiencing and becomes strongly associated with conditions of worth. By expanding on the example above we can show how the conditions of worth have greater potency when the emotion component is fully considered. If the caregiver in the above situation not only scolds but also attaches a value to the conditional regard, such as 'stop that, *that's dirty*', then the child introjects this too and may then instead of experiencing pleasure may experience the emotion of disgust. In all later instances of potential opportunity for enjoyment when exploring their genital area, the child will instead experience a sense of disgust at their behaviour. What was once a pleasurable experience has now become confused with a feeling of disgust at oneself. There is now an internal sense of tension between what is experienced by the organism as satisfying and pleasurable and yet is experienced in awareness as disgusting. This may then lead to avoidance of feeling disgust and the emotion of shame might then be experienced as a secondary response to experiencing any sexual desire or attraction later in life. In the next chapter we will explore how a similar experience may lead to tension that can be understood in terms of the phenomenology of depression.

Within PCE theory, at the basis of the self is a continuous flow of experiencing that has many elements that interact with each other. This is shown to be the case as the person develops their self-concept and the various sub-systems for processing experiences communicate with each other. This includes when emotion schemes, and conditions of worth are forming within the self-structure, and how we can understand the person's best attempt to process experiences when developing through play and exploration. In the next section the conditions of therapy will be explored, and these will be set against this theory of development.

Theory of the conditions for therapy

For most readers, the next few paragraphs will be familiar territory. Rogers' paper entitled 'Necessary and sufficient conditions for therapeutic change' (1957b) and his chapter (1959) detailing the same conditions must be two of the most widely read and cited works on counselling and psychotherapy. Rogers boldly proposed that six conditions were needed in a clinical (or other) relationship before therapeutic change could take place, and most contentiously that *no other conditions* were needed. Rogers (1957b) also stated that it was his way to communicate his positive regard for the client through empathic understanding responses. However, he also acknowledged that it was quite possible that the condition might be communicated through other means and in this sense his statement of 1957 was an integrative statement relevant to all psychotherapies. It remains the classical person-centred theorists' claim for the communicating of positive regard through verbal empathic understanding responses. It is that others have been more flexible in expressing their empathic understanding through a wide range of ways which has led to divisions and factions emerging in the field of PCT. For some, this means that PCE, never mind PCE-CfD, will be considered as a deviation rather than an expression of the same set of principles. However, this notion was contested (Bohart, 2008; Bozarth, 2008): specifically when working with client's experience of depression, PCE-CfD can draw from a range of insights and practices from Focusing or EFT that it can help facilitate experiential processing without compromising the core person-centred relationship conditions.

Wyatt (2001: iii) combined Rogers' 1957b and 1959 versions[2] of the therapeutic conditions, with the 1957 variations in italics:

1. That two persons are in *(psychological)* contact.
2. That the first person, whom we shall term 'the client', is in a state of incongruence, being vulnerable, or anxious.
3. That the second person, whom we shall term 'the therapist', is congruent *(or integrated)* in the relationship.
4. That the therapist is experiencing unconditional positive regard (UPR) toward the client.
5. That the therapist is experiencing an empathic understanding of the client's internal frame of reference *(and endeavours to communicate this to the client)*.
6. That the client perceives, at least to a minimal degree, conditions 4 and 5, the unconditional positive regard of the therapist for him, and the empathic understanding of the therapist. *(The communication to the client of the therapist's empathic understanding and unconditional positive regard is to a minimal degree achieved.)*

Some accounts of PC theory talk about 'core[3] ' conditions of empathy, unconditional positive regard and congruence, and others refer to these as the 'therapist-provided conditions'. Whilst this might appear to make some sense, it is both unnecessary and problematic since it gives the impression that PCE therapy is something the therapist does to the client. It is better to think of the six conditions as a whole, not least because the relationship is central to therapeutic change, with both client *and* counsellor bringing essential elements. So the client and counsellor *together* make the change possible.

This forces practitioners to think about helping as a relationship from the start and is different from those therapeutic approaches in which the client is seen as someone in receipt of *treatment* by an *expert*: the therapist. Seeing the client as being in need of treating can prevent the client from being seen as a person, and instead they are seen in a rather detached way as a thing, a machine or computer to be fixed in a step-by-step procedure. These ways of thinking about counselling do not fit in with the fundamental principles of PCE- CfD. When it comes to the practical activity of PCE-CfD, it makes more sense to see the counsellor as holding a set of attitudinal qualities within one complete helping relationship, not a collection of separate conditions.

---

[2]In a quirk of history, it is worth noting that Rogers wrote the 1957 version *after* the 1959 version, but the 1959 chapter was delayed in the production schedule of the book edited by Sigmund Koch (1959) *Psychology: A Study of a Science.* Thus, the 1957 paper represented Rogers' revisions of the conditions.

[3]Some writers have suggested that Rogers 'never' used the term 'core conditions'. However, in a chapter he did describe the three therapist conditions and then referred to them as 'core elements of therapeutic success'. For details see Rogers (1966, p. 188).

Nevertheless, in order to try and understand the constituent parts of this relationship it is necessary to take a more detailed look at each one at a time.

Psychological contact

Rogers' (1957b) first condition states that therapy requires two people to be in psychological contact. Person-centred theorists are not the only ones nor the first to locate contact at the centre of human psychology, and although Whelton and Greenberg (2002: 107) declare that 'The type of contact that is called "psychological" is the type of contact that a human self has with another human self', this must not be taken for granted.

In circumstances of extreme acute or chronic distress, some clients withdraw from psychological contact, and indeed contact with the world. Although most frequently connected to anxiety attacks and trauma, some clients diagnosed with depression might experience episodes of dissociation or depersonalisation. Clients whose depression is linked to trauma might experience dissociation and even enter a fugue state within a therapy session. Rather than assume that the client is permanently in psychological contact, it is better for therapists to keep this first condition in mind and be ready to congruently and empathically help the client reconnect and maintain contact if it becomes impaired or lost (Prouty, 1990; Traynor, Elliott & Cooper, 2011).

Client incongruence

This second condition identifies the client as a person in need of help and is the simplest expression of person-centred psychopathology. Earlier in this chapter we explained how classical person-centred theory understands the root of psychological tension as a discrepancy between self and experience and the formation of conditions of worth. In the classical literature (Rogers, 1951, 1959) this is referred to as 'incongruence' between the introjected elements of the self-structure and the self-related organismic experiences of the individual. It is the single, universal source of anxiety, depression and all symptoms of distress which are uniquely expressed by each person. In classical person-centred practice it provides the rationale for empathy – the method for understanding the narrative of the world of experience of the client.

Therapist congruence

The third condition is one which demands we read carefully the phrase that the therapist is congruent 'in the relationship'. In classical theory this means that in relation to the client the therapist is more integrated as regards the (inevitable) discrepancy between self-structure and experience. In this relationship at least, the counsellor must be more congruent or integrated than the client. In simple terms Rogers means that whilst the client *in this moment* may be feeling distressed and in need of help, the counsellor *in this moment* is not and is prepared to help.

Therefore in a structured helping relationship the counsellor needs to be prepared to be the counsellor, and there are several ways of understanding 'be prepared to be'. This condition refers, at least in part, to the counsellor's *fitness* to help, and in contemporary professional helping this includes:

- that they have appropriate training, qualifications and supervision
- that they have not done anything which might impair the carrying out of their professional responsibilities
- that they feel psychologically prepared and able to be the therapist (i.e. congruent as the therapist) with that client, and this includes having sufficient personal therapy.

In PCE-CfD we expect this to comply with Rogers' statement:

[T]he therapist should be, within the confines of this relationship, a congruent, genuine integrated person. It means that within the relationship he is freely and deeply himself, with his actual experience accurately represented by his awareness of himself. (1957: 97)

Wyatt (2001: 84–5) elaborates the concept further and identifies the following features of therapist congruence:

- Being authentic and 'real' rather than putting on a professional facade.
- Psychological maturity, indicating the degree to which the therapist is open to their experience.

These clearly are restatements of some of the qualities of being psychologically healthy, confirming the concept of congruence as a statement of the therapist's fitness to practise, *with that client, at that time.* She further *explains that being authentic takes into account the personal style of the therapist* – referring not to *what* the therapist does, but *how* they do it. Requiring them to interpret the ground rules of being a person-centred therapist in their own way, whilst remaining ethical and adhering to (in this case) PCE-CfD competences.

Unconditional positive regard

Unconditional positive regard has sometimes been over-simplified and therefore inaccurately referred to as 'acceptance'. Whilst acceptance is a word that Rogers did use occasioanlly, the term itself clearly indicates that here are two components to the concept, unconditionality and the positivity of regard, both of which have raised criticisms from various quarters in the psychotherapy community over the years.

The positive regard element of this condition is not the same as 'liking' or 'being nice to' (Mearns, 2003: 3–5). Nor does it have anything to do with having similar values or beliefs to the client. In some texts, Rogers described positive regard as 'prizing', and warmth and respect also convey the positive nature of the attitude. These terms all convey something about the depth or genuineness of the attitude that, as Tony Merry explained, 'can't be turned on and off like a tap' (2002: 80). It is virtually impossible to affect a display of prizing or respect towards someone without appearing false.

There can be no *guarantee* that the therapist will feel warmth towards a client, but it can help if we invoke the cliché 'love the sinner, not the sin'. This permits, or possibly even *instructs*, the therapist to prize the client as a human being worthy of their warm attention without having to condone their behaviour. The key to prizing clients lies in the self-awareness of the therapist. The more self-aware the therapist is, the more they will know their own prejudices, based as they are on fear. The fewer prejudices the counsellor has, the less judgemental they will be.

Few areas of person-centred theory have attracted more criticism than the idea of the *unconditionality* of positive regard, to the point that many critics confidently assert that it is both philosophically flawed and impossible to practise. Rogers writes:

> It is the fact that he feels and shows unconditional positive regard toward the experiences of which the client is frightened or ashamed, as well as toward the experiences with which the client is pleased or satisfied, that seems effective in bringing about change. (1959: 208)

Of interest to PCE-CfD practice is the idea of 'configurations of self' (Mearns, 1999; Mearns and Thorne, 2000). Mearns notes that a client might have different internal selves or configurations, each with its own distinct characteristics. A client might say they have different selves within them: a 'depressed loser', 'controlling careerist' and an 'optimist'. The person-centred therapist must display UPR towards all of these, or put another way, create a level playing field for the configurations within the client's self-structure. However, it is easy to see how a therapist, even without intending to, could tilt the playing field and favour one configuration at the expense of the other two. This might be good practice in some therapies where the configuration with, for example, the rational resolution to a difficulty might be favoured. However, in PCE-CfD the therapist is creating the conditions in which the client's actualising tendency can resolve the tension and move forward regardless of which internal facet of self might hold the key. For this to take place, inviting 'dialogue' between any or all configurations is possible and may even be necessary. It is clear then that each must be equally valued, and indeed prized, since in person-centred theory terms all configurations must be acting for at least survival, and possibly maintenance and enhancement of the organism, even though one or more might appear to be acting against growth, when viewed from the external frame of reference.

Empathic understanding

The relational nature of therapy consists mainly in this condition – a unilateral experiencing of empathy is almost certainly impossible, since implicit in the experience of empathy is the idea of checking that you are accurate. Therefore, experiencing empathic understanding is the experience of checking that your understanding is accurate. So communication is an essential ingredient, as attested by Rogers' explanation of the conditions 'and endeavours to communicate this to the client' (Rogers, 1957b, in Kirschenbaum & Henderson, 1990: 221). Empathy experienced by the therapist, without communicating it to the client is of little or no use.

'Internal frame of reference' is a term used to describe the client's private world of perceptions, experiences and meanings and is only available to the therapist via empathy. According to Rogers, 'It can never be known to another except through empathic inference and then can never be perfectly known' (Rogers, 1959: 210).

Rogers continues:

> being empathic is to *perceive* the internal frame of reference of another with *accuracy*, and with the emotional components and meanings ... *as if* one were the other person, but without ever losing the 'as if' condition. (p. 210, italics added)

Rogers' last major statement about empathy 'Empathic: an unappreciated way of being', available in his book *A Way of Being* (Rogers, 1980), was a defence against the critics who called it 'wooden' and 'parroting'. Here he writes about the *process* of empathy, rather than the *state* of empathy, as 'being sensitive, moment by moment, to the changing felt meanings which flow in this other person' (p. 142) and that we have to 'lay aside [our] own views and values in order to enter another's world without prejudice' (p. 143).

Sanders (2006: 69–72) summarised the developments and extensions of definitions of empathy since Rogers' death:

> *Godfrey 'Goff' Barrett-Lennard* (2003: 34–50) summarised the traditional idea that counsellor empathy facilitates self-empathy or 'listening within' in the client. Self-understanding in a non-judgemental atmosphere begets self-acceptance which facilitates integration of previously difficult areas of experience.
>
> *Eugene Gendlin* proposed that empathy moves the client's experience forward by allowing the client to monitor their experience through the repeated reflections and checking of the counsellor (see Purton, 2004).
>
> *Fred Zimring* (2000/2001) proposed that empathy helps us shift our way of processing from an objective 'me' self-state to an inward-looking subjective 'I' self-state, making internal self-structure change more possible.
>
> *Margaret Warner* (1997), in a similar vein to Gendlin, writes of how empathy fosters the ability to hold experiences in attention in ways that stimulate personal growth (self-understanding depends on our ability to stay with or 'hold' an experience for long enough for us to engage with it). This is particularly important in infancy (and parenting) and has a crucial role in healthy personality development.
>
> *Jerold Bozarth* (1984/2001: 138) stated unequivocally that 'reflection is not empathy' – that empathy is the *state* of *effort-to-accurately-understand* that

the therapist is trying to communicate to the client. Reflection is just one of the responses, according to Bozarth, through which empathy may be communicated, and he goes on to make a case for a very wide set of responses such as using metaphor, personal reactions, mimicry and jokes.

Peter Schmid (2001) explains the dialogical definition of empathy as the art of naïve not-knowing. Empathy as a human attribute comes without a particular intention but always as an expression of the personal quality of solidarity. We are empathic because we *must be* in order to be human and relate to others. Thus empathy in a therapy relationship is an expression of a flourishing human being, and restores this quality in others.

These various understandings of empathy reveal some common themes:

1. Therapist-experienced and communicated empathy facilitates the development of self-empathy, self-monitoring or self-reflection. This is seen as an essential prerequisite for perceiving and accepting previously 'difficult' experiences.
2. Empathy is not only achievable through reflection, but also by creatively communicating in any and all possible ways.
3. Empathy is not a one-way event, tool or instrument. It is a two-way relational process.

These principles are central to the practice of PCE-CfD.

Client perception

This subheading is an attempt to summarise the final condition which underlines the relational nature of person-centred psychology. In Rogers' (1957b, 1959) words, cited in Wyatt (2001: iii) with Rogers' 1957 variation in italics:

> That the client perceives, at least to a minimal degree, conditions 4 and 5, the unconditional positive regard of the therapist for him, and the empathic understanding of the therapist. (*The communication to the client of the therapist's empathic understanding and unconditional positive regard is to a minimal degree achieved.*)

The intent of this condition is clear: to clearly state the importance of communication in therapy. The client must experience empathy as being accurately understood and must feel prized and not judged. That the therapist intends to offer these conditions is not sufficient. The conditions cannot be seen to be fulfilled unless the client experiences these conditions, therefore the therapeutic outcome cannot properly be judged.

Godfrey Barrett-Lennard realised that the 'conditions theory' hinged upon the client's experience of the therapist in the counselling relationship. In 1962 he devised a questionnaire instrument that would reliably measure the client's perceptions of the therapist. This resulted in the Barrett-Lennard Relationship

Inventory and, following subsequent work, he concluded that there was a plausible causal connection between the client's perception of the therapist-provided conditions and change in the client. Successful communication of the therapist-provided conditions is a precursor to being able to evaluate the effectiveness of therapy. However, causality between the relationship conditions and outcomes is yet to be evidenced, and this might be difficult to achieve as it would possibly involve the unethical manipulation of the therapist's attitudes towards the client. Elliott, Bohart, Watson and Murphy (2018) have attempted to offer a scheme for approaching the issue of causality through the application of a set of principles to the research process. Further research is needed to address this critical issue.

This condition also points to the importance of the evaluation of skills and microskills in training. Debates amongst counsellor trainers regarding the role of microskills training and assessment will not be rehearsed here, but suffice to say that communication skills figure as central to being a competent therapist. It is also worth noting that Rogers does not mention the communication mode through which these conditions are transmitted and received. Bozarth (1984/2001) makes the case for idiosyncratic empathy, but we are certain that *all* of the therapeutic conditions will be offered idiosyncratically[4] in a counselling relationship with any life in it. This is also explicitly addressed above in Wyatt's (2001) understanding of congruence as comprising authenticity which is dependent on the personal style of the therapist – *how* the therapist says or does things as well as *what* they say or do. Naturally, this includes non-verbal communication, and can be as varied as the creativity of the counsellor will allow.

Theory of change

In 1961, Rogers further shifted the understanding of personality from a state to a process and similarly moved from an events-based understanding of therapeutic change, from a *mechanism* (a pre-morbid state to a resolved state, or from a 'sick' state to a 'healthy' state) to a continuous *process* (see Figure 2.1). This process is best understood as one of development or unfolding – continuous assimilation of unfolding experience and adaptation to new situations.

Rogers describes the process of change in a completely arbitrary array of seven stages. There is nothing in Rogers' description of the process of change that implies stages or the number seven – he simply gives a structure to what would otherwise be a rather difficult description of a fluid process. Rogers condenses the six therapeutic conditions into one process, 'that the

---

[4]This means the way the counsellor must respond personally and authentically to the unique experiences of the client: idiomatically, colloquially, and in a way that is congruent with the emerging micro-culture of the relationship. It is not possible to specify this as a series of mechanistic call-and-answer interventions. This way of being is covered in the metacompetences.

Stage 1	Stage 2	Stage 3	Stage 4	Stage 5	Stage 6	Stage 7
process is so fixed and stuck that the person is unlikely to come for therapy – they think everyone else has a problem			⇨ process of change ⇨			process is so spontaneous and fluid that almost continuous change happens outside the session as much as in the session

Figure 2.1 Rogers' seven stages of process

client experiences himself as being fully *received'*, calling this the 'basic condition' (Rogers, 1961: 130):

> By this I mean that whatever his feelings – fear, despair, insecurity, anger, whatever his mode of expression – silence, gestures, tears, or words; whatever he finds himself being in this moment, he senses that he is psychologically *received*, just as he is, by the therapist. (p. 130–31, original emphasis)

It is the totality of the continually changing therapeutic relationship comprising this 'basic condition' that ensures the client feels *fully received.* Here again, the relational nature of therapy, dependent upon the communication skills of the counsellor, is stressed; in Rogers' words, 'it is the client's experience of this condition which makes it optimal, not merely the fact of its existence in the therapist' (1961: 131). Hence the therapeutic relationship conditions make the therapeutic change possible, but they are not synonymous with it. The change process is something that happens within the client's own internal and interpersonal world. To this end, the therapeutic relationship itself can be changed by the client's own experience of therapy.

The change process continuum is arranged by Rogers between two polarised positions, one in which process is stuck, rigid and fixed, and the other in which it is appropriately and completely fluid, flowing and adaptable. Within the continuum, Rogers marks thresholds in the seven stages that are important in our understanding of what may or may not be achieved in the counselling and may require subtle nuances in the counsellor's behaviour.

In Stage 1, Rogers describes the person as not likely to come for therapy because their self-structure is so rigid, their self-perceptions so controlled through denial and distortion that they do not perceive themselves to have any problems – all problems are external. Rogers concedes that traditional therapy has little to offer the person in Stage 1, not least because they do not present themselves for therapy.

In Stage 2, the client will notice patterns of experiences in their life, but are likely to see no significant connection to themselves, saying, for example, 'Chaos just follows me around' or 'The boss always had it in for me, that's why I was sacked this time'. Any self-perceptions are experienced as immutable facts, for example 'I'm a depressive' or 'I can never get anything right, it's all my fault'.

From Stage 3 onwards we find a general loosening of process, so that once-rigid perceptions are more likely to change as a result of being fully received. Now therapeutic change has a foothold and all manner of characteristics and self-perceptions become more fluid. However, this more fluid process is fragile, and clients may experience a high degree of anxiety as they approach the possibility of change. A key moment in Stage 3 is when the client realises that their self-perceptions are constructs or ideas, rather than facts about themselves. This signals the client's further realisation that ideas can be changed, and personal change becomes at least a possibility, albeit one which may seem frightening.

The remaining stages see the client able to increase the sophistication of their self-reflection and the flexibility of their self-structure. Rogers documented this continuum of change in a number of dimensions of processing. Here we have summarised the most important – for our purposes – dimensions and the changes predicted by Rogers:

Feelings: The person moves from hardly recognising feelings at all, to describing feelings as objects in the past ('I was feeling desperate'), then tentatively acknowledging feelings but being frightened of them, to fully experiencing feelings in the present. Feelings are no longer feared, nor do they feel 'stuck'. In the later stages, Rogers (1961) says that feelings flow to their full result, meaning that they don't get strangled or halted before the full expression leads to a feeling of being cleansed.

Personal constructs: In Stage 1, ideas about the self are not even entertained. The person gradually becomes aware of personal constructs but only thinking of them as facts. Then at a key moment in Stage 3, they are recognised, albeit rigidly, as ideas not facts, and therefore potentially changeable – so the client can now believe that change is possible. As self-related ideas become increasingly acknowledged and flexible, the whole self-structure becomes fluid and eventually open to being revised frequently.

Internal dialogue: The person starts off having little or no internal dialogue and being largely fearful of paying too much attention to him/herself ('you think too much'). As their fear of looking inside at themselves lessens, they slowly experiment until they are able to have almost constant, mostly comfortable, internal dialogue as a matter of course in daily life.

Expression: People in the early stages of process are largely inexpressive. They don't talk about themselves much and are embarrassed or nervous when doing so, thinking it is pointless. Loosening of their process leads to free expression, including expression of feelings. In addition, in the final stages, individuals welcome and trust this flow of expression.

Differentiation and elaboration of experience: People in the early stages of process see things (their experiences of others and themselves, moral issues, etc.) in highly contrasting, right/wrong categories – there are almost no 'grey areas'. As they begin to differentiate and elaborate an increasing proportion of their experiences of themselves, others and the world, they begin to see the complexity in experience. This leads to discovering diversity and plurality *in themselves*, amongst others and in the world. Eventually they not only experience this diversity and plurality without fear, they welcome it.

Perception of problems: People start off believing that they couldn't possibly have any problems. Everyone else has the problem, not them. They gradually begin to be able to look at and understand themselves (see 'personal constructs' above) with less and less fear, eventually being comfortable with the idea that they are a mixture of lived possibilities, some of which they experience as positive, some as negative; none of which necessarily generate feelings of great fear.

Attitude to change: Where it was once denied even as a possibility, change becomes an accepted, welcome part of the process of living. Clients might start with a 'if it ain't broke, don't fix it' or 'a leopard can't change its spots' attitude, but end up relishing change as a challenge. Along the way, the client will move through times of being afraid of change to varying degrees, depending upon how central the focus of change is to their self-concept. The client remains open to change in the future as a result of getting to the later stages of this process.

Bodily changes: The psychological changes described above run alongside what Rogers (1961) described as 'physiological' changes. What he described included the increasing tendency to suffer from fewer bodily (embodied) symptoms of anxiety (headaches, irritability, digestive problems etc.) on the one hand, and more physical manifestations of ease, contentedness and feeling at one with things and happy with oneself (muscular relaxation, bright eyes, free breathing, physical responsiveness) on the other.

It should be remembered that these stages or phases don't exist and never have done in any real person's change process – they are completely arbitrary signposts to help us put some structure to the abstract theory. In the lived experience of real people, the process of change is unique. It has an irregular, halting trajectory not always appearing to move forward when observed from the external frame of reference. Furthermore, it is quite likely to proceed at different rates in different areas of a person's life. It is useful as a theoretical construct but caution should be applied if the temptation is to think about these stages when with a client.

PCE-CfD competences covered in this chapter

- **B1** – Knowledge of the philosophy and principles that inform the therapeutic approach
- **B2** – Knowledge of person-centred theories of human growth and development and the origins of psychological distress

(Continued)

(Continued)

- **B3** – Knowledge of the person-centred conditions for, and goals of, therapeutic change
- **B4** – Knowledge of the PCE conceptualisation of depression
- **B7** – Ability to experience and communicate empathy
- **B8** – Ability to experience and communicate a fundamentally accepting attitude to clients
- **B9** – Ability to maintain authenticity in the therapeutic relationship
- **S1.1** – Ability to identify the ways in which clients manage and process their emotions, including the ability to recognise when clients are finding it difficult to access these
- **S1.6** – Ability to help the client differentiate between feelings that are appropriate to (and hence useful for) dealing with a current situation and those that are less helpful to them, for example:
  - because they are emotional responses relating to previous experiences rather than the present context
  - because they are reactions to other, more fundamental, emotions

(Competences are listed in Appendix 1)

3

The Person-Centred Experiential Theory of Depression

The previous chapter provided a general grounding in the development of PCE therapy as an evolution of the person-centred paradigm and specifically introduced the core theory and elements that go into making up this approach. This chapter assembles and examines in more depth those aspects of theory which relate directly to the practice of therapy with clients who experience depression.

Before looking at the theoretical underpinning of the experience of depression, we must remind ourselves that although the PCE theory of personality and psychological distress is a universal theory, this does not prevent us selecting a set of client experiences (the phenomenology of depression) and turning our attention to examining the specific elements of theory which help us understand those experiences, how they are formed and what might be useful to clients experiencing such phenomena.

This chapter[1] first presents the description of experiences that are most commonly clustered together and given a label of 'depression'. It then describes the theoretical basis of PCE-CfD by presenting four cornerstones of the approach to the experience of depression:

- the nature of the self
- self-discrepancy
- self-configuration
- the nature of emotions.

These are elucidated further by proposing ten hypotheses that can be empirically tested.

The phenomenology of depression

The term 'depression' is commonly used within everyday language and is generally understood to refer to persistent low mood that is accompanied by a feeling which is experienced as hopelessness and helplessness in anticipating a change in the low mood. However, whilst common features prevail many people will experience the phenomenology of depression as quite specific to them. As we have outlined in Chapter 1, the PCE approach does not rely on the use of diagnosis and is instead premised on a growth metaphor. Nevertheless, for practitioners working in healthcare settings where the language draws upon a medicalised vernacular it is useful to be able to understand what is meant by such terms as major depressive disorder (MDD). MDD is described in the DSM-5 (APA, 2013: 160–61) as:

a. Five or more of the following symptoms have been present during the same 2-week period and represent a change from previous functioning;

---

[1]This chapter also draws on the first edition of the textbook and therefore acknowledges Sanders and Hill (2014) as the creators of much of the content.

at least one of the symptoms is either (1) depressed mood or (2) loss of interest or pleasure.

  i. Depressed mood most of the day, nearly every day, as indicated by either subjective report (e.g. feels sad, empty, hopeless) or observation made by others (e.g. appears tearful). (Note: In children and adolescents, can be irritable mood.)
  ii. Markedly diminished interest or pleasure in all, or almost all, activities most of the day, nearly every day (as indicated by either subjective account or observation).
  iii. Significant weight loss when not dieting, or weight gain (e.g. a change of more than 5% of body weight in a month), or decrease or increase in appetite nearly every day. (Note: In children, consider failure to make expected weight gain.)
  iv. Insomnia or hypersomnia nearly every day.
  v. Psychomotor agitation or retardation nearly every day (observable by others, not merely subjective feelings of restlessness or being slowed down).
  vi. Fatigue or loss of energy nearly every day.
  vii. Feelings of worthlessness or excessive or inappropriate guilt (which may be delusional) nearly every day (not merely self-reproach or guilt about being sick).
  viii. Diminished ability to think or concentrate, or indecisiveness, nearly every day (either by subjective account or as observed by others).
  ix. Recurrent thoughts of death (not just fear of dying), recurrent suicidal ideation without a specific plan, or a suicide attempt or a specific plan for committing suicide.

b. The symptoms cause clinically significant distress or impairment in social, occupational, or other important areas of functioning.
c. The episode is not attributable to the physiological effects of a substance or to another medical condition.

Note: Criteria A–C represent a major depressive episode.

Note: Responses to a significant loss (e.g. bereavement, financial ruin, losses from a natural disaster, a serious medical illness or disability) may include feelings of intense sadness, rumination about the loss, insomnia, poor appetite, and weight loss noted in Criterion A, which may resemble a depressive episode. Although such symptoms may be understandable or considered appropriate to the loss, the presence of a major depressive episode in addition to the normal response to a significant loss should also be carefully considered. This decision inevitably requires the exercise of clinical judgement based on the individual's history and the cultural norms for the expression of distress in the context of loss.

d. The occurrence of the major depressive episode is not better explained by schizoaffective disorder, schizophrenia, schizophreniform disorder, delusional disorder, or other specified and unspecified schizophrenia spectrum and other psychotic disorders.

e. There has never been a manic episode or a hypomanic episode.

Note: This exclusion does not apply if all of the manic-like or hypomanic-like episodes are substance-induced or are attributable to the physiological effects of another medical condition.

Within the DSM-5 there are in fact a number of 'depressive disorders' that are considered specific and differentiable conditions. These include 'disruptive mood dysregulation disorder, major depressive disorder (including major depressive episode), persistent depressive disorder (dysthymia), premenstrual dysphoric disorder, substance/medication-induced depressive disorder, depressive disorder due to another medical condition, other specified depressive disorder, and unspecified depressive disorder' (APA, 2013: 155). The DSM-5 claims that all these variations of experience share the experiencing of sadness, emptiness or irritable mood that come with somatic and cognitive changes to the capacity to function properly. However, as is typical of medicalised models of distress, the root causes of such experiences are considered to stem from various sources. It is also the case that these different experiences of depression can last for a variable period and might have specific times in the life cycle when they appear.

Here we are primarily concerned with what is described above as the major depressive variation on experience. For the sake of theoretical integrity, any attempt to help a client is reasonably expected to be preceded by an adequate explanation of the phenomenology of the client's experiences. This might be in the form of a heuristic description as to how the experience might have arisen, and this is set in accordance with the theory. The theory must also be mapped directly on to a coherent rationale for therapeutic practice. In the sections that follow, this heuristic is presented for PCE-CfD to account for the experience of depression within the context of the theory of distress that informs the therapeutic practice.

The nature of the self

The term 'self', as used widely in psychology and everyday life, has many meanings. It has been pointed out by many writers that the self is an ethnocentric construct originally accepted uncritically by Western psychology (see Cushman, 1995). Non-person-centred psychologies view the self in ways with varying degrees of overlap in understanding; self-psychology, developed by psychoanalyst Heinz Kohut in the 1960s, whilst of peripheral interest, is too firmly rooted in the 'deficiency' model of psychoanalysis to be helpful in an explication of PCE-CfD theory (Kohut, 1971). Tudor and Merry (2002/2006: 125–6) identify three ways in which the term is used in person-centred psychology and provide over 30 entries with 'self' as part of the entry. Tudor and Worrall (2006: 101–135) also comprehensively explore the wide range of meanings of the term and their implications in person-centred and experiential psychologies. Here the construct of self is presented through descriptions and discussions only so far as to lay out the foundations of the PCE-CfD conceptualisation of depression.

The self as a concept

As stated in Chapter 2, Rogers (1951: 497) described the self in developmental terms as a portion of the perceptual field of the infant which is concerned with awareness of being, the pattern of perceptions of the 'I' or 'me', plus the values attached to the emerging concepts and perceptions. In 1959 (p. 200) Rogers reinforces the perceptual nature of the self with important consequences for personality and change: the self is i) a concept, a stable, consistent,[2] durable set of I/me-related perceptions; ii) a perception, a concept, a *process*, primarily an experiential response to the world,[3] including the internal world (so it is reflexive); and iii) therefore amenable to change, since its 'natural' state is adaptation.

> *PCE-CfD Theory of Depression*, Hypothesis 1: The phenomenology of depression can result from rigidity within the self-structure arising as a result of threat to the integrity of the self-concept.

Since a well-functioning self is a fluid and adaptive process, assimilating and accommodating experiences and organising responses to them, any rigidity will restrict the potential range of experiences and consequent responses to the world. This rigidity will affect both the range of possible perceptions which can be admitted to awareness and the range of responses which might be made as a result. The structure of the self may become rigid because of threat. This can arise in several ways, not only in sudden intense moments of threat, such as accidental trauma or deliberate abuse, but also by the drip-drip of negative comments and criticisms from others. Threat can also arise from within the self-structure, as suggested in Chapter 2. The self as a reflexive process can and will turn experiences back upon itself, so healthy, fluid self-processes can be impeded and curtailed by other impaired self-processes, such as intrusive thoughts, anxiety and so on, especially when these specifically target elements of the self (e.g. when intrusive critical thoughts recur whenever the individual experiences pleasure).

At a quite simple and straightforward level, these threats (both intense and repetitive) can result in patterned restrictions of perception and response

---

[2]It is important to explain that the self is both permanently fluid and adaptable, yet consistent and stable. That is to say that I experience myself as being the same person this morning as I was when I went to bed last night. There is a day-to-day, week-to-week, year-to-year consistency in the self. The self is fluid *and* stable.

[3]Note: whenever the term 'world' is used in this chapter, it will be meaning both the external environment (including relationships) and the internal world of meanings of the person.

which become configured and experienced as depression. Further detail on problematic psychological factors will be given later, but at a general level, threat can result in the following processes which can create a fertile psychological substrate for depression:

- limited and limiting outlook, leading to a feeling of loss of agency and helplessness
- reduced range of responses which can be experienced as restricted capacity for experiencing emotions
- pervasive feelings of negativity (e.g. self-blame) when experiences are variously selectively filtered and targeted
- social and experiential withdrawal resulting from these restrictions on experiencing.

The self as organism

Rogers also uses the term 'self' in relation to the organism; indeed, Tudor and Worrall (2006: 125–6) assert that Rogers conflates the concepts of self and organism. Some writers (although not Rogers himself) use the term 'organismic self' – originally Seeman (1983) in his work describing organismic integration as the epitome of health – and it is often popularly used to mean the true self, one that is inherent or originating in the organism. The problems associated with this cluster of concepts are carefully dissected by Tudor and Worrall (2006: 125–6); however, for the purposes of laying down the theoretical foundation of PCE-CfD, there is no need to reproduce them here.

The notion of self as part of an integrated organism does allow us to establish the importance to PCE-CfD of the internal and physiological, or in this case we might say 'integrated' wisdom of the client.

> *PCE-CfD Theory of Depression*, Hypothesis 2: Some aspects of depression can result from the embodied self.

Locating the self as an organismic phenomenon allows us to emphasise the *embodied* nature of the self. As a result, we can see two processes important to the understanding of the genesis of depression.

First is the inclusion of bodily feelings in the palette of experiences available for work in therapy. Since the individual is an integrated organism, with all domains acting in concert (whether this is clear to an observer or not), psychological tension can be embodied. Elements of experience are embodied with a psychological referent, a tag, clue or handle, which points to the meaning of the bodily sensation. There is no formula or taxonomy of embodied feelings in PCE-CfD. Each is unique and is even likely to change from moment to moment. Given the commonality in the descriptive vocabulary, figurative language and metaphor used by clients when asked to describe the feelings of 'depression', we might speculate that when people talk of 'pain', 'heaviness', 'lack of energy' or 'feeling dead inside', they are expressing their undifferentiated and fuzzy awareness of embodied experience. It is also the case that the experience of depression can include more direct, concrete somatisation of distress, such as weight loss or weight gain. This is explained in PCE-CfD as the human organism acting as an organised whole; clients and their experiences are best understood as an indivisible entity. Somatisation such as weight gain or loss can itself add secondarily to the distress experienced, and we find people experiencing a downward spiral of helplessness and feeling out of control.

Second is the straightforward notion that experiential elements of the self-structure can involve embodied feelings. So, for example, there might be an alignment of distressing elements, some of which might be embodied. In some cases, people ascribe more credence, importance or even 'wisdom' to embodied feelings. A client might feel unable to get out of bed because they have no physical energy and their feelings of helplessness would be redoubled if they believe there is nothing to get out of bed for. Of course, some people give bodily sensations less importance or are likely to dismiss them altogether, thereby reinforcing the injunction to empathically follow the client in question rather than taking ready-made recipes for understanding into the therapy session.

As easy as it is to see the reinforcement of distressing self-related experiences, there is also the possibility of discrepancy between a bodily sensation and a thought. So, in contrast to the example above, a client might feel unable to get out of bed because they have no physical energy, whilst becoming further distressed by thinking 'this is not like me, I am never like this, I don't feel like myself any more, why can't I do the simplest of things like getting out of bed?' This most basic example of a discrepancy between parts of the self is used here simply to illustrate a possible dynamic involving an embodied element of the self.[4] It is also an example of a much larger category of intrapersonal events which are called 'self-discrepancies' and will be detailed below.

It is possible to see how these most simple of individual intrapersonal processes might aggregate to form an experience specific enough to be labelled as depression and severe enough to bring a person to their GP. Since a very high proportion of people experiencing depression have suicidal thoughts, the aggregation of more 'simple' processes clearly is sufficiently severe to make people think about killing themselves.

The pluralistic self

Although not explicitly addressed in Rogers' original work, the notion of the self as a pluralistic system or matrix rather than a unitary entity is of central importance not only to PCE-CfD theory, but also to the developing PCE theory of the 21st century. There are several strands of PCE theory which rest upon understanding the self as comprising subselves, parts, configurations, voices, schemas

---

[4]Client statements can be understood to be *signposts* to specific intra- and inter-personal problems, in this case pointing to embodied self-discrepancies.

and so on. There are both similarities and differences between the PCE under-standings of what Mearns (1999; Mearns and Thorne, 2000) calls 'configura-tions', and, for example, constructs such as 'objects' in object relations theory and 'ego states' in transactional analysis, but no comparisons are made here, limiting ourselves to the range of PCE understandings. For the purposes of sim-plicity and unifying vocabulary in PCE-CfD we will use the term 'configura-tions' to describe this phenomenon. Although this is Mearns' term, concepts very similar if not identical to configurations of self have been developed in parallel over many years in different strands of PCE psychology.

We need go no further than an everyday conversation to seek validity for the construct, since there can be few conversations in which a person does not spontaneously say something like 'I can't decide: a part of me wants to and a part of me doesn't', 'Sometimes I enjoy it and other times I don't, I'm like two different people', or 'When asked to do it, I always have this debate inside: one me says "do it", another me says "don't do it", and the me that often wins is the one that says "wait and see, it'll blow over"'.

The experience of several parts of the self, or even several selves, is a com-mon one with which almost everyone can identify, as is the experience of these parts in conversation or dialogue, often representing different points of view, different options or different aims.

> *PCE-CfD Theory of Depression*, Hypothesis 3: Symptoms of depression can result from problematic dialogue between parts of the self.

This general statement about everyday experience of parts of the self is neces-sary to draw attention to the differences between PCE-CfD and more classical person-centred theory. PCE-CfD deliberately posits the notion of a pluralistic self and takes elements of emotion-focused theory to support and explain the symptoms of depression, as described below. From classical person-centred theory, PCE-CfD takes the notion of discrepancy between self and experience sometimes written about as the discrepancy between the real and ideal self. These elements of theory are consonant to the extent that it is easy to present this as a coherent theoretical position requiring little adjustment for most counsellors encountering PCE-CfD practice for the first time. This will be explored in more detail in the section on 'self-discrepancy' below.

Self-discrepancy can also be linked to the broader tradition of experiential therapies and EFT, as in the notion of dialogue between different self-configurations. There is a variety of dialogue dynamics between the aims or modus operandi of different self-configurations other than simple conflicts. Discussions, argu-ments and disagreements are commonplace and whilst possibly less immedi-ately disruptive than discrepancies, they can set a distressing, tedious or hopeless backdrop to day-to-day life, or aggregate feelings in a drip-drip fashion which eventually and dramatically break when the load gets too great. These are explored in detail in the 'other self-configuration dialogues' section.

On the other hand, psychotherapy has little concern for agreements between self-configurations. It could be argued that subselves develop by necessity to provide us with psychological balance (e.g. an individual needs a balance of self-criticism and self-belief to stop themselves from becoming narcissistic). This would be a natural expression of a well-developed holistically functioning organism. Problems arise when subselves get out of balance or become fixed and polarised in their positions.

This discussion of the nature of the self gives us the general platform from which to understand the detail of the PCE-CfD conceptualisation of depression. It also contributes the basic intrapersonal architecture within which distress can arise in the form of symptoms of depression. Now let's look inside this structure to the more detailed intrapersonal dynamics that may lead to depression.

Self-discrepancy

The term 'self-discrepancy' is taken from the work of Neill Watson (Watson, Bryan & Thrash, 2010), who in turn took the term from 'self-discrepancy theory' developed by Edward Tory Higgins (Higgins, 1987). Watson and his colleagues further developed the notion by integrating the ideas of Rogers and Higgins.

Self-discrepancy is a succinct phrase under which to gather the various – sometimes subtly different – expressions of discrepancies within the self-structure which lead to psychological tension as outlined originally by Rogers (1951) and later elaborated by others in PCE theory. Rogers used the term 'incongruence' to describe the single source of psychological tension (see Chapter 2), but in PCE-CfD it is acknowledged that a more broadly-based range of self-discrepancies are considered to be precursors for experiences which might be diagnosed as depression. Watson and his colleagues particularly aligned self-discrepancy with depression and developed instruments to measure how levels of self-discrepancy might be associated with depression.

The PCE-CfD conceptualisation of depression embraces the self-discrepancy definitions used by Watson et al. (2010) at a conceptual level. Watson and his colleagues first restate Rogers' theory: introjection of conditions of worth leads to undifferentiated psychological tension (anxiety and/or depression) generated by a real–ideal discrepancy. Let us look now at the self-discrepancy theory in more detail.

Higgins' self-discrepancy theory

Higgins (1987) distinguishes between domains of self and standpoints on the self to create a complex matrix of possible self-objects and their interactions. Domains of the self are:

- *the actual self*: representations or experiences of the attributes you (or someone else, another) thinks that you possess
- *the ideal self*: experiences of the attributes that you (or another) would like you, ideally, to possess (hopes and aspirations for you)
- *the ought self*: experiences of the attributes that you (or another) believes you ought to possess (a representation of your duty and responsibilities).

The standpoints on the self are:

- experiences from your own standpoint
- the standpoints of another or others.

So, the domains of the self (actual, idea and ought) can be seen from either of the two standpoints (own and other). Importantly, we can translate both the domains and standpoints into Rogers' personality theory by understanding that all 'own' representations are congruent symbolisations of experiences, while all 'other' representations are possible introjects leading to distortions.

Thus, Higgins' self-discrepancy theory uses a matrix of self-objects based on the experiences of the owner of the self (authentic experience) versus the perceptions or demands of a significant other (introjected values). The matrix of possible interactions is a more detailed, systematic elaboration of Rogers' notions of congruence.

Higgins' self-discrepancy theory and depression

Within the matrix Higgins proposes two types of discrepancy important to PCE-CfD: i) actual or real self vs. the *ideal* self: the self you or others *want* you to be (real–ideal: RI); and ii) actual or real self vs. the self you think (or have been told) you *ought* to be (real–ought: RO).

He then goes on to propose a link between sets of discrepancies and concomitant outcomes, for example:

- own ideal self/other ideal self is associated with depression
- own ought self/other ought self is associated with shame and anxiety.

Higgins' contribution of the RO discrepancy and discriminating the differences between the discrepancies and the experience of anxiety or depression is an interesting and useful elaboration of theory. Furthermore, both RI and RO discrepancies have been measured in, and validated by, a number of studies (see Watson et al., 2010).

Finally, and parenthetically, it is acknowledged in theory literature, diagnostic manuals and clinical settings that many clients receive mixed anxiety and depression diagnoses and report overlapping symptoms and experiences of depression and anxiety. This is entirely concordant with PCE-CfD explanations of idiosyncratic combinations of client experiences being due to unique elaborate patterns of introjected values discrepant with authentic experiences.

The entire edifice of Higgins' self-discrepancy theory is unnecessary for understanding the PCE-CfD conceptualisation. As a perceptual theory, PCE-CfD takes the key notion that conflict between the way we experience ourselves and the way we ideally want to be is an important archetypal self-discrepancy in the genesis of depression and that there is some evidence to establish the validity of this (Watson et al., 2010). As a phenomenological theory, PCE-CfD does not adopt Higgins' discrepancy theory as a diagnostic or treatment tool. The experience of the client is paramount, and the therapist follows the client in order to understand the unique network of associations and meanings that go to make up their lived experience of depression and works with that, even though it might contradict any and all theories.

In summary, PCE-CfD theory proposes that self-discrepancy is one starting point, a template from which to build possible understanding, or a signpost from which to explore the client's world. The signpost points to a theoretical starting point from which we consider the idea that personality is composed of many self-aspects in relation to each other. That starting point in theory leads to a number of possibilities, including distressing intrapersonal processes where one aspect is, for example, excessively critical of another, constantly suppresses another, regularly interrupts another, or experiences the absence of another.

> *PCE-CfD Theory of Depression*, Hypothesis 4: Symptoms of depression can uniquely result from the discrepancy between a person's real or actual self and their introjected ideal self.

Discrepancies or incongruence between parts of the self can be experienced by the individual person as a fixed state, in the same way that some people describe depression as a global and permanent state of being. PCE-CfD practice accepts the client's fatalistic apprehension of their world, whilst understanding that these global, totalising experiences are often maintained by micro-processes that can fix our general mood or sense of who we are. In both Chapters 4 and 5, it is shown how this translates into the PCE-CfD therapeutic stance.

The purpose of identifying and working with self-discrepancies of this type is to reduce the tension by any one or a combination of means – many of which will be managed by clients themselves. Sometimes awareness alone is sufficient; sometimes the origin of the ideal self or ought self can be uncovered, revisited and revised, effectively removing the tyranny of who the client wants to be or thinks they ought to be. We will explore the practice issues involved and again look at examples in Chapters 5 and 6.

Higgins' (1987) and Watson et al.'s (2010) contributions through the self-discrepancy theory are valuable extensions to the theory of personality and distress. It should be noted that when developing conditions of worth within the self-structure there will be many sources from which they can be introjected. What this means is that the 'other' source is often initially likely to be caregivers but soon the sources can extend to include friends, other authorities such as teachers in schools, then peer groups and aspects of culture including popular and more traditional elements such as religion and attitudinal prejudices including all forms of discrimination which may be interpersonal or institutional. Hence, the discrepancies that people might experience are often likely to be multiple in kind and form a complex set of intrapersonal relationships. For the PCE-CfD therapist it is essential to remain open to the complexity and not rush to assuming that the 'reason' for the client's distress is easy to understand and/or formulate. Humans are complex beings and there are always more intricate and highly differentiated ways of knowing ourselves.

There are other types of discrepant dialogue between configurations of self that make significant contributions to the PCE-CfD conceptualisation of depression, and these can be grouped under the heading 'other self-configuration dialogues'.

Other self-configuration dialogues

As has been shown, there is a common-sense basis for understanding dialogues between two or more configurations of self. These configurations are not 'multiple personalities' in the clinically accepted sense of the term (for detailed analysis of the difference, see DSM-5, compared with a discussion in terms of EFT, see Elliott, Watson, Goldman & Greenberg, 2004), but they can be experienced as distinct entities with their own agendas, aims and characteristics. Nor are they 'voices' as in the commonly used term 'hearing voices' describing a symptom of psychosis, but they are often experienced as having a voice, and they might even generate subvocal expressions, particularly negative ones. However, there is an immensely helpful metaphor of voice that was used by Stiles, Meshot, Anderson & Sloan (1992) in conceptualising these self-configurations that refer to 'problematic experiences' where each experience has a representative voice that is difficult to assimilate into the gestalt of the self-structure. It does not require a leap of imagination to appreciate the reality of dialogue between these elements, since i) practitioners with scant experience will have encountered clients describing such experiences, and ii) most people with a modicum of self-awareness will in some sense share the experience.

In some psychotherapeutic approaches we find a taxonomy of configurations of self. The most basic of these is to sort them into 'pathological' and 'healthy', 'adaptive' and 'maladaptive' or, in PCE terms, those that are 'for growth' and those that are 'not for growth'. PCE-CfD does not assign a value to self-configurations from an external frame of reference. In PCE-CfD, the 'problem' resides in the lived distress which follows from the level of tension and nature of the incongruence itself and any further value is attached by the client; that is, the client decides on the importance and meaning of the tension. Many, if not most people live with some level of tension due to self-discrepancy or incongruence. The degree and type of conflict and the resultant amount of disturbance is what brings people to seek help.

As a phenomenological approach, the first position in PCE-CfD – both in theory and in practice – is to let the description of the nature and explanation of the function reside with the client in question. Furthermore, in the context of the in-session practice of PCE-CfD, 'off the shelf' psychiatric diagnoses are regarded as potentially stigmatising and antitherapeutic. However, it is instructive to understand that there are some well-defined, commonly experienced patterns of self-configuration and resultant dialogue which are associated with the experience of the symptoms of depression. Hence PCE-CfD incorporates the concepts of conflict splits and self–inner-critic dialogue derived from EFT (Elliott et al., 2004).

Conflict splits

To acknowledge the origin (EFT) of the importance of this cluster of processes, the vocabulary is retained and the term 'conflict-splits' is used, as it is almost self-explanatory. Some theorists and approaches understand the dynamics between differing aspects of the self as 'splits', and when two elements of the self are in opposition this is known as a 'conflict-split'. PCE-CfD theory does not identify any self-elements as maladaptive or adaptive per se. Rather, it is the emotional responses to conflict between self-elements that produce distress or can be 'maladaptive' in terms of EFT theory.

In PCE-CfD, a conflict split is most simply expressed as an oppositional clash between two aspects or elements of the self. Rather than look for specific self-elements (ideal self, ought self and real self) in a conflict split, we just acknowledge and accept that two aspects are in conflict without naming or valuing either of them more than the other. Conflict splits are often out of, or barely on the edge of, the client's awareness so the first step is to help bring them more clearly into awareness if possible. Sometimes the client is readily able to do this themselves when they experience therapist empathic understanding and clarification. However, simply becoming aware of the conflicting configurations is often not sufficient to resolve the conflict. The therapeutic task is to clarify and differentiate the oppositional configurations and then encourage contact and dialogue between them. In the subsequent chapters on practice, this is shown through process-facilitative responses by the therapist to actively help clients process these conflicts.

> *PCE-CfD Theory of Depression*, Hypothesis 5: Symptoms of depression can result from conflicts between parts of the self that result in shutting down of experiencing, withdrawal, and feelings of guilt, unworthiness, hopelessness, helplessness, blame and so on.

Some conflict splits are more characteristic of depression, particularly those that result in the client shutting down experiencing or feeling guilty, blameworthy, unworthy, helpless or any of the other long list of experiences associated with the phenomenology of depression. For example, the critical self can beat down on the experiencing self to the point where the latter feels defeated and hopeless or totally collapses. Under these circumstances, the critical self can be experienced as the part that verbalises the 'shoulds', 'oughts' and evaluations of the self. This is one way Rogers' constructs of introjections and conditions of worth play out in the plural self.

This conflict and tension, which is a continuing process that maintains depression, is not a static state. Again, we see a relentless process of both wearing down resistance of adaptive parts of the self and aggregation of psychological tension over a prolonged period. The following are highly stylised examples, but for illustration, conflict splits expressed in everyday language might include:

'I am ambitious and want to apply for the job – you're too useless to get anywhere or do anything.'

'I feel bullied by her – you're not a real man – a real man can't be bullied by a woman.'

'I am being suffocated in this relationship – you are no good on your own.'

And the mechanics of the links between conflict splits and depression can work like this, for example:

'I am ambitious and want to apply for the job – you're too useless to get anywhere or do anything.'
- Can lead to paralysis, fear of rejection and a feeling of hopelessness: 'It's useless applying for jobs, I'll never get one.'

'I feel bullied by her – you're not a real man – a real man can't be bullied by a woman.'
- Can lead to a feeling of self-loathing: 'If I can't stand up to her I'm not a real man, I'm a useless feeble, excuse of a man.'

'I am being suffocated in this relationship – you are no good on your own.'
- Can lead to a feeling of helplessness: 'I have stopped thinking about the future because I know I'll not be able to change anything for the better.'

PCE-CfD holds that depression may result when the relationship between different aspects of the self is hostile (e.g. where a person experiences a punitive 'inner-critic') or oppressive (e.g. where an aspect of the self is suppressed or silenced). And to all these possible outcomes we can add the feeling of failure. It is not uncommon for people to have more than one conflict split and for these to have been persistent and pervasive, seeping into everyday life over many months.

Self-critical dialogues

A self-configuration that is relentlessly, negatively, evaluative is a common experience. Like other experiential therapies, in PCE-CfD this is called the 'inner-critic' or 'critical-self'. It is highlighted because, although several therapeutic approaches consider it a simple matter to 'reframe' the criticism as concern, exaggerated protection and so on, in PCE-CfD it is acknowledged that the unyielding, universal taint that can be brought by a critical-self can be a foundation for depression. Such a foundation can be long-standing and particularly stubborn. Even when brought into full awareness it can persist as an obstacle to fulfilled living unless actively worked with employing specific interventions.

Most experienced therapists will have encountered clients with vigorous inner-critics and might have wrestled with their own in personal therapy. It is a common experience and one that is occasionally alluded to in everyday conversation, for example 'Stop beating yourself up' and so on.

Examples of self-critical dialogue include:

> 'I know I passed my exams – but it was only just a pass; that's not good enough.'

- A double-edged sword and can lead to a pervasive feeling of being not good enough. This can lead to perfectionism – useful up to a point, but beyond this can lead to a self-destructive spiral.

> 'My boyfriend says he loves me but I'm not attractive. In fact when I look in the mirror I wince, I'm so ugly. He must be blind or stupid.'

- The client's inner-critic puts down the client and, importantly, significant others in order to maintain the logic of the negative self-image. This invalidates positive messages from outside as well as inside – represented in theory by Rogers' processes of denial and distortion of experience (Rogers, 1959: 205).

> 'I just can't get that voice that says "you are a failure" out of my head.'

- A stubborn and relentless feeling of failure will wear the client down and lead to feelings of hopelessness and helplessness, preventing them from being able to move on and self-heal.

> 'I wanted to be a dancer but wasn't disciplined enough. I'll never be really happy, but it's my fault.'

- Self-blame can be generalised to taint the future as well as explain past failures. It also sets up failures in the present.

A common feature of these critical-self messages is their totalising nature. They put a negative, unpleasant spin on the past, present and future, defeating hope and agency, and limiting the range of experiences – not only are positive experiences made less likely, but the palette of experience is reduced from vivid colours to plain grey. They invalidate all sources of affirmation from inside the person and from others. Having such an overactive inner-critic can also be a lonely, isolating experience, especially if the critic is shaming.

Shafran, Cooper and Fairburn (2002) suggest that a degree of self-criticism provides essential balance to the personality, a basis for self-improvement, and prevents the individual becoming complacent. From a PCE-CfD perspective the problem is the imbalance between elements of self-structure, not the fact that there are several self-configurations: an inner-critic configuration balanced by a resilient and self-believing configuration would not necessarily lead to psychological tension and distress. On the other hand, classical person-centred theory has it that people with little incongruence in the self-structure have a natural balance between the individual and the social and are inherently 'more understanding of others and ... more accepting of others as separate individuals' (Rogers, 1951: 520). This understanding of Rogers' original work renders the notion of the adaptive, or balancing, inner-critic unnecessary.

Either version of theory is supported by PCE-CfD practice in which the client's lived experience of psychological tension, their self-generated therapeutic tasks and collaborative, creative work with the counsellor are the drivers for therapeutic processes.

Other problematic psychological processes related to depression

PCE-CfD embraces a range of process-facilitating responses that are organised into a coherent theoretical framework. A further group, taken mostly from EFT, do not obviously spring from dialogues or discrepancies between self-configurations. In PCE-CfD most of these are best thought of simply as problematic psychological processes which have been identified through client observation and research (Elliott et al., 2004). They range from uncomplicated psychological processes which can block progress and suggest a simple method of resolution, to more fundamental processes requiring more extensive work.

These processes are listed here to give theory coordinates for specific potential features which commonly occur in experiences of depression. This will then allow us to map the theory on to practice in later chapters.

Emotional overwhelm

> *PCE-CfD Theory of Depression*, Hypothesis 6: Depression can be the result of, or exacerbated by, emotions that are too overwhelming to be faced or worked with in therapy.

Starting at the more theoretically elementary end of the continuum, PCE-CfD specifically acknowledges that people can get stuck, in life and therapy, in the face of overwhelming emotion (e.g. as a result of grief or a reaction to trauma etc.).

This overwhelm can present problems in two ways. First, the person may get frozen like a rabbit in headlights, unable to engage with an emotion because they sense the sheer scale of the emotional response that awaits them and then, quite reasonably, avoid it at all costs or simply come to an emotional standstill. In PCE-CfD theory and practice we do not cast an individual's behaviour as 'avoidant' or 'resistant'. We understand that we are all doing the best we can to survive and maintain ourselves in the face of difficult experiences. From Rogers' (1961: 125–59) 'process conception of psychotherapy' we know that until Stage 5 (out of seven) the immediate, present experience of feelings is mistrusted and feared.

This gives the first set of theory coordinates for which PCE-CfD practice must have a strategy.

Second, we know that sometimes people do try to engage with their emotions. They know that feelings are important and somehow represent a road to health if only they were not so scary, dark and simply huge. They make repeated attempts to let their feelings flow, and indeed they might spend hours weeping, but seem unable to move on – on each attempt they experience the full depth of their feelings, only to feel brief relief and return to square one.

The difficulty here is that whilst they have experienced their emotions, they have not worked with them, no change has taken place, no realignment or other adjustments in the self-structure have spontaneously occurred. In PCE-CfD theory, experience itself is not necessarily a change process – it might be for a few people, but for many more, some other change process must be engaged. One problem is that the sheer depth and size of the emotions involved mean that they are too big to be worked with – they need to be cut down to a digestible size.

Another problem can be the masking of a helpful, adaptive emotion by a more intense unhelpful maladaptive emotion. What is 'helpful' or 'unhelpful' is uniquely determined by the context and personal responses of the client in question. PCE-CfD practice provides appropriate ways of working with both scenarios of emotional overwhelm, which will be explored throughout the next few chapters focusing on practice.

Problematic reaction points

> *PCE-CfD Theory of Depression*, Hypothesis 7: Some aspects of depression can be the result of, or exacerbated by, puzzling, unexplained experiences which feel exaggerated or out of character.

There is the tendency for some clients to get stuck in the experience of having an unexplainable, uncharacteristic reaction to a situation. This experience can be understood at two levels. First is when the client feels a deep sense of their reaction being *absolutely* uncharacteristic, behaviourally or emotionally, indeed so out-of-character that the reaction doesn't seem to belong to them. Such experiences can be frightening to the extent that the person will avoid them, often at great cost in terms of shutting off areas of experience, avoiding activities and situations. Feeling inauthentic, incongruent, and having the immediate sense that everyone can see that you are not who you say you are, may lead to intrapersonal, interpersonal and social withdrawal. This simply adds to the common experience of feeling that they are watching their lives from a third-person position. Problematic reaction points can also result in self-criticism, possibly adding further fuel to an already active internal inner-critic (above). The problem is that when the client is not inhabiting their experience, that is not agentically in touch with it, the client cannot gain any purchase on the problematic behaviour in order to change it.

Rogers (1951) connects this kind of experience with a self-structure based on the introjection of values and the subsequent denial of 'organic experiences and needs which have not been symbolized' (p. 509). This links to the PCE-CfD understanding of the embodied self – organic needs and experiences can be thought of as bodily needs and experiences. In the case of problematic reaction points, the client is unable to inhabit their experience. There is such dissonance between the bodily needs and the lived sense of introjected self that the bodily experiences seem so alien as to be 'not me', and the shock of this can stop a client in their tracks. This raises an immediate anxiety and a sustained shadow is cast over the trustworthiness of experience, leading to withdrawal on many levels, as explained above.

Second is a much more superficial experience where the reaction may be puzzling, nagging or unclear, feel somewhat uncharacteristic, over-exaggerated, and can cause a persistent anxiety or cast a dark shadow of doubt on a situation, relationship or any life event, causing the person to avoid thinking about or otherwise engaging with the experience. In EFT these problematic reaction points are considered to be not only a driver of some symptoms of depression, they can also be an obstacle to progress in therapy or a presenting problem; that is, the client begins therapy by bringing this puzzle, possibly one that has been nagging at them for some time, making them feel low.

Meaning protests

> *PCE-CfD Theory of Depression*, Hypothesis 8: Some aspects of depression can be the result of having a cherished belief about the world destroyed.

Many readers will recognise that moment in our lives when something challenges or destroys a cherished belief about the world or life. The more central the belief is to our sense of self or identity, the greater will the reaction be. The feelings of shock, surprise, injustice, outrage, violation and anger can feel overwhelming and disabling. Sometimes it is such a violation of our understanding of life that the feelings can persevere for a long time, taint almost all experiences and shake our faith. The resultant constellation of feelings is called a 'meaning protest'. Nothing short of the meaning for living has been shaken.

In terms of personality theory, it might be that such a belief has been incorporated into the self-structure by a process of authentic organismic evaluation. In such cases the belief would be expected to be flexible and therefore reviewable in the light of subsequent changes in circumstance. Alternatively, beliefs can be introjected: that is, taken in under threat, whole, from the experience of significant others, along with the values put on them by others. With regard to meaning protests the key point is not whether the belief is introjected or the result of organismic evaluation. The problem arises simply because the belief is 'cherished' (i.e. central to the self-structure). Whilst we might expect authentically incorporated experiences to remain reviewable, up to a point, we also know that the whole self-structure can become rigid as a result of threat, so we must expect a reaction of distress when any cherished belief is destroyed. How flexible the self-structure is at the time of the challenge is the important matter.

Beliefs that provide a foundation against which the unfolding narrative of our lives is set might be something like: 'true love lasts forever'; 'a job is for life'; 'good people do not get ill and die'; 'the world is a safe place'; 'parents die before their children'. A belief about the world that is central to our identity might be: 'every man in this town has worked in the widget-making trade'; or 'a woman is only fulfilled when she has children'. Redundancy, bereavement, illness, disability, trauma and so on are the typical triggers for challenging such beliefs.

If such a belief is at the centre of our self, then the whole self-structure can feel shaken and collapse, and although we might refer to the result generically as 'psychological tension', it often leads to the experience of depression. For many people, the symptoms are also intractable. The psychological balance engendered by a cherished belief central to our understanding of justice, relationships, life itself, is not easily restored once destroyed. Even if the meaning protest is not a keystone in the self-structure, essential to its structure, it can still unleash a temporary tsunami of outrage. At the peak of this tidal wave of feelings, there can be a collapse, resulting in symptoms of depression which can outlast the outrage. Other clients may not be fully aware of exactly what the cherished belief is that has been violated. They just have a dull sense that something is wrong. Naming the meaning protest then expressing outrage and upset are often sufficient for the client to experience release and resolution, facilitated by empathic following. Meaning protests often leave lasting impressions, and sometimes these are sufficiently distressing to be a cause of depression that needs attention in therapy.

Unfinished business

> *PCE-CfD Theory of Depression,* Hypothesis 9: Some aspects of depression can be the result of particular types of incompletely processed life events.

'Unfinished business' is used to describe any issue which remains unresolved, coupled with associated unresolved emotions. Clients often report symptoms of depression beginning after distressing life events that have not been processed sufficiently to render them benign and allow the person to move on (e.g. redundancy, neglect, abandonment, bullying or other abuse, relationship breakdown, bereavement, etc.).

Many unfinished business scenarios involve another person, such as a deceased friend, partner or relative; a work colleague, manager; friend; current or ex-partner; parent; or authority figure such as a past teacher.

Some therapeutic approaches propose that unfinished business in adult life is a replayed archaic dynamic, a vestige of a past relationship, most likely a poor care-giving relationship in infancy that resulted in an attachment injury. In PCE-CfD theory it is unnecessary to ascribe any particular cause to unfinished business since, when offered the therapeutic conditions, some clients will be able to describe the circumstances surrounding unfinished business and let any meaning unfold. Resolution can follow spontaneously. For those whose experience remains unresolved and painful, more active techniques can be offered. These are explained further in the next few chapters focusing on the practice of PCE-CfD.

The nature of emotions

> *PCE-CfD Theory of Depression*, Hypothesis 10: Some aspects of depression can be the result of inappropriate and unhelpful learned emotions.

PCE-CfD conceptualises depression as resulting from particular types of emotional experience and emotional processes. This means that in practice the therapeutic focus should be on the client's feelings and emotions.

The relationship between emotion and psychological growth and wellbeing has been carefully established in the previous two chapters from a theoretical point of view and is worth briefly repeating here in our discussion of depression and PCE concepts. Regardless of the depressive processes experienced by clients (self-discrepancy, self-critical dialogues, unfinished business etc.), a core issue is how clients relate to their emotional experience. From the PCE-CfD point of view, greater openness to feelings is associated with lower levels of depression and better psychological health, but in supporting clients, counsellors should be alert to the nuances and subtleties of how feelings are expressed. For example, to regularly experience core maladaptive feelings of worthlessness is likely to result in unsatisfying, unpleasant responses and behaviour sets that will beget further unfulfilling, uncomfortable and noxious cycles of experience, reinforcing depressive symptoms. Similarly, to express unhelpful secondary reactive emotions, such as guilt as opposed to helpful, adaptive anger, can deprive clients of the resources necessary to assert themselves and get their needs met. Using emotional expression to manipulate others can also have negative consequences, such as the type of unhappy interpersonal relationships that are often associated with depression.

In EFT it is understood that there is an optimal level of emotional arousal for processing emotion, and difficulties in achieving this are often associated with anxiety and depression. These elaborations of understanding of emotions are of interest as the background to PCE-CfD theory and practice. It is important for PCE-CfD practitioners to understand that being emotional does not itself necessarily have any therapeutic benefit for clients: the quality and the kind of emotional arousal is important. The PCE-CfD definition of emotional wellbeing is a client restored to open, authentic processing of fluid adaptive emotions – a life facilitated by fit-for-purpose emotions which change according to circumstances. PCE-CfD puts the definitions of such value-laden terms as 'maladaptive', 'satisfying' and 'fulfilling' firmly in the control of the client. In terms of emotion, the prime therapeutic task of the PCE-CfD practitioner is to try to enter the client's world of emotions and their meanings without any hint of judgement.

This chapter has provided a coherent and accessible theoretical account for the phenomenon of depression. The sections above also offer the coordinates for practice and articulate the theory with the action of the PCE-CfD therapist. In summary, this chapter has considered the theoretical account of depression for PCE-CfD and reviewed the application of the theory to practice. The theory of depression as developed by Sanders and Hill (2014) is robust whilst the evidence base might be said to be emerging.

Competences covered in this chapter

- **B1** – Knowledge of the philosophy and principles that inform the therapeutic approach
- **B2** – Knowledge of person-centred theories of human growth and development and the origins of psychological distress
- **B4** – Knowledge of the PCE conceptualisation of depression
- **S3** – Ability to help clients reflect on and develop emotional meanings
- **S4** – Ability to help clients make sense of experiences that are confusing and distressing

(Competences are listed in Appendix 1)

4

First Meetings and the Initial Phase Sessions

Chapter overview

- Case vignette: Alan and Jill
    - Meeting your client
    - Making an assessment (generic and of risk or harm)
    - Completing measures
    - Establishing the relationship
    - Agreeing the tasks and goals
- Working briefly

So far in this book the core theory of PCE-CfD has been introduced, followed by the PCE-CfD theory specific to the phenomenology of depression. In the next few chapters the practice of PCE-CfD will be explored across a course of sessions using a range of case examples. These case examples will track a selection of the many factors that therapists and clients experience over the beginning, middle and final phases of therapy. In this chapter the first meeting and subsequent few sessions of therapy will be explored by following one client–therapist relationship. The chapter will look at some of the issues faced when first engaging with a client experiencing depression. These issues will be considered in the context of a PCE-CfD therapy relationship.

Exploring these case examples will bring many of the theoretical and conceptual issues discussed so far into a more tangible and real-life perspective. Short case examples in the form of vignettes using fictionalised therapy transcripts will convey the challenges presented for PCE-CfD therapists. For example, in PCE-CfD we need to consider issues related to working in a time-limited context, completing outcome measures such as the National Minimum Data Set (NMDS), or facing and addressing the responsibility of risk of suicide within a client group where risk is significantly increased. These vignettes are symbolic of the real world of therapy and, whilst they are idealised scenarios created to make a point, they do not pretend to be able to convey the degree of complexity that is often involved in the work. The real world of PCE-CfD is often going to be far more complicated and much less straightforward than presented here. However, the vignettes should give some idea as to how many of the prominent issues might be faced and can be addressed and overcome.

In this chapter we will follow the case of Alan who is working with a therapist called Jill. The text for the vignettes is set out in a tabulated format divided into three columns. In the far-left column is the annotation for the speaker where T = Therapist and C = Client; a number is also added to show the speaker turn, which can be helpful for supporting discussions and orienting to specific responses when using the vignettes for group work in training courses. The middle column is the actual client–therapist dialogue and in the right-hand column there will often be reflective discussion about the therapist's internal process, therapeutic task, or indicators for when and how the therapist might be providing evidence for the approach based on the PCEPS (more discussion on the PCEPS later in the book). The first edition of this book also listed competences within the dialogues, however, in this edition the competences are provided as a full list together with the competence map in Appendix 1 and at the end of each chapter where they have been identified.

The transcripts are sometimes fictionalised and edited from the first edition (Sanders & Hill, 2014) or will have been freshly created for this latest edition. The case examples were all based on many years of experience of working with clients who were depressed and consider the way that PCE-CfD might be practised. The aim is to offer a 'how to' approach when working in a PCE-CfD way but not a prescription for how others 'should' do it. Therapist styles vary significantly and as much as there are competences to be adhered to there are innumerable ways that these can be expressed by therapists. The reflective commentary on the other hand is an opportunity that offers the chance to develop insight and understanding of the therapists' thinking and feeling process as they engage in therapy with the clients. It is intended to shed light on complex decisions that might be faced in a therapeutic setting, such as helping the client to determine what they might wish to focus on at the start of therapy, when and how best to introduce the minimum dataset, or consider issues of risk and suicide. Over the next few chapters we shall explore these and much more.

Case Vignette: Alan and Jill

Client Alan – Therapist Jill

Alan is a white, British, 55-year-old engineering equipment salesman, married with two grown-up children. He arrives at his GP's surgery in something of a personal crisis. He has been sleeping poorly, has difficulty concentrating, is constantly tired, has lost interest in sex and has a persistent low mood. He has also lost interest in his work, which has previously been a source of interest and pride. He went to the doctor on the insistence of his wife who on two occasions found him asleep at his computer whilst working at home during the day. The final straw for her was when she found him weeping in the kitchen without being able to explain why. Alan's GP, Dr Clayton, has been the family doctor for 15 years and a quick look through Alan's records showed that he was an infrequent visitor to the surgery, with a good level of general health. It was clear that Alan is intelligent, active and takes an interest in his health, so Dr Clayton immediately referred him to Prit in the IAPT services for assessment.

At the assessment Alan was not thought to pose any risks to himself or others and met the diagnostic criteria for PCE-CfD. Prit referred him to Jill, an experienced PCE-CfD therapist working for a service commissioned to provide therapy within the surgery.

Session 1

T1.	Hello Alan. My name's Jill. I see you've got the leaflet there explaining PCE-CfD. Have you had a chance to read it?	Jill likes to make sure that clients are given the Department of Health booklet as part of the assessment process or by the service receptionist.
C1.	Yes, yes.	Although not all the therapies are offered by her service, she finds that most clients do read through it. It can lead to productive discussion about what will happen in the sessions: for example, it gives her an opportunity to get some basic information about the client's expectations and later, for example, to introduce the time-limited nature of PCE-CfD. Jill is also checking that PCE-CfD is going to be a suitable approach for Alan.
T2.	OK, there are a couple of things I need to go through with you before we get to talk more about why you're here.	
C2.	[*Nervous smile.*] OK.	
T3.	Did you choose PCE-CfD yourself, or did someone tell you it would be right for you? Maybe you looked at what was available and thought it would be the best for you?	

C3.	Well, I don't know what would be best. The guy I saw before asked me and I didn't know then either. He told me about one other treatment, but the waiting list was shortest for this and it looked OK. I think I want to talk about things, not read books about … well … you know …	
T4.	No, of course, it is difficult to choose, it sounds as though the short waiting list was important and you wanted someone to actually talk to rather than get advice from a book or a computer, is that right?	Jill is spending the first part of the first session 'structuring' (see later in this chapter in sections on working briefly), establishing the ground in both what she says and how she says it.
C4.	Well, I went to the doctor's because my wife was worried and I agreed with her that I needed to sort myself out. She was worried, so I thought I'd better get going as soon as possible. Is that OK?	
T5.	Right, you wanted to do something about how you were feeling as quickly as possible because your wife was worried. And you agreed with her, that there was something to be concerned about, by the sound of things.	She responds empathically to get a clearer sense of what has brought Alan to the service in his own words.
C5.	[Nods.] Yeah.	
T6.	That's what brings you here today. So you've seen the leaflet, yes? [Alan nods] and you might have read that we've got up to twenty sessions to work together.	Jill uses the fact that Alan has seen the leaflet to introduce the idea of his aims for the sessions and to find out, even at this early stage, that his expectations about PCE-CfD are in line with what she thinks is possible.
C6.	Mm, hmm.	
T7.	Do you have any questions about what this counselling involves? Anything at all?	
C7.	I've not been to counselling before so I don't know what to do. I suppose you'll give me suggestions about what to do, erm … to feel, you know … better.	
T8.	OK, it sounds as though you're a bit nervous, and you're guessing that I'll be giving you suggestions about how to deal with depression.	

(Continued)

(Continued)

C8.	I suppose so.	
T9.	OK, well, let's see, in PCE-CfD there are a couple of important things to know. One is that though you might not think it right now, I think that you will have some good ideas about what might work for you. Another is that I will give you plenty of time to talk about what's going on for you that you might think is important. That's where we'll start, me listening and you talking. In fact, that is what we will do for most of the time. There might be a few times when I think of something that might be useful to do here in the session, and I'll say so. It'll be up to you if you think it's a good idea or not ... Also, talking like this can often bring up a lot of feelings, sometimes strong ones ... and that's completely normal.	This is direct structuring – Jill is explaining what is likely to happen in PCE-CfD, and again is taking the opportunity made by what Alan has said. Many such opportunities might arise in the first session. It is important that Alan knows from the outset that PCE-CfD will probably bring up strong emotions – the therapist needs to allow time to work with this. In PCE-CfD the capacity of a therapist to help the client regulate their emotional arousal is a key competency and is a feature on the Person-Centred and Experiential Psychotherapy Scale (PCEPS).
C9.	Can I be honest?	
T10.	Of course, please do. That's important. I really want to hear what's going on for you ... whatever it is ...	Jill is emphasising and demonstrating that it's both safe and important for Alan to be honest and that she will treat his honesty, along with everything else he says, respectfully.
C10.	I don't see how that will work. I erm ... I don't know. I don't know what would work.	
T11.	You don't think just talking will work, is that it? And you sounded really, er, hopeless then ... not knowing what would work.	Jill is aware that feeling hopeless is also a common experience in depression and uses this knowledge to check if that's something she could hear in Alan's voice. This is showing good emotion specificity.
C11.	Did I? Yes, maybe. I need this to work.	
T12.	It's very important that these sessions actually help. You need this to work. And right now, it just doesn't look as though it's going to.	Jill is achieving a number of things in these simple responses: she is making sure Alan is clear about what to expect from PCE-CfD, checking whether the therapy is really suited to him. She is making no attempt to 'shoe-horn' him into the therapy. She is leaving the decision making up to him and, when he has made his decision, she affirms this.
C12.	Well, I ... I think ... I, er ... I'll give it a go. Like my Dad used to say, don't do it if you can't do it properly. I'll give it a go.	

T13.	OK Alan, what I can I hear is that this is so important for you, it *must* work, and you will give it your best shot.	
C13.	Yeah, that's it. So what's next?	
T14.	OK, it sounds as though you want to get on. That's OK with me. And we can take a minute or two, well actually a few minutes at the end of each subsequent session to see how *we* think things are going – what, if anything, has been helpful and what has not. I'll also ask you to do a set of questionnaires at the start of each session – this is the official way of keeping track of whether the counselling is helping or not. Does that sound OK?	Again, Jill takes her lead from issues raised by Alan. This time to introduce the fact that it is important to continuously evaluate the sessions, including what Alan does *not* find helpful. She also introduces the fact that there will be some formal measures to evaluate progress.
C14.	Erm, OK, right, that's fine, but what if it's not working straightaway?	
T15.	Well, it's a good idea to give it a bit of a time, a few sessions, because sometimes things can take a little while to change. Also, if you're concerned that we'd just stop after the first session or two just because the forms tell us it's not working, there's no need to worry. We'll give it plenty of time. The forms are also to collect information to research the best ways of helping people. [*Pause.*] I've been given the assessment report from your meeting with Prit, and it's got some detail of the things that you discussed. How about we complete the measures for this first session and then we can carry on talking about why you are here.	
C15.	[*Alan nods in agreement and the forms are completed. Jill checks them quickly to check whether any suicide or serious risk has been indicated.*]	

(Continued)

(Continued)

T16.	Right … it's important we start off on the right foot, and what I would prefer to do is for you to tell me why you're here in your own words. It means I get to hear it from you, in your own words, since you know best why you're here, and second it might be that things have changed since you saw Prit, what, three weeks ago? You might feel better or worse, or no different. Would that be OK?	This is more structuring – here Jill is explaining and demonstrating that for her, Alan's story is paramount, his experience is the fuel for the therapeutic process, and that things can change. It also continues to show him that he is in control of the process.
C16.	Fine by me … Now?	Jill thinks that she and Alan have made good psychological contact and quickly formed the impression that he was able to actively engage with the therapeutic process – he was keen to 'sort himself out' as he put it on introducing himself.
T17.	Yes, in your own time, there's no need to rush.	
C17.	[*Pause of about 30 seconds.*] Erm, it's difficult to know where to start. I don't really know where … right now I feel OK, but that's because I'm here, talking to you. When I get home I'll just feel crap …	

After a hesitating start, Alan talks about his experiences in terms that can fit well into the PCE-CfD theory for depression. Nothing much has changed for him since the assessment interview. Jill is empathic, genuine and accepting. She notices that Alan sticks to his task. He is comfortable with the way Jill is empathically helping them both find their way into the sessions. After about 10 minutes of Alan describing his experiences, in fairly distanced terms, Jill says …

T18.	I hope I've followed you there [*Alan nods.*] and I can really tell just how much you want to get from this session. It feels that there is a kind of sense that you have of what you'd like to get from the counselling. But this isn't really, clearly, formed for you yet, is that right?	
C18.	[*After a short pause.*] I want to just get better, back to the way I was. But I can't see a way of doing that. I used to be organised, you know, get things done, enjoy going out … the whole thing. Now I can't think straight and can't or don't even want to do anything. So … just get back my old self, really.	Statements like 'get back to the way I was' and 'get my old self back' can be signposts to self-discrepancies – between ideal (old) self and experienced self. Jill makes a mental note but thinks it's too early to dive in to more direct work on processing these

T19.	You put it very simply 'to get better', and 'get your old self back' – that's what you want, and at the same time, it seems almost impossible to you. You can't see how you can do it, and more than that you can't find either the right direction to go in, nor the motivation, the 'get-up-and-go'.	discrepancies in a more explicit way. Sometimes helping to really unpack a person's goals helps them get a better handle on the problem, helps them get more detail and a clearer understanding can emerge. Jill won't use any goals Alan comes up with to tie up the therapeutic process or make it completely goal-oriented. The goals Alan sets are a way into Alan's world and might provide useful signposts for them both as things unfold.
C19.	No, that's right, I don't know what to do and even if I did, I'm not sure I'd actually do it when I get up in the morning. Don't know what to do ... it's like being in a fog, stumbling around.	
T20.	In a fog. You have to go slowly in a fog and sometimes you get lost. Is that how it feels?	Jill is helping Alan work with his own metaphor to help him articulate his feelings.
C20.	Well not slow, but, yes ... just lost and ... then hopeless. Like there's no way out.	Jill is patient and empathic, helping Alan elaborate and clarify his experience until a more specific goal emerges. Sometimes this doesn't happen, and a client is left with an indistinct or global goal. Alan has goals 'to feel better' and get his old self back, but grinds to a halt.
T21.	There's no way out. [*Flat reflection, not a question.*]	
C21.	Like ... in a maze that's it, in a fog and in a maze. Just no way out, no point in looking, so just go to sleep. Well, I wish I could ... but ...	

Alan continues to talk until just over 10 minutes before the end of the session, Jill carries on experiencing and communicating the therapeutic conditions, empathically understanding Alan from within his own frame of reference and focusing on catching the core meaning that Alan is expressing. Jill has found it easy to experience and demonstrate an accepting presence towards Alan and she feels warmth for him. Continuing to explore tentative goals and aims, Alan talks about work, especially how much pressure the whole sales team is under. Now the job is completely different from when he started. He started off talking about how everyone was suffering and moved on to talk about his own difficulties, just not having the time to get the job done the way he wants to – too much paperwork and not enough time talking to customers. He talked about being snowed under, putting jobs to one side and not fulfilling his quotas. He said the job was impossible.

He didn't talk at all about his family, except to say that he loved his wife and grown-up children. He then brought up the topic of his 'old self' again.

(Continued)

(Continued)

T22.	Yes, you mentioned 'your old self' earlier, but I didn't give you a chance to say much more about it. There seems to be an 'old you' you've lost touch with that used to be organised and get things done.	Jill thinks there's sufficient time left to at least start to work with this, so she returns to Alan's need to get back to his old self. It turns out to be a clear signpost to a discrepancy between the way he experiences himself now and the way he wants to be (his old self).
C22.	Yeah, I used to be 'Mr Organised', planned everything, and to be honest, I got it all done as well. I was good at that sort of thing. Everything sorted, you know.	
T23.	Mr Organised … sounds trustworthy …	
C23.	Yes, but not now …	
T24.	Not now. Now … you say you can't think straight and don't want to do anything … this new you seems quite different from Mr Organised.	Empathic responding allows Alan to describe and clarify different configurations – bringing them into thoughtful awareness possibly for the first time. This in itself can be part of the therapeutic change.
C24.	Yeah. Just no comparison .. like two different people. Can't imagine what it was like …	
T25.	So, on the one hand there's the organised trustworthy, old you, and now, today you feel all over the place, no get-up-and-go, can't think straight.	
C25.	Yeah … that's me.	

Jill empathises, which helps differentiate further the discrepancy between the old Alan and how he feels now to get a clearer sense of what 'getting my old self back' means to him (having more energy, being more organised, going out more and having fun). Alan and Jill tentatively set these as more specific goals for their time together. Then with just a few minutes to go …

T26.	I promised that we'd have a chance to see whether you think it's been useful today, whether anything in particular has helped, or anything has not helped. Have you got any thoughts?	Experienced practitioners know that sometimes, having the time and space to talk can help. The feeling of relief or 'lightness' might be short lived, or enduring – it's impossible to predict.
C26.	Erm, er … yes, er … well I've got something out of just talking. I just realised that I hadn't actually talked to anyone. I didn't want to worry my wife, didn't want to admit to this feeling, you know, at work.	

T27.	OK, so talking …
C27.	I can't say it's … made me feel, let's see … better. No, but I do feel a bit, lighter. I thought at the beginning that it would be a waste of time, but I'll come back. Yes, it's been OK. Better than I thought.
T28.	OK, so better than you thought it was going to be and you feel lighter. Anything that wasn't helpful?
C28.	No, not really. [*They agree a time for their next meeting and say goodbye to one another.*]

Session 2

Alan arrived on time for his second session and started by telling Jill that he felt as though he had gone 'back to square one' the day after the first session. He was flat and disappointed, and it only made him feel more hopeless and beyond help. This opening had led to him being able to talk more about his symptoms of depression, and he talked about them as though they were 'out there', things that had happened to him in the past, albeit only yesterday, and he described his experiences in rather precise language, almost as though he was describing something out of a textbook.

Jill listened empathically. She reflected the fact that he sounded flat and disconnected from the things he was talking about, but Alan did not take this up. She realised that there were several opportunities to use a technique to help Alan be more in touch with his experience, such as going inside and making a space, but she thought it was more important to build a strong relationship and just as important to take any opportunities to tentatively enter Alan's world when invited.

About 35 minutes into the session, Alan returned to talking about work. Again, he compared the past and the present, how much things had changed and how the company piled on the work. He was caught in a vicious cycle: the better he was at his job, the more they gave him to do, and although he was on commission, he didn't enjoy his work anymore. Then he paused, obviously deep in thought and distracted.

(Continued)

(Continued)

C1.	Work ... [*Deep sigh.*] I ... I feel beaten by it. I'm ... useless. [*Looks at Jill, then out of the window, looks uncomfortable and a little fearful.*]	
T1.	[*After a pause.*] Beaten by work and useless. ... That's some combination ...	
C2.	And I don't know what to do about it. Bloody useless!	
T2.	You've talked much about work in this session and the last, and you sound a mixture of, almost angry, and then as you've just said, beaten and useless. In your voice you then sound angry with yourself for being useless. Would that be right?	Jill is tentatively empathically responding to Alan's implicit feelings – carefully checking that she is accurate in her reflections. These thoughts and feelings that Alan is expressing don't make a logical whole picture, but Jill isn't concerned. She's not looking for logic or reason, nor lack of, either. She's really empathically following Alan, making sense where possible, or letting things hang where they are left. Therapists can feel pushed to 'do something' when there are a specified number of sessions available, but Jill thinks that patience, empathic understanding and building her relationship with Alan is the right thing to do. She has seen some small changes already in what he is talking about and the way he talks about it. For now, she is standing beside Alan in his 'not knowing what to do'. She doesn't judge this or suggest any solutions.
C3.	Well, I, erm, yes, work is ... work is important isn't it? What else, well, the kids, of course, but you have to earn money don't you?	
T3.	It's important to earn money for your family. But you feel useless.	
C4.	Yes. And I don't know what to do. That's why I'm useless.	
T4.	So, it's important for you to earn money for your family, but you feel useless because ... it sounds like you're at the end of your tether when you say you don't know what to do.	
C5.	No, it's hopeless. I mean yes, I don't know what to do. It doesn't make sense. I get stuck thinking about it. I can't sort it out, make sense, do anything. What's the point? If it wasn't for the kids ...	
T5.	That's a real dead end by the sound of it – nowhere to go – and if it wasn't for the kids ... ?	Jill continues to be aware that Alan's sense of hopelessness is a prominent experience for him and is ready to pick this up if and when necessary.
C6.	No, that's when I pull myself up short, there's a part of me that thinks I have a responsibility for them still, but then I hit the deck again and still can't get anywhere.	

T6.	There's a part of you that thinks you have a responsibility for your children, even though they're grown up, and that part of you stops you from really, seriously thinking about … killing yourself? Is that what you were not saying?	At this point, it would be routine for NHS therapists to risk assess and if appropriate give advice about sources of support for episodes of suicidal ideation. In this case, Alan's risk factors are not that severe or critical.
C7.	Well, yes, but it sounds worse when you say it like that. I've thought about it. I think about it a lot, but it's just thoughts. Really, I'm a coward. Then I say to myself – don't be so stupid. What about the kids! I can hear my Dad's voice saying, 'It's the coward's way out – be a man Al. Bloody pull yourself together' … He would think I was useless.	Although he is male, his age is not a risk factor, he is in a stable relationship and employed (and so is not socially isolated), has no history of self-harm or drug/alcohol abuse. He is talking in measured terms about self – configuration dialogue, rather than clear suicidal ideation. Jill notes this and will keep a watchful eye on any developments.
T7.	It sounds like there's a part of you that gets really defeated, hopeless and helpless, then another part of you that thinks of the kids and pulls back from the brink. Is there another part of you that almost speaks with your Dad's voice, saying 'Be a man, Al. Bloody pull yourself together!'?	Jill can hear the parts of Alan's self – his configurations of self – in dialogue here and thinks it might help to make this a little clearer in her reflections.
C8.	Yes, and you know what? I just get lost in the middle. Lost …	
T8.	And in the middle of it all you get lost – not knowing which one to listen to, maybe, or what to do.	
C9.	[*Alan nods in agreement with Jill's reflection.*]	
T9.	OK, Alan it's never a good time to draw things to a close, and it might feel like it's all hanging in mid-air, but if you would like me to, after we've completed the dataset, I can remind you where we finished off today and see if any of these feelings are still around for you at the beginning of the next session. What do you think?	

(Continued)

(Continued)

Jill draws the session to a close. Things are hanging in mid-air a little. She finishes off by asking whether anything has been particularly helpful or unhelpful and whether Alan thinks the work they are doing is meeting his goals. He says he still doesn't know yet but will be back next time. Jill asks if there's anything Alan would like to say or do to help him finish off before he goes back outside into the 'real world'. He smiles and says he'll be fine. They book another appointment.

Session 3

T1.	Okay, thanks Alan for completing the forms. I'm here to listen to whatever you want to talk about, and I promised at the end of the last session to remind you of where we left off. Do you still want me to do that?	
C1.	Yes, I remember. You don't need to remind me, I was thinking about it all the way home and for the next couple of days. What I was thinking about was my Dad. I think about him a lot.	
T2.	Uh, huh. I see, would you like to talk more about that?	
C2.	Yes ... I suppose I haven't actually talked about him since he died. But, then I, er, I don't really know why I should have.	
T3.	You just saw no need to talk about your Dad.	Alan's feelings about his Dad looked as though they caught him by surprise, and they caught Jill by surprise too (she noted this and almost as soon as she spoke she realised that her reflection about being taken by surprise might have been her own surprise coming out a little and decides to take it to supervision. Jill also realises that Alan's feelings are not clear at this moment. Strong, yes, but even though it looks like it, she doesn't want to jump to a conclusion that he might be sad or grieving. She waits for his feelings to become clear.
C3.	No, right but anyway, the thing is, I, I, [Eyes moisten and catches breath in almost a sob.] I, [Strangles a sob tries to compose himself, but tears stream down his face.]	
T4.	Feelings about your dad are still very present, Alan, and very strong by the look of things ... and you seem to be taken by surprise ...	
C4.	Yes, I, no, not really, just that I don't want to get into this [Sobs more.] ...	

Alan struggles for some time with expressing his feelings. Every time he tries to talk about his Dad, he breaks down. Jill sits with him for several minutes while Alan continues to struggle and return to speaking about his Dad. Jill reflects that he is determined to talk about his Dad, even though it is very difficult. After about 10 minutes, Alan says that this is exactly why he never talks about his Dad – he just can't without crying uncontrollably. He says that he crumbles and becomes afraid that he might never stop crying, so he puts it all away and gets on with life. He has a respite from crying ...

T5.	It seems just too overwhelming to even try to talk about your Dad, and yet at the same time, you want to. The feelings are just too big, too much, too ... something, right?	Here Jill has helped Alan clarify a therapeutic task (but there is no need for her to name it as such). He wants to talk about his Dad without being stopped in his tracks by the wave of emotion that accompanies every effort to talk. One possibility would be to wait until Alan is ready in his own time. This might take more time than is comfortably available in time-limited work like PCE-CfD.
C5.	Yes, I want to but it's like a big wave ...	
T6.	And you can't stand up to it.	
C6.	Right.	
T7.	So, would you like to try something to try to get those feelings to a level so you can feel the feelings, but be able to talk about your dad as well?	What follows is an example of Jill helping Alan with emotion regulation and is specifically aimed at helping Alan manage the overwhelming emotions so that he can work on his issues about his Dad. Jill makes a tentative offer.
C7.	Yes, but I can't see how I can do that.	
T8.	Well, if you want to give this a try, we can see how you do ... first, can you think of a safe place, may be from your childhood, it could be anywhere, any place ... there's not a correct answer, just a space or place that for you signifies safety ...	
C8.	[*Pauses to think.*] Er ... yes, I don't know if it's right, erm ... shall I say? [*Jill nods 'uh-huh'.*] Well, it's not from when I was little, but when I was about 14 or 15, we had a shed in the yard that had just junk in it, and I made a kind of workshop, with my engines in it – I used to have a few steam engines. It was my own place ... heaven.	

(Continued)

(Continued)

T9.	OK, can you get a sense of it, what it was like, remember what it looked like, felt like?	Visualising or bringing to life a past experience can sometimes cause emotional over-arousal. Here, Jill is creatively helping Alan visualise an experience to help him regulate the feelings. In contrast, solid, straightforward empathic following keeps the emotional arousal at the level controlled by the client. This may be the preferred option in some situations but in this case Alan is finding the visualisation useful.
C9.	Oh yes, easily. No problem! [*Enthusiatically.*] I can smell it!	
T10.	OK, so in your imagination, now you can get a clear feeling of being there? [*Alan nods 'Mmmm'.*] And those strong feelings that come when you try to talk about your Dad, perhaps you can sense them, get a hint of them and how big and unmanageable they are? [*Alan nods 'Mmmm'.*] Try putting them somewhere safe, in that shed, it's up to you, erm, maybe in a cupboard if there are any, or … what seems good to you?	
C10.	Yes, a tin box, in a tin. I used to put my bits in tins, old biscuit tins, and I think they can go in there. [*After a pause of about 15 seconds.*] Shit! Oh, bloody hell, that's actually worked. I can feel a relief.	
T11.	So, the feelings are safe in the tin, do you want to check to see that they're still there? Now can you put the tin somewhere handy, but far enough away so as to be not in the way.	
C11.	Yeah, on the shelf, easy. I can still … no really, this is great … God, what a relief, yeah.	
T12.	OK, a real relief, that sounds good, yes? And, so how about, now that they're there, safe, thinking about talking about your Dad a little …	It's not necessary for Jill to give the emotion regulation idea a name (since there isn't any element of explicit psychoeducation in PCE-CfD) or extend it beyond the task of helping Alan work on the material relating to his Dad. He seems to adopt the idea very easily and so Jill can return to empathic following and counselling as usual.

C12.	OK, let's see, right well, I was 25 when he … died … and [*takes a deep breath*] I still feel, actually, OK, so I was 25 when he died and it was a shock for everyone. I was completely knocked for six, just flattened. He was my rock.

Alan spends the remaining time in the session talking about his Dad. He occasionally exclaims his surprise at being able to do so and Jill checks how he is doing with the feelings. A couple of times during the session he begins to cry a little and Jill stays with that, neither encouraging him to contain his feelings and put them away, nor get immersed in them. Alan seems able to regulate his feelings without any assistance or instruction, though Jill is ready to help with either, should Alan get overwhelmed again.

Alan begins to talk about his conflicting feelings about his Dad, love and grief, and frustration bordering on anger. His love and affection for his Dad is tempered by Alan's growing sense of burden about his Dad insisting on Alan 'being a man'. It is a start. Jill's contribution is genuine, non-judgmental empathic following – nothing more, nothing less.

At the end of this session, Alan says that this time he does feel helped. He is very positive about the session. He is still incredulous that he can manage the feelings that he has been afraid of for so long.

Session 4

T1.	Hi Alan, thanks for completing the forms. There seems to be some improvement according to the score on this measure. I'm ready to listen to whatever you want to talk about today.
C1.	Well, I actually felt better at the end of last week and it has stayed with me, sort of, so I'm feeling better. Know what I mean?
T2.	You felt better at the end of the session, and that feeling didn't die down like in previous weeks, and now you feel, erm, better about, and on top of, feeling better. Is that it?
C2.	Exactly. Yes. And I talked to Mary [Alan's wife] about it too.

(Continued)

(Continued)

Alan goes on to talk more about his Dad, specifically, wanting his Dad's approval and trying to 'be a man' in his Dad's terms, but resenting this. He realises how much he carries his Dad's values and voice inside him and how he admonishes himself if he fails to live up to his Dad's expectations. At the same time, he finally grieves for his Dad.

Jill is empathic, genuine and non-judgmental, accompanying Alan as (in theory terms) his self-structure restructures after realising how much he is influenced by his Dad's aims for him. This sounds easy, but took time and Alan hit a few very rough patches. Jill didn't intervene actively or immediately with techniques or suggestions of how to correct this experience. Alan was doing the work himself, after quickly realising that his powerful emotions didn't have to overwhelm him he was able to experience these more fully and begin to process the meaning they have for him.

Freed from his Dad's expectations, he decides to ask his employer if he can take his retirement package early. They agree to this and Alan and Mary decide to 'downsize' and see if any part-time jobs come up to keep them active.

In this vignette, the client Alan has begun to identify what is a significant factor in his life (his relationship with his father) and consider how this impacts his functioning and sense of self. The internalised messages about being a man, being able to cope and be capable were very strong conditions by which he experienced a sense of worth. Grief of his father's death, the pressure of work and life and these negative self-evaluations all contributed to his sense of worthlessness and hopelessness. The therapist was skilful and able to identify his motivation for change (get back to his old self) and the tension and incongruence between this and how he currently feels.

Jill was a patient therapist and was able to draw on her experience and trust that the PCE-CfD approach is a powerful therapy that can help clients make significant and meaningful changes in their lives without needing to rush in or push the client to achieve these. However, working in time limited settings, specifically those in IAPT, there is the added pressure of the 'effectiveness ideology' where the emphasis is on outcome. The sections below look a little more closely at some of the important issues for PCE-CfD in a healthcare setting or service where the number of sessions might be limited. The recommended number of sessions for PCE-CfD in an NHS or IAPT setting is 20, as per the training manual. The concept of working briefly will be considered next.

Working briefly

The sections below will consider the concept of working briefly. The aim is to highlight some of the issues that a PCE-CfD therapist, such as Jill, might have been considering around the work with Alan when the issue of time and limited session numbers form part of the therapeutic frame.

The parameters of time and limits bring several theoretical and practical matters into sharp focus. Tudor (2008: 19–20) asserts that structure, focus and direction in therapy are frequently conflated in our understanding and need to be looked at separately. He discusses the degree to which certain types of structure, focus and direction of therapy, and/or each session, are *encouraged* by limits. Consideration of time and limits also requires therapists to develop a contextual awareness of the notions of goals, accurate, ongoing, collaborative assessment of the client's needs and an understanding of when therapy is 'happening' and when it is 'finished' or completed. These words are put in quotes to indicate that each term signals a somewhat contentious idea. PCE therapies' identification of the client as the 'owner', and therefore driver and manager of the therapy process means that understandings of both progress in therapy, and when the client has achieved sufficient movement to feel able to discontinue therapy, are held by the client.

When relaxed service limits apply, and the client is put at the centre of the entire process, the therapist will follow the client in all respects – content, pace (including getting stuck), direction, limits (including duration of relationship, within ethical and safety boundaries) and so on. Whilst an idealised position, and unattainable for many, this is an important theoretical therapeutic position, validating the client's agency and encouraging the client's internal locus of evaluation. With the client in control, the PCE therapist would not diagnose 'resistance', 'denial' or 'avoidance' as client devices, nor would they have any strategy save congruent reflection. There would be nothing pressing the therapist to proceed at a pace any quicker than that set by the client's actualising tendency or to ask why the client is not (in the view of the therapist) attending to the salient problematic issues. The therapist would understand the client's actualising tendency to be directing the process for the maintenance and enhancement of the client. The therapist's strategy, if they cannot understand the client's process, would be to strive towards becoming more fully empathic.

A number of generic principles that underpin PCE-CfD as a brief model are worth bearing in mind:

- Therapists should be responsible for holding the therapeutic frame; that is, contractual issues should be clearly negotiated in the early stages and thoughtfully adhered to – the duration and number of sessions would obviously form a part of this.
- The importance of collaboration cannot be over-emphasised, to ensure the client can exercise the highest levels of autonomy and agency in both shaping the frame and engaging in the process of therapy.
- Remember that the client has come to therapy for a reason, something has prompted them. In exploring this, the therapist should work with the client, alert to and willing to agree a focus for the therapeutic work as it emerges for the client, and if/when this changes during the process of therapy, this should be discussed and made explicit. This creates shared understanding and clarity about what therapist and client are trying to achieve in therapy, maximising the likelihood of a meaningful outcome for the client.

- Regular in-session feedback can be used to review progress and to make collaborative decisions about any changes to the therapy and when the therapeutic relationship should come to an end. This feedback can include the client's feedback to the therapist about any aspect of their work and relationship and data produced through using outcome measures.
- Due to external circumstances, therapy may sometimes have to come to an end before the client is ready to finish. In such circumstances therapists should discuss with the client alternative sources of support that can be accessed post-therapy, and work to make the ending as constructive an experience as possible for the client.

Working briefly and assessment

In psychological helping, practitioners have three ways of apprehending the clients' needs for treatment: diagnosis, formulation and assessment. Whilst these procedures appear to share a general aim, they tackle the issue from quite different philosophical positions.

Diagnosis is the most formal of these procedures and is also the term most popularly used by the public at large. Some clients can find a diagnosis something of a relief, as they find it reassuring to have a name for, and validation of, their distress, and furthermore, diagnosis gives access to treatment. It implies a level of medicalisation and categorisation that makes it a contentious notion for probably the majority of PCE therapists. Bayne, Horton, Merry, Noyes and McMahon(1999) list the main PCE objections to diagnosis, and these help us tease out the differences between diagnosis and assessment. Then, incorporating Jerold Bozarth's (1998) comments on assessment, it is possible to assemble an approach to assessment suitable for PCE-CfD. Bayne's criticisms of diagnosis and labels are comprehensive and include:

- diagnostic labels are often poorly defined and meaningless
- labels can become self-fulfilling prophesies
- labels beget formulaic treatments
- labels focus on history rather than present experience and potential for future change
- practitioners can become preoccupied with pathology and underestimate a client's strengths
- diagnosis can lead clients to become dependent upon experts
- diagnostic labels have a superficial appearance of scientific objectivity.

However formidable these objections appear, they do help us understand that assessment does not equal diagnosis – assessment can be a process which facilitates therapeutic engagement rather than stifling it. Indeed, research shows that assessment interviews can have a therapeutic effect in and of themselves (Poston & Hanson, 2010). Appropriate explanations from the therapist set in a genuinely collaborative way of working, the therapist as companion rather than expert, and emphasis on the client's experience and narrative rather than diagnostic manual language, all contribute to constructing assessment positively as an assistance to therapy, not an obstacle.

In classical person-centred practice, the status of assessment is not clear-cut, since Bozarth (1998: 127) on the one hand declares that 'Psychological assessment as generally conceived is incongruent with the basic assumptions of client-centered theory', yet on the other hand goes on to discuss situations in which assessment may be considered by person-centred therapists, in the service of the client's 'self-authority' (p. 128). He lists three circumstances where person-centred therapists could engage in assessment by the use of measures:

- the client requests assessment or the use of measures
- the agency or professional setting may require assessment
- the client and therapist might have to make a decision regarding future treatment suggested by such mediators of therapeutic possibilities as agency protocols, funding or the law. Assessment or diagnostic tools might afford an 'objective' view which could inform the client's and therapist's decision. (pp. 128–31)

We can also adapt Bozarth's (p. 130) axioms for a model of person-centred careers counselling to PCE-CfD, to be applicable to assessment thus:

- the PCE-CfD practitioner has attitudes and behaviours which focus on promoting the inherent wisdom of the client
- there is an initial emphasis on a particular area of client concern, in this case, depression
- there are opportunities for the client to test their emerging concept of self with outcome measures
- the PCE-CfD practitioner has certain information and skills available to the client through which the goal of ameliorating depression can be implemented.

So, in psychological therapy services associated with PCE-CfD, assessment involves getting a sense of the problem from the client's own point of view, looking at the history and development of the problem(s), getting a sense of the client's resilience and vulnerabilities and collaboratively agreeing a course of therapy. It is hoped that this short section does more than render assessment barely acceptable: something that practitioners do – only because they *must*. The intention here is to lay the foundation for assessment to be creatively developed and implemented by PCE-CfD practitioners within their local service framework. It is a principal element of good practice when working briefly in NHS settings.

Working briefly with the experience of depression

PCE-CfD necessarily presses the client and therapist to work with the primary presenting issues associated with the experience of depression. It appears to impose a limit, a focus on the entire therapeutic endeavour: namely, to work with depression. However, we have seen already how varied the experiences of depression can be, both between clients and from moment-to-moment in the same client. Depression can be thought of as a complex set of experiences within a complex matrix of life circumstances. The client's experiences are often distressing and they will most likely be seeking relief from them, but the prime task of PCE-CfD is to identify and understand these experiences and seek resolution, rather than simply work specifically to ameliorate the distress at a relatively superficial level at the expense of changes to the experiential process of the client.

PCE-CfD may begin with the focus of 'working with depression', but with its modus operandi of following the client, the therapist will, together with the client, discover the salient intra- and inter-personal factors which are implicated in the psychological distress, and there is no telling where this will lead. We must remind ourselves that the client's internal wisdom – on which therapeutic movement in PCE-CfD is predicated – will most likely not absolutely follow diagnostic categories or theoretical systems, even though PCE-CfD does propose some tentative conceptual hypotheses (see Chapter 3). Therapists must not be distracted by the nature of, for example, time limits, focusing the therapeutic relationship on the limits themselves, rather than the experiences and therapeutic process of the client. Appreciating the internal wisdom of the client includes appreciating the client's ability creatively to engage with the world – specifically, creatively to engage with the limits of the current therapeutic relationship. Following the client is not simply the first position in PCE-CfD, it must be an enlightening omnipresence, even when practice becomes task-focused and specific. Following the client and trusting their actualising process will remind therapists just how creatively 'self-righting' (Bohart & Tallman, 1998, 2010) clients can be.

Working briefly and structure

Keith Tudor (2008) discusses how the imposition of time limits might lead the counsellor to think that it is necessary to impose some or more structure (in the sense of framework) on therapy sessions; that is, that formatting or sequencing the work makes it more time-efficient. Tudor makes it clear that he does not think that increasing structure necessarily follows from working in a time-limited way. However, he uses classical non-directive PCT as his baseline. With this as the baseline, any structure would be seen as an iatrogenic imposition, drawing power and control to the therapist and away from the client.

Discussion regarding the degree of structure that is acceptable always returns to drawing a line, creating a limit or prescribing a degree. It is difficult to maintain a discussion of the possibility of *no* structure without stretching the feasibility of practice beyond what most would consider practicable in anything other than private practice. What is clear though, is that neither PCT, EFT nor PCE-CfD has a required implicit processional framework or works in ordered stages, so the mindful application of any such framework by the therapist would be a definite and deliberate change in the architecture of the therapeutic relationship. The first task of a therapist so minded would be to explain the theoretical basis for the introduction of structure and how it would improve the therapy. Within existing PCE-CfD theory, there is little to suggest that structure would make a positive contribution. The imperative to work with the client's idiosyncratic structure, or lack of it, remains intact.

The only construction implicit in PCE-CfD is that imposed by the limited number of sessions. The therapist's first imperative is to structure the relationship positively and hopefully. Next the therapist is advised to keep the fact of the limited number of sessions on the table, so to speak. This requires a degree of sensitive awareness which should be well within the skills set of a good therapist. One practice would be to review the therapy in as non-intrusive a way as possible at reasonably regular intervals. Miller (2010), for example, calls this feedback-informed treatment (FIT) and makes concrete suggestions for integrating into practice gentle enquiries such as 'How is this going?', 'Are you finding these sessions helpful' and 'Has anything been especially helpful?'

Working briefly and direction

Directivity is a contentious issue in the context of working briefly. Whereas Tudor (2008) cautions against letting time limits push the therapist to be more directive, Gibbard (2004, 2007) explains how an increase in directivity is necessary to help the client achieve their goals within a limited number of sessions. The degree to which the therapist directs elements of the therapeutic hour is a matter of significance for PCE-CfD therapists. An aim of therapy is for the client to develop a greater internal locus of evaluation and a key factor in this process is letting control of the therapeutic process rest with the client. The therapist taking control of aspects of therapy or being the expert is considered antitherapeutic – simply adding to any possible feelings of helplessness and loss of agency felt by the client. In PCE-CfD, the therapist seeks to release the client's self-agency by arranging the helping relationship around the central pillar of trust in the client's experience, internal wisdom and personal power, however fragile the client might initially feel it to be. This control can be taken from or left with the client in many ways and by many degrees. PCE-CfD practice is based on a non-categorising, non-judgmental attitude; establishing a collaborative relationship; following the client's experience and respecting their preferences and choices as wise; not leading them to 'expert' solutions; sharing knowledge when requested; making tentative offers of ways of working in a cooperative relationship. With these characteristics the PCE-CfD practitioner constructs the level of non-directivity in the helping relationship in sharp contrast to one where the therapist is a consultant, diagnostician, advisor or expert administrator of psychotechnology.

In later chapters, how PCE-CfD offers the client a range of possible task-oriented ways of working will be considered, some of which are derived from focusing, or EFT. In PCE-CfD practice, this involves noticing issues and processes that the client finds problematic, checking with the client that these are areas of significant importance and offering to focus empathically on what is important for the client at their own pace, rather than *introducing* techniques. These strategies are offered in PCE-CfD in the spirit of facilitation of the therapeutic process and on the understanding that they are part of the collaborative venture of therapy as a whole – one person making suggestions informed by experience in the moment-to-moment relationship in the service of helping the other. They should be offered in such a way as to make it equally possible for the client to consider them, take them up, refuse them or put them aside to be tried later – so it is entirely possible that the client will eschew any offers of task-oriented elements, negotiated or otherwise. In this case, the therapist proceeds with therapy as usual, since for some clients, freedom from direction and external loci of control are the very key to removing the threat which is locking the self-structure in incongruence. The therapist continues to trust the client's internal wisdom to choose or refuse offers, whichever feels most helpful.

This 'default position' of trusting the client's internal wisdom is in stark contrast to approaches which might require therapists to interpret the client's behaviour as 'resistant' or 'avoidant' and implement designated interventions. When suggesting that therapists work with limits positively, this is no more than a manifestation of the theory-derived obligation to understand all of the client's behaviour as being the best they can do at the time and that they know their own experiences better than the therapist. In Rogers' terms, the client behaves at all times 'as an organised whole' with 'one basic tendency ... to maintain and enhance ...' themselves (1951: 486), or put even more simply, 'It is the *client* who knows what hurts, what directions to go, what problems are crucial, what experiences have been deeply buried' (Rogers, 1961: 11–12).

PCE theorists and practitioners identify two important domains of direction in therapy: the direction of content and the direction of process (see Sanders, 2011). These continue to be vigorously debated, and each will be briefly described and their implications considered.

Directing content

The content of a session literally means the topics of conversation, client narrative or what the client talks about. It is easy for a therapist to influence this content, and this can happen in several ways, for example:

- by choosing which elements of the client's narrative to reflect
- by being simply and atheoretically curious about certain elements, or saying 'tell me more about ...'
- by believing that certain topics are more germane (e.g. to the issue of depression) and asking the client to follow them – a therapist might have an idiosyncratic theory regarding the importance of, for example, certain feelings or past experiences.

It hardly bears repeating the elements of PCE literature, which assert that there is nothing in PCE theory to suggest that directing the content of the session is a good thing. Indeed, as alluded to above, content direction establishes the therapist as more of an expert in the client's experience than the client themselves and this is seen as antitherapeutic. The difficulty is that in extremis or when under pressure due to time limits, the therapist might feel pushed to be more active and 'do something'. This urge can be assuaged by taking control of the content of the session and directing the client to areas of experience that the therapist thinks more useful. However, in PCE-CfD there is no evidence base to back up such direction of content and the basic PCE-CfD therapeutic stance is to avoid content direction in general and certainly not to resort to it in desperation if either the client, or worse still the therapist, is anxious about time limits.

Directing process

Process direction is a different issue and some of the evidence base of PCE-CfD is provided by the more active elements of EFT ,and it is in approaching these process-facilitating responses of the therapist that the therapist will be considered as directing the therapeutic process.

In PCE-CfD, we expect many clients to identify specific therapeutic aims in collaboration with the therapist. These general aims are likely to point to more specific therapeutic needs which in turn suggest process-facilitation responses. Some of these responses have the effect of helping the client move more quickly to a nexus of energy, stuckness or opportunity in their experiential process and orientation. The rationale for making such an offer would be therapeutic, but the intervention might well have the secondary – hopefully welcome – effect of moving the process along towards a satisfactory resolution.

As explained previously, process-facilitation responses are invitations, not instructions. They are made as part of a collaborative stance, the nuances of which depend upon the attitudes and skill set of the therapist. PCE-CfD good practice dictates that the offer of appropriate responses is seen by the client as a facilitative opportunity to achieve their self-determined goals, not expert prescriptions which must be followed to meet externally set outcome criteria.

Competences covered in this chapter

- **G1** – Knowledge and understanding of mental health problems
- **G2** – Knowledge of depression
- **G6** – Ability to engage client
- **G7** – Ability to foster and maintain a good therapeutic alliance, and to grasp the client's perspective and 'world view'
- **G10** – Ability to undertake a generic assessment
- **G11** – Ability to assess and manage risk of self-harm
- **B5** – Ability to explain and demonstrate the rationale for counselling
- **B6** – Ability to work with the client to establish a therapeutic aim

(Competences are listed in Appendix 1)

5

Early Sessions Phase of PCE-CfD

Chapter overview

- Case Vignette 1: Habiba and Steph
- Case Vignette 2: Aileen and Mira
- Reflections on the early sessions phase

In the previous chapter the beginning of therapy was considered. In this chapter, two further case examples will be used to explore the early sessions phase of PCE-CfD. These case examples will be drawn from vignettes like those in the previous chapter, although the focus this time is on a series of sessions reaching across the early phase of PCE-CfD. The aim within these two case examples is to further demonstrate how distress experienced in the self-concept is explored and processed through deep empathic following of the moment-to-moment experiencing. Close empathic understanding responses will be shown to be the primary therapeutic response of the therapist within PCE-CfD. In addition, we see how process-facilitative responses that can help the client process experiences can be creatively and skilfully incorporated into the dialogue even at an early stage, in such a way that supports the client's agency and autonomy. As will be shown below, such therapist responses can facilitate the change process and help further the release of the client's actualising potential. The vignettes give an opportunity for trainees to start to understand more about facilitating change in a way that supports experiential processing directly and explicitly while remaining true to the notion that it is the client who sets the pace and direction for change in PCE-CfD. As per the previous chapter, the material for the vignettes are a fictional account of therapy and developed from examples within the first edition. The layout of the transcripts is the same as the last chapter and process reflections are added to highlight the competency and adherence to the PCEPS.

Case vignette 1: Habiba and Steph

Habiba is a 45-year-old woman whose parents came to the UK in 1954. Her father worked in heavy industry in the West Midlands and her mother was a full-time houseworker and mother to Habiba and her two brothers. Her parents were considered liberal Muslims who, given the somewhat precocious white British teenage culture at the time, and after much debate and negotiation, did not subject Habiba to an arranged marriage – she wanted to marry for love. She went to nursing college and met and married a doctor in her first year as a nurse. Her husband Rafiq, also Muslim, had come to England to train as a doctor and work in the NHS. They had two children, a girl and a boy, in quick succession, and a very happy family life.

Five years ago, Rafiq suddenly left her and moved to a different part of the country to a new job. Habiba went into shock and was intensively supported by her mother, who moved in with Habiba and her teenage children. Since then, Habiba has not recovered. She lives like a robot, no joy, no pain, just going through the motions. She is unable to concentrate, sleeps poorly and her children complain about her moods. Her husband is still separated from her, although not divorced, and this sham (her word) preserves a veil of honour and dignity for the extended family. She now works in an old people's home in a job that doesn't challenge her and where all that is required is that she goes through the motions.

Habiba was referred for PCE-CfD with Steph (recently qualified as a PCE-CfD therapist but with ten years' experience as PCE therapist in the NHS setting). Steph learns that Habiba wants to feel more energy and get some zest for life back, and together they set that as her first therapeutic goal. She spends the first two sessions painstakingly going through all her complaints about her husband but finds it impossible to talk about anything in any depth. We pick up the dialogue at the start of session three.

Session 3

T1.	Thanks for completing the forms Habi, what would you like to talk about today?	

(Continued)

(Continued)

C1.	I've spent all week trying get him [*She always refers to her husband as 'him' or 'the children's father'.*] to sort the children's savings accounts out. We started them when they were born and now Aisha's 17 we have to think about university fees. I hate having to ask him for anything, but it's a complicated investment in his name; I really hate having to talk to him [*Her face is mask-like, expressionless.*] and I ... I ... [*Trails off.*]	
T2.	It sounds difficult, a real hassle to get Aisha's fees sorted. With all the things you have complained about the children's father, I've never heard you look frustrated or angry or get angry, no angry tone in your voice at all. Of course, you may not feel frustrated or angry, I realise that. It would help me understand if you could say some more about it ...	Habiba is not sufficiently emotionally aroused in order to do any productive work with regard to emotionally processing her feelings about the situation being discussed. Steph has respectfully, empathically stayed with Habiba for over two sessions. Steph gives her some feedback about how she looks whilst talking about her husband. Habiba might access some feelings if she can experience the discrepancy that Steph sees.
C2.	[*Pause of 20 seconds, looking blank.*] Not really. Just numb. No, I used to, I think, at the beginning, I'm not sure, no, just nothing. Dead, really.	
T3.	Numb, dead, nothing – sounds detached and distant from all feelings.	Steph keeps looking at Habiba, and occasionally meets her gaze without demanding anything. She waits attentively, conveying interest and concern.
C3.	[*Habiba sits quietly, looking blank, unfocused and detached from what is being said.*] Yes, I suppose so. [*Silence for 55 seconds, then.*] So anyway, I finally got him to talk to Aisha about it, but I don't like her having to ask. He should just have it there ready without all this; she shouldn't have to worry about the fees. She has her exams to worry about.	

T4.	You talk about the children's father being, erm, obstructive, and not wanting Aisha to be worried. And somehow, you still seem to have no feelings yourself.	
C4.	No. Not really. Just get through the … what happens each day. Feelings get in the way. And anyway, what's the point? He's gone.	
T5.	There's no point in feelings, you just get through each day. Feelings will only get in the way of getting things done, is that it?	
C5.	Yes, I suppose so.	
T6.	In the first session, we talked about getting some energy back, some zest for life. When I listen to you, you seem so detached, disengaged. I wonder if there's anything you can imagine that would help you feel more of those emotions that you talk about.	Steph takes it a step further reminding Habiba of the therapeutic goal they negotiated in session 1.
C6.	Yes, I remember. I don't know what to do, I don't. It's not your fault. I should just give up.	
T7.	I hear how very, very difficult it is, and that you're at a loss as to what to do … at the end of your tether. Would it be OK for me to make a suggestion? You can tell me if it's not OK.	Whilst continuing to wait patiently and respectfully is an option, Steph decides that since they have a reasonably strong relationship she will risk a more direct response.
C7.	Yes, alright.	
T8.	This numbness you feel when you think about the children's father, can you feel it now?	
C8.	I don't know.	
T9.	Okay, try turning your attention inside, you might close your eyes if it helps but it's not essential, and in your imagination find a place that's safe for you. You don't have to tell me where it is or what it's like. Just nod when you can feel safe inside. [*Habiba nods.*]	Steph decides to invite Habiba to focus on clearing a space to help Habiba identify a specific feeling she might have.

(Continued)

(Continued)

		OK, now take a moment to think about the children's father, maybe some of the conversations you've had with him this week.	
	C9.	Oh. OK.	
	T10.	What comes into your awareness?	
	C10.	Just numb. Well, no, right next to the numbness is irritation.	
	T11.	Numbness and irritation right next to it.	Steph is ready to work with numbness as the main feeling, and is preparing to ask Habiba to inhabit that numb feeling to see if it has any meaning when something else happens …
	C11.	Yes, that's it exactly, and when I remember what … [*Habiba opens her eyes with a start and bursts into tears, sobbing uncontrollably.*]	

Clearing a space is often a helpful process-facilitative response for the client finding it difficult to focus on a specific issue in therapy. In the example above, Steph knew that Habiba really wanted to work on getting her zest for life back but also that she seems unable to move into exploring this and keeps returning to her feelings of frustration towards her husband. These feelings were varied and included feeling dead, numb and being frustrated with the sense that feelings 'just get in the way'. In addition to this, Habiba didn't seem to experience emotions congruently and instead was very flat whilst saying she was really annoyed. Having a set of confused or even conflicting feelings is common, and so Steph helped Habiba focus on just one thing for a while. The invitation into clearing a space is a very well-attuned response as Habiba quickly accessed a different experiential process. For the next 10 minutes Habiba is aroused with a mixture of feelings. Habiba is unable to talk about them coherently, since she seems to have gone from under-arousal to approaching over-arousal very quickly. Steph tries to help Habiba get the strong emotions down to a safe size by supporting Habiba with her emotion regulation. To do this Steph supports Habiba in being able to see the raging feelings in a glass bottle safely put about 100 yards away in an orchard. That helps to identify the emotions in a more clear and differentiated way and very tentatively begin to work with them by looking into the bottle without risk of anything escaping. She identifies terrible humiliation, hurt, betrayal and raging anger.

T12.	You feel kind of confused by all the feelings …	
C12.	I just don't know where to begin with these feelings. I feel too confused by it all, them all, everything. I want to just blank them all off again. It's best. Honestly.	
T13.	It really does seem best to put it all away out of reach. You're not quite saying 'life would be simpler' if you could shut it all away again. Get back to being numb?	Steph notes that Habiba's visualisation of the feelings in a glass bottle at a distance in an orchard indicates the strength of the feelings. It is a visualisation of a *very* safe place.
C13.	Yes. [*Looks down, shaking her head.*] No, no, that's not … no. I need, I want to … I don't know what to do with these feelings, but I must do something. This is just ruining everything.	
T14.	These are really difficult feelings to understand, to experience without being afraid and overwhelmed. And let me check, first you want to somehow get to grips with them, whatever that means [*Habiba nods.*], and second they all, or most of them, started when the children's father left?	Steph is again gently checking that Habiba still wants to work actively with the goal she set in session 1.
C14.	More like when he said he wanted to leave … well, no let's see …	
T15.	Will it help to try going back to that day, and, with me here with you, walking through it again, like a re-enactment of a crime.	Steph's empathic responses at T16 become more emotionally evocative and this is helpful because Habiba has been finding it difficult to be in touch with her experiential process. This evocative empathic responding helps Habiba get in touch with her feelings and starts to stretch her ability to experience difficult feelings.
C15.	It was a crime! The swine! Why? What had I done? Nothing, that's what. He even said 'It's not your fault'.	
T16.	OK, Habiba, you feel angry and a sense of injustice, feeling that he did wrong by you and you didn't deserve to be left like that.	

(Continued)

(Continued)

C16.	I remember it as though it was yesterday. [*She starts getting upset and takes a deep breath.*] He waited until the children had gone to my mother's house for the weekend. It was Friday night and I'm sitting down on the sofa, just finished the washing up …	
T17.	Yes, okay this is when he left …	

The evocative empathic responses help and in a short while Habiba keeps hitting the notion that 'it's just not *fair* for him to leave'. She couldn't get past the idea that he wasn't fair, him leaving wasn't fair, life wasn't fair. He must have lied when he said he loved her when they first met. She could see no point in anything amid all this injustice and broken dreams. Except her duty to the children.

C17.	He *said* he loved me, but what changed? That doesn't change, does it? [*Looks imploringly at Steph.*] You can't fall out of love with someone can you? He *lied*! He never loved me, but I loved him.	To Steph, this sounds like a meaning protest. It sounds like Habiba has had a cherished belief about love and marriage, and how people in love conduct themselves, shattered by Rafiq's behaviour and the things he has said.
T18.	So love is forever? Is that a good way to put it? It never changes? You said a session or two ago that you married for love. Your parents weren't convinced at first, but *you* believed in love, is that it?	
C18.	Yes, well, of course it's natural to think that isn't it. I was in love, I made a promise. I stuck by him, but he … he …	
T19.	It's really important to you that *you*, *Habiba* believe in love everlasting, loyalty, keeping promises. It sounds as though it's right at the centre of you at this moment.	The therapeutic task associated with meaning protest is meaning creation, which looks similar to a cognitive therapy on paper. However, in this PCE-CfD context, there is no judgement of rationality or refutation of cherished beliefs. Indeed, meaning creation begins with accepting and valuing the cherished beliefs that have been violated.
C19.	It is … it just doesn't seem right … how could he? He ruined everything.	

T20.	In that one moment, all that you held dear, and still hold dear, was ruined.	In PCE-CfD meaning creation can be simply being genuinely, respectfully empathic to the extent that the client can loosen their constrained introjects about, e.g. love, under their own agency. Sometimes, it might involve a slightly more active, persistent examination if the client's needs suggest.
C20.	That's it.	
T21.	And there's no going back.	
C21.	No. Of course not. Not now. But it still hurts. Like a broken heart. It sounds like a Disney movie, but it's true. It hurt my heart. It was … is … broken.	
T22.	Your heart was broken that day and it remains broken. You believe that love lasts forever, but he spoiled that forever.	
C22.	Yes, he did. [*Habiba's eyes moisten and she catches her breath.*]	
T23.	You fought hard for that belief, with your parents. You fought hard for love, rather than tradition and an arranged marriage. So, the stakes were high.	Many therapeutic moments of movement are fleeting and as Steph follows Habiba she takes the opportunity to quickly move on to respectfully examine the details of Habiba's beliefs about love and the possibility of healing.
C23.	Yes, I did. Everyone must think how stupid … humiliating, totally humiliated and … how could he do it? I *loved him.*	Steph still follows Habiba. She doesn't challenge the rationality of Habiba's beliefs, since she understands that Habiba's beliefs will have been forged at a time when they were important and helpful. Questioning their rationality would be non-therapeutic in that it would further threaten Habiba's self-structure. That doesn't preclude gentle, respectful exploration of their continued viability, though this is a difficult line to tread.
T24.	You were shamed, all that effort and arguing, was open to ridicule.	
C24.	Yes, that's right. But what hurts most still is the fact … how could he do it? It was supposed to be forever.	
T25.	It still hurts, and it can never be mended.	
C25.	Broken is broken. Like a nice vase, or, erm, well, I suppose you *can* mend a vase, but it never looks the same – always looks, you know, like it's been broken.	

(Continued)

(Continued)

T26.	You feel that your heart might mend but will always have a mark or scar, or is that just about vases?	Steph continues to tread this line and take opportunities to examine possible beliefs about healing and how Habiba feels about these ideas.
C26.	[*Smiles.*] Ha ha. I see what you're saying. I don't know. Maybe. I don't know.	
T27.	When you think about that possibility, of mending or changing your ideas about love, what happens inside, to your feelings?	

The remainder of the session, and the next two sessions, are taken up with similar meaning creation work in which Habiba gradually develops a different idea about her ability to heal. She does not have to remain broken but might carry a scar. This work in PCE-CfD uses the term 'meaning creation', borrowed from EFT. It describes in another way the process of revising personal constructs. A social psychologist named Janoff-Bulman (1992) also writes about this using the term 'shattered assumptions' and it is a widely understood phenomenon in social psychology. These cherished beliefs are basically assumptions about the world and part of the client's social cognitive dimension to the personality. As we can see above, the close and evocative empathic responses work with both these cognitions and the underlying and accompanying emotions involved. In PCE-CfD this active, yet gentle and respectful, collaborative process engages the client in the meaning creation process.

In the session above, we have seen Steph help her client in at least three ways: first, she helped Habiba identify and experience her emotions more strongly; second, she helped her associate the feelings with specific events when Habiba felt lost; and third, Steph responded to a meaning protest with non-intrusive meaning creation. Therapeutic tasks are identified and met with process-facilitative responses in a fluid way.

Case Vignette 2: Aileen and Mira

Aileen is a 25-year-old white Irish woman. Until she became pregnant 18 months ago, she worked for a national chain of fast food restaurants as a kitchen manager, and she intends to return to work soon. She was a keen hockey player, having played for her school team, she also played in the local town's team in the second eleven. She is married to Tim, also 25. She gave birth to Aisling, a healthy full-term baby, 9 months ago.

Everything was fine for the first couple of months, even though Aisling was demanding and didn't sleep particularly well. Aileen started out very confident – Aisling was a planned baby and things couldn't have been better – but, in Aileen's own words, she slowly lost interest in being a mother. It wasn't dramatic, but the more distant and uninterested she became, the lower she began to feel. Over the next two months she felt guilty and useless, irritable and increasingly overwhelmed with responsibility.

The health visitor was the first to notice things weren't quite right and suggested that Aileen saw her GP, who referred her for CfD. Aileen's counsellor is Mira, an ex-health visitor herself. Aileen was clear in the first session that her aim was to start feeling happy again so that she could be a good mum.

The first four sessions comprised Aileen telling her story in a hopeless, detached way. She has felt isolated at home because she's been unable to talk to Tim about how she feels – not because he is unsympathetic, but because she felt guilty and did not want him to know that she was struggling. So far it has been a relief to share it with Mira.

Session 5

T1.	Okay Aileen, thanks for completing the measures. What would you like to talk about today?	As this session gets under way, Mira is ready to follow Aileen empathically, and at the same time is conscious that Aileen has been struggling to find a clear direction. In this instance Mira senses the building frustration for Aileen so is open to offering some structuring of the session. She has no idea where Aileen will go or if it will be accepted but is ready to gently make suggestions if Aileen continues to experience the feeling of pointlessness and detachment. In this active way of being, Mira will always take her lead from Aileen and any suggestions made are empathically attuned responses to Aileen's experiences.
C1.	Well, I don't feel any better really. I nearly talked to Tim on Thursday, but I thought there'd be no point. It'd only worry him.	
T2.	There's no change in your mood or feelings, and though you thought about talking to Tim, you then thought that it probably wasn't worth it because you didn't want him to worry.	Aileen's level of emotional arousal is low and therefore makes working on feelings in PCE-CfD less possible. In PCE-CfD, the therapist can decide whether to wait, patiently following Aileen empathically,

(Continued)

(Continued)

C2.	[*In a flat, lifeless tone.*] Yeah. I mean there is no point, is there? I do feel a, well, a *tiny* bit better, I mean I feel better *here* and just after talking to you, but …	or make an empathically attuned response to facilitate greater experiential specificity. Mira knows that helping Aileen access emotions and then to help her increase her emotional arousal *might* be useful and holds the thought in readiness as the session unfolds.
T3.	So, just a little change, maybe feeling up a bit when you've been here and for a while afterwards. Then … back down to earth – bump … but … no, not 'bump!' [*Accentuated in tone.*] You sound *flat*, low, really flat.	
C3.	Yeah, That's how I feel. Nothing to … [*Tails off.*]	
T4.	Right now it looks pretty bleak. Nothing to …? I'm not sure if you wanted to finish that.	
C4.	No not really. I just feel like a tyre that's been punctured. Useless. Not fit for … what do they say?	
T5.	Erm, not fit for anything?	
C5.	Yeah. Fit for nothing, useless. A disappointment.	
T6.	A disappointment. [*Said in a level tone, not as a question implying 'A disappointment to whom?'*]	Talking about negative feelings is movement. Aileen's flat tone has gone. She *feels* disappointed and shows it. In this moment she *is* the disappointment. And the metaphors and images she is using are engaging and expressive.
C6.	Yeah. Inside I just feel I've let everyone down.	
T7.	You've been a disappointment to everyone. And that has punctured your tyre. You can't get very far on a punctured tyre.	Mira wonders if Aileen can extend this slight emotional specificity to gain greater clarity of what might be happening inside for her, to come closer to any felt sense of this experience of disappointment. The empathic reflections that follow can help Aileen get a clearer emotion focus.
C7.	No. Useless and oh, I don't know.	
T8.	You *sound* punctured. A disappointment. [*Pause of 30 seconds.*]	
C8.	To *everyone*. Yeah. That's what I feel inside.	

T9.	Inside, right now?	Here Mira is helping Aileen get
C9.	Yeah.	clearer on her emotion focus.
T10.	It's like a physical sensation …? The sense or physical feeling, to be a disappointment?	
C10.	Well, I suppose it's like a colour that stains everything. I look at myself and there's a stain and mark, a black spot. Like a black mark against me.	Helping give the experience more dimensions, or make it more embodied, can help bring experiences that are just on the edge of awareness more into awareness. Mira hopes that this expressive imagery that Aileen is developing will help in this process.
T11.	Like at school? A bad report.	
C11.	Yeah, like a criminal record.	
T12.	That's strong stuff, a criminal record. More than just blotting your copybook. A criminal record. What did you do to get that?	
C12.	I couldn't love my baby.	This is the first time Aileen has touched upon anything that is a discrepancy between the expectations embedded in her identity and her lived experience. This is 'straightforward' incongruence in terms of the person-centred theory underpinning PCE-CfD. The question Mira has to deal with is 'How to work with it?'.
T13.	And that's a crime. [*Said as a statement.*]	
C13.	Yes. Sort of. Yes. It's what I've always wanted. It's what it means to be … a Brennan. A Brennan woman. Brennan's my maiden name.	
T14.	I see. That's a powerful tradition. Something to live up to, and it is such a disappointment to not be able to live up to it.	
C14.	Yeah. Of course, my mother was a saint.	
T15.	I'm not sure whether you are being ironic when you say that, 'a saint'?	
C15.	No, really, she was just a great mum. I love her, but blooming heck, what an act to follow! And she still is now. She's been so supportive.	

(Continued)

(Continued)

T16.	So, your mum has been a great mum all the way through – all your life. And you really appreciate that.	
C16.	I do. I don't know what I'd do without her. But I can't tell her. Oh no. No! I couldn't stand her *understanding*. She is so blooming *perfect*. It ... it's not her fault. It's me. I'm disappointed in myself.	
T17.	So, let me see if I can get this ... the weight of tradition, of family expectations and your mother's ability to apparently embody those traditions and be everything you think a mother should be on the one side and then you, the realities of your life and your real experiences of motherhood on the other.	
C17.	Yeah, that's about it. Shit, oh sorry! Such a disappointment.	
T18.	Oh, and the disappointment. Like a drip, drip.	In theory terms this is a particular form of discrepancy between self-structure and experience. A self-critical part of Aileen's self-structure takes shape. It coalesces around quite a catalogue of introjected expectations. Mira could wait to see if Aileen unpacks the bits herself or works with the whole in some other way. But, since these implicitly self-critical statements of family expectations are so well-formed, she decides to see if Aileen can give them voice now and dialogue with them.
C18.	Nagging at me. [*Sounds irritated, even a little angry.*]	
T19.	So, it's not a drip, drip, it's nagging. And you sound angry when you say that. Is it nagging now?	
C19.	Yes, right now. And yes, I am bloody cross, fed up with it. Just go away!	

T20.	You're fed up and want it to go away right now. Can you hear it saying anything?	
C20.	Yes, like, the Brennan women do this, do that. Are *quiet* and *good* wives. And *loving mothers*. And never want anything for themselves.	
T21.	Right. Does the nagging voice have anything else to say?	Mira is pursuing this work with the self-critic quite actively. She tries to bring the dialogue into the room – making it a spoken dialogue between parts of Aileen's personality and her lived experience.
C21.	It just repeats itself.	
T22.	Does it have a tone?	
C22.	Well it's a kindly scolding. Sort of soft but insistent. It's a proud voice.	
T23.	When you hear it now, inside, do you feel anything?	
C23.	Actually, it's me. It's my voice. Like a young me.	
T24.	The disappointed voice is you. A young Aileen. [*Statement, not question.*]	
C24.	Yes.	
T25.	Anything else?	
C25.	Yes, she's so *certain,* so sure of herself. So sure she's got it right. But she hasn't.	
T26.	She hasn't got it right. You want her to know that. And your voice as you speak is now gentle, not angry any more. This is a conversation with that part of you, by the sound of it. Is that right, or have I got that wrong?	Although this is a very active demonstration of PCE-CfD practice, Mira is always respectful and doesn't push anything past the point at which Aileen is presently experiencing. She checks her understanding and ...
C26.	No, that's right. I'm not cross with her ... me.	
T27.	So you know what that part of you has to say [*Aileen interjects: For now! She's got plenty more to say.*] ... and ... she has more to say, what do you want to do now? I was wondering if there was anything you wanted to say back? To tell her.	... is tentative in making suggestions to continue to move things along. She wonders whether encouraging dialogue in the session between Aileen and her 'younger self' configuration would be helpful. She is ready to let this pass or follow Aileen somewhere else if this is not acceptable or useful for Aileen.

(Continued)

(Continued)

C27.	Erm, yes, well, OK ... I want her to know that it's not that simple. Life is miles more blooming complicated than that. You can't just say, 'You're a Brennan woman and Brennan women get married, have kids, live like it's the 1950s or something. It's not like that now.'	
T28.	The world is not like that anymore. *I'm not like that* anymore.	Mira uses a first-person empathic response as she is now very much inside Aileen's frame of reference and this kind of empathy can be very evocative for the client.
C28.	That's right I'm *not* like that. I just thought, actually I remembered, well, I didn't forget, ... well ... maybe ... anyhow I, I [*Catches her breath and eyes fill up with tears.*]	
T29.	Take a minute ... these are strong feelings ... when you are ready ...	Now Aileen moves out of the process of dialogue and returns to disclosing a discovery from her immediate experience. Aileen is now emotionally processing feelings associated with the self-critical aspect of herself and the hurt she feels. Then something sort of bubbles through in her experiencing and she makes a disclosure about her feelings of becoming a mother. These therapeutic tasks, processes and the facilitative techniques move fluidly, unannounced and without comment.
C29.	[*Composes herself slightly.*] I, I feel frightened saying this [*Lowers her voice as if telling a secret.*] ... I was not ready, really. Not ready to have children. Actually, I'm not sure I really wanted children. When I think of all the things I used to do and then BAM! I hit a brick bloomin' wall. Hit the bloody buffers good and proper.	
T30.	You ...	
C30.	I've never said that before. I'm too ashamed, too guilty. Didn't ... want ...	
T31.	Something you've kept inside ...	And now Mira slots into respectful empathic following, and continues to the end of the session, making no more suggestions.
C31.	Yes, I don't think I even really told myself. [*Laughs a weak laugh.*] Until now, the younger me, all certain there, well, bugger off! Life's just not like that! And before you ask, I don't feel anything, really. Just 'So go on, what do you think of that, little miss perfect!'	

The remainder of the session, and two further sessions, carry on in a similar vein, with Aileen gradually and increasingly exploring her immediate thoughts and feelings about the experience of motherhood. This is an alignment of the discrepancy between her self-structure and experience. In this case, some of her experiences of being in the world and not fully symbolised experiences of her self-structure were initially on the edge of awareness. A combination of the safety of the therapeutic relationship and facilitating responses supported greater emotional specificity and focus around self-critical parts of her personality. This enabled and encouraged the dialogue between discrepant elements of her self-structure and organismic experience, allowing alignment and some restructuring.

Aileen was also able to talk about the things she missed and resolved to get back into some sort of sport. This was her incentive to tell Tim that she wasn't coping as well as she had led him to believe. This relieved some pressure from her.

Aileen returned in session 7 to talk more about her 'young self' and discovered that the intention of the younger 'configuration of self' was to protect her and equip her for a successful and contented life. A brief, calm, even respectful dialogue between self-configurations ensued for a few minutes before the younger Aileen just disappeared. Aileen believed that this was because she had done her job, so to speak.

After eleven sessions, Aileen and Mira decided to finish the counselling. Aileen was feeling much more in touch with her feelings and was able to talk to Tim, who helped more with the childcare in small but important ways. Nothing spectacular, but a positive result.

Reflections on the sessions

This chapter has considered two case examples of the early sessions of PCE-CfD. We have seen two clients, Habiba and Aileen, both begin to move towards greater consistency in their self-structure and alignment of self and experience. This is the essence of PCE-CfD work. In both examples we saw how the therapists were able to approach the client's difficulties in accessing and processing their emotions. To support the clients, both therapists drew upon process-facilitative responses. These are always responsive and empathically attuned with the client's immediate experiences. As such, they are aimed at supporting the client's autonomy and self-directing capacities whilst removing the blocks to processing emotions, the result being greater congruence for the client. The therapist is always respectful and never pushes the client but, in inviting either clearing a space or engaging in dialogues between self-configurations, the therapist is demonstrating their trust in the client's capacity to accept the invitation or decline and to follow a different track. Bohart (2012) has argued previously that person-centred therapists are able to incorporate such process-facilitating responses into therapy without compromising the principles of being person-centred. Bohart's position is that if we are to truly trust in the client's capacity for self-determination, then we can trust the client's capacity to decline or reject any such invitation to engage in more focused process facilitation offered by the therapist. This position is one that supports the maxim, 'It's not what you do but how you do it that matters'.

It is worth noting that in the first edition of the book use of such process-facilitation responses from the therapist was presented in terms of being a more auxiliary feature of the therapy. However, in this edition they are presented in more synergistic terms. The therapeutic use and place of process-facilitative responses can be quite difficult to understand for some classical non-directive client-centred therapists, such as those who follow the Frankel and Sommerbeck (2008) stance. However, this need not be the case and other prominent theorists within the person-centred approach have stated the rightful place for a very wide range of therapist response modes that are able to convey the attitudes of empathy, unconditional positive regard, in a congruent manner (Bozarth, 2008; Bohart, 2008; Brodley & Brody, 1996). These authors have proposed that at various times therapists' use of techniques are a legitimate feature of person-centred therapy. This can be most easily understood as being in direct response to the clients' needs, or techniques can be used to support therapists in further conveying their empathic understanding and unconditional positive regard for their clients. In the next chapters there will be more examples of process-facilitation responses.

Competences covered in this chapter

- **G5** – Ability to work with difference (cultural competence)
- **G6** – Ability to engage client
- **G8** – Ability to work with the emotional content of sessions
- **B4** – Knowledge of the PCE conceptualisation of depression
- **B6** – Ability to work with the client to establish a therapeutic aim
- **B7** – Ability to experience and communicate empathy
- **B8** – Ability to experience and to communicate a fundamentally accepting attitude to clients
- **B9** – Ability to maintain authenticity in the therapeutic relationship
- **S1** – Ability to help clients to access and express emotions

(Competences are listed in Appendix 1)

6

Middle Phase Sessions

Chapter overview

- Prescribed psychiatric drugs, therapy and depression
- Case Vignette 1: Sam and Cath
- Process-facilitation responses
- Case vignette 2: A return to Habiba and Steph
- Case vignette 3: Alicja and Victor

The change process within therapy does not follow a straightforward linear path, easily and neatly divided up into stages whereby one stage is completed and followed by another and so on. However, person-centred theory of change suggests that there are some observable characteristics to the directions of change and the behaviours and processing styles of clients who are going through these changes. These can be identified and are often more apparent at some rather than other points during therapy. As previously stated in both Chapters 2 and 3, Rogers' (1961) theory of the therapeutic process of change provides detailed description of the process directions in which people move as they begin to change. Clients can enter therapy at any stage of a process of change and will also leave at various stages too. Changes that might be indicative of taking place between the third and fifth stages of process will be considered below. At stages three and four it is common to see a loosening of the structure in symbolic representations of experiences and within the self-structure more generally. An example of this was the restructuring that Habiba experienced through the meaning-making process following the cherished belief that 'love is forever' being breached. In the fifth stage, we see a further shift into a more immediate expression of feelings in the present moment. This was evidenced in the previous chapter when Aileen was expressing emotions in the moment in relation to her mother. Of course, it is not possible to predict what process direction of change will be. Rogers' (1961) description of the process of change was an attempt to find the structure that is present within the process of change rather than to impose one on to people, and that is how we should consider these following examples of therapeutic dialogue.

There are several factors that can impact the process of change. One of the most likely to be encountered in PCE-CfD is the impact of medication on the therapeutic work. The issue of using medication during therapy raises critical issues for therapists to consider. Therapists need to feel comfortable and confident in being able to engage in a dialogue with their clients about their use of prescribed medication. In the sections below several critical issues related to medication are introduced. This is followed by a short vignette where client and therapist consider the impact of medication use on their therapeutic work together. The second and third vignettes then consider the use of a range of process-facilitating responses in PCE-CfD. These are to further show how the techniques often used in EFT and focusing can be helpful to support the client through a process of revising personal constructs and making significant changes to their emotion processes and changes within the self-structure.

Prescribed psychiatric drugs, therapy and depression

This section on prescribed psychiatric drugs is included since many, if not most clients will have direct or indirect experience (via relatives, friends or colleagues) of antidepressants, and GPs will prescribe antidepressants alongside psychological therapy. The term 'psychiatric drugs' is being used over 'medication' as medications are specifically targeted to treat the causes of an illness. As there is no known conclusive evidence for a biological root cause to experiences of depression, the term psychiatric drugs offers a better fit than does medication. Other than provide the briefest of summaries, it is not intended to cover in detail the history of the use of antidepressants for depression or the pharmacology of antidepressants. For more information on these subjects, readers are directed to Healy (2005) and the NICE Guideline's chapters on pharmacological and physical interventions in depression, which is currently being updated (NICE, 2009). Similarly, the NICE depression pathways website[1] has general information on medication and associated clinical decisions describing antidepressant treatment in adults. However, readers should progress to these sources with a critical outlook as there has been criticism about the information given in the NICE guidelines concerning psychiatric drugs and some researchers suggest that there has been underreporting of their potential harmful effects and difficulties with withdrawal (Sharma, Guski, Freund & Gøtzsche, 2016). This section will provide a basic introduction to some of the prominent issues

---

[1]http://pathways.nice.org.uk/pathways/depression (accessed 24/11/18).

that are then considered in the context of a scenario common to PCE-CfD therapists in their practice.

There are three classes of antidepressants: monoamine oxidase inhibitors (MAOIs), tricyclic antidepressants (TCAs) and selective serotonin reuptake inhibitors (SSRIs). Healy recounts that the 'original' antidepressants were discovered in the 1950s during the search for neuroleptics or 'antipsychotics'. The first MAOIs and TCAs were developed in 1957 and, during testing as antipsychotics, were found to have mood-altering effects. Complex syndromes of side effects limited these drugs to the treatment of what was then known as 'major, biological or endogenous depression'.

SSRIs were discovered in the 1960s as a result of more detailed understanding of the action of TCAs in blocking the reuptake of certain neurotransmitters. Subsequently, it has been found that SSRIs have a noticeable anxiolytic (anti-anxiety) effect and that indeed this may be their main action. Whilst these findings are further examples of attending to the diversity of individual responses to prescribed psychiatric drugs, they also have some implications for psychological theories of distress which understand anxiety to be the underlying factor in the majority of psychological disturbance.

Choice of frontline treatment

It is broadly recognised that there is a tendency to medicalise a growing number of aspects of everyday experiences. One feature of this tendency is the fact that antidepressants receive considerable media attention, and SSRIs have been described as 'smart' drugs. These trends do nothing to highlight the fact that psychological treatments are also promoted as frontline treatments of choice by NICE. Furthermore, whilst the evidence of effectiveness for antidepressants for depression has been critiqued (Doshi, Dickersin, Healy, Vedula & Jefferson, 2013), the evidence base for certain psychological treatments of mild to moderate depression continues to strengthen (Sharbanee, Elliott & Bergman, 2015). In a systematic review of counselling in primary care, Brettle, Hill and Jenkins (2008: 212) found 'clear evidence that among primary care patients, for the treatment of depression, there is a strong preference for counselling as opposed to medication'. They continue in the report of their findings, 'The preference for counselling is unaffected by factors such as age, ethnicity, the presence of mental health problems, or problem severity' and 'The receipt of a preferred intervention improves treatment take-up and compliance but there is no clear evidence that the receipt of a preferred treatment improves clinical outcomes'. Clearly, patients prefer counselling and are more likely to complete the treatment when this preference is honoured.

The use of prescribed psychiatric drugs

The use of prescribed psychiatric drugs for experiences diagnosed as depression continues to excite vigorous debate. Although the aim here is not to engage with these debates, some of the contentious areas will arise briefly or tangentially and, when this happens, signposts to relevant reading material will be provided. The following sections cover several issues worth highlighting.

Prescribed psychiatric drugs to match the diagnosis

The medical model of mental illness is predicated on the idea of a unique diagnosis providing clear indication of a unique treatment. We have seen how this ideal is confounded in real life, not least in the diverse diagnostic category of depression, with its subdivisions and flexible interpretations of experiences. Nevertheless, when it comes to the prescription of psychiatric drugs following NICE guidelines, very careful attention is paid to the severity and persistence of the symptoms.

Antidepressants are not recommended for people with what is considered simple first-onset subthreshold symptoms or mild depression. They may be considered if (i) the patient has a past history of moderate or severe depression, (ii) the subthreshold depressive symptoms have been present for two years or more, (iii) the symptoms have persisted following completion of other treatments, or (iv) the patient has a chronic physical condition, the treatment of which might be complicated by depression.

In all of the cases above, the prescription of antidepressants should be considered in comparison with or, in some cases alongside, approved psychological treatments, of which PCE-CfD is included in IAPT. The treatment of severe and complex depression is the domain of specialist mental health services.

Wide effects of psychiatric drugs

There is no disputing that antidepressants cause a wide range of effects, some of which are so objectionable and intolerable as to compromise treatment compliance and obviously this renders treatment useless. Whilst for many, some adverse effects are minimal, for others they are only tolerable as an option in a desperate situation but may be sufficiently debilitating and unpleasant that they can exacerbate low mood, hopelessness and other symptoms of depression. Prescribing clinicians are expected to monitor side effects, but it is also the case that clients might feel more comfortable disclosing problems with antidepressants to counsellors.

All professionals working in primary care share responsibility in helping patients access appropriate treatments and support, including responsibility to monitor the effects of medication and prescribed psychiatric drugs, both positive and negative. It goes without saying that *hunting* for wider effects has no place in PCE-CfD, and any mention of possible such effects by the client should be the basis of empowering the client to disclose appropriate concerns to the prescribing clinician, rather than the counsellor immediately reporting the problems on behalf of the client. This is, however, always an option if the client's safety is thought to be in danger.

The Pharmaceutical Services Negotiating Committee website (PSNC, 2019) is a good resource for clients who want more information; for a comprehensive list of wider side effects, see the NHS website (NHS, 2018). It is clear from the list that persistent severe adverse effects would make anyone feel low, let alone a person already suffering from the distress of depression. Finally, it is also recently reported that there can be a significant increase in risk of suicide, aggression and homicide in all ages when taking antidepressant medication treatment and specifically related to SSRIs (Gøtzsche, 2017). PCE-CfD practitioners should be alert to the implications of this and be willing to act if they are concerned about a client.

Prescribed psychiatric drugs and talking therapies in tandem

NICE make it clear that it is acceptable to prescribe both frontline treatments – antidepressants and psychological therapy – simultaneously, although the evidence is mixed regarding the degree of improvement, if any, over either treatment prescribed individually. PCE-CfD therapists might encounter some medical practitioners who are persuaded that psychological treatment combined with antidepressant therapy is indeed associated with a higher improvement rate than drug treatment alone, but that the active contribution of the psychotherapy is to help keep patients in treatment. Furthermore, patient preference also has to be taken into consideration. It would be disappointing if the only rationale for combined treatment is to use psychotherapy as a compliance-enhancing factor.

PCE-CfD practitioners will have clients referred to them who have been given prescriptions for antidepressants. In the majority of cases, the prescribed psychiatric drugs will not have a deleterious effect upon counselling unless adverse effects are severe, whilst there is an equal chance that medication might energise a client sufficiently to be able to attend and benefit from the PCE-CfD sessions. So, it is possible that the treatment compliance hypothesis might work both ways.

Withdrawal and discontinuation effects

In the natural course of events, people who experience mild to moderate depression come to the end of antidepressant treatment most often due to the sustained remission of symptoms. When the cessation occurs during PCE-CfD work, practitioners need to be aware of some of the issues which may become active. Proper advice and support during withdrawal and discontinuation should be sought due to the likelihood of significant effects (Guy, 2018).

Stopping antidepressants of any sort must be done under the guidance of the prescribing clinician, or where the prescriber is unwilling to support withdrawal, but the person who is taking antidepressants is certain they want to stop, then they should seek advice and support from a different clinician. Withdrawal symptoms or discontinuation effects are common to all classes of antidepressant (Davies & Read, 2018); however, PCE-CfD practitioners are most likely to be referred clients who are prescribed SSRIs. There are well-documented discontinuation effects associated with SSRIs (Haddad & Anderson, 2007). The phenomenon includes experiences such as dizziness, headache, nausea, lethargy, sleep disturbances and less commonly, mania and hypomania. The onset of these experiences is usually sudden and within hours or days of abrupt discontinuation of prescribed psychiatric drugs, and highlights the need to discontinue SSRIs carefully and slowly with full medical support. However, there are many reasons why clients might abruptly discontinue taking antidepressants without consulting the prescribing clinician, and the discontinuation effects can easily be mistaken for relapse or recurrence. If the PCE-CfD therapist is knowledgeable about these effects, it can help the client from having their experiences of withdrawal misunderstood as experiencing a return of their depression.

It is good practice for PCE-CfD therapists to be aware of the symptoms associated with SSRI discontinuation and alert to the possibilities of the client mistaking these experiences as signs of depression returning. Even if discontinuation is conducted with medical support as part of a change in the profile of treatments for a particular client, the client should be made aware of possible withdrawal symptoms and supported appropriately. In the ideal scenario, the client will have been made aware of the possible withdrawal effects at the point they were originally prescribed. The duration of the adverse experiences is usually quite short, and often simply being aware of their likelihood and timely support from relatives, friends and therapist is sufficient.

PCE-CfD therapists can have a role in supporting clients who have decided to discontinue prescribed psychiatric drugs under medical supervision. Regular counselling sessions can help sustain the client through the difficulties of withdrawal effects and counsellors can, if asked by the client, help monitor these effects and collaboratively develop coping strategies. Recently there has been work completed to provide guidance for psychological therapists working with clients who are considering, currently taking or stopping antidepressant medication. The section below provides some further details on these issues.

Guidance for therapists

There has been a substantial rise in the use of antidepressants and more recently the potential harm of antidepressants has become more widely considered. In the UK, the number of prescriptions being issued has doubled in the last decade alone. According to an NHS report (NHS Digital, 2017), between 2015 and 2016 the rate of prescriptions increased by a further 6% (3.7 million prescription items), giving a total number of prescription items as 64.7 million. Considering this increase, work has been done to develop more support for therapists working with clients taking antidepressants whilst in therapy. Specific guidance has been developed for working with clients who are considering starting antidepressants, or who might be considering coming off antidepressants or who have reduced/stopped and are managing a withdrawal process when already engaged in therapy. The UK government, supported by the professional associations in the field, established an All Party

Parliamentary Group (APPG) specifically to look into the use of prescribed psychiatric drug dependence (APPG, 2019). One feature of the APPG's work was the development of guidance for therapists in their work with clients taking prescribed antidepressants. This guidance has been informed by recent reviews of literature and other research findings and will be published in 2019 (https://prescribeddrug.org/).

Recent research published in a systematic review of studies suggested that the adverse effects of antidepressant withdrawal are much more severe and longer lasting than was previously thought and are much more prevalent (Davies & Read, 2018). Therefore PCE-CfD therapists should consider this latest information and be ready to work with the client if such side effects are identified or suspected. Many clients who take antidepressant medication will at some point want to stop using them, and for many this may prove difficult. The most recent research that has looked at the experiences of antidepressant use has shown that stopping can be difficult, and for many they try but fail to stop (Read, Gee, Diggle & Butler, 2019).

Thinking about coming off antidepressants after taking them for a long time is a delicate and important issue for therapists to face with their clients. Therapists may be anxious about engaging in discussion with their clients about their prescribed psychiatric drug use. This might in part be because in the recent past therapist's actions around the issue have become subject to complaints and further ethical scrutiny (BACP, 2004). One example of the risks involved is that therapists might find themselves subject to disciplinary action being taken; for example, there was a case where a therapist's 'facial expressions' formed part of the subject of a complaint heard and upheld by the British Association for Counselling and Psychotherapy (BACP, 2004). With so many clients in therapy now taking antidepressants, it is imperative that counsellors feel capable and secure enough to engage in dialogue with clients about their medication: what it means to them, how the client feels about taking it, and what if any impacts it might have for therapy. The guidance developed by the APPG will be an essential source of information for PCE-CfD therapists.

Case Vignette 1: Sam and Cath

In this case example and vignette, the client Sam, a 46-year-old woman and mother of three children, has been taking antidepressants for 18 months. She began to reflect upon and question her initial decision to start taking the drugs. Sam is now considering what her options are concerning continuing to use the antidepressants, stopping altogether and the impact either of these might already have had, or potentially could have on her experiences in therapy. The therapist is Cath, who has worked in the NHS service for around ten years and prior to training in PCE-CfD she had trained as a PCE therapist. Before that she worked as a psychiatric nurse for eight years. We pick up the work at about 15 minutes into session 9.

(Continued)

(Continued)

Session 9

C1.	... so it's hard having sort of dulled emotions and just being flat most of the time, no matter what happens or how angry I think I should be or something, I just feel sort of flat and dead.	
T1.	You feel flat and I can really hear this now, you feel kind of flat and dull and it's in your voice right here.	Cath focuses on the 'here and now' experience of Sam. As PCE theory tells us, as the client expresses their experiences 'they are the experiences'. In this instance Sam 'is' the dullness she expresses and this can be heard in her tone of voice.
C2.	Yeah, I am, I just kind of feel flat, dead, like there's nothing going on when I know really that there is.	
T2.	Like, some of what you experience isn't quite all it might be ...? There's something missing for you?	Cath empathises with the idea that Sam is missing a part of who she feels that she can be if she were experiencing more fully.
C3.	Yes, I sort of feel that, that I am more than this flatness. There's more to me, I've more to say or to think or something but I really, I just can't seem to get a hold on it.	
T3.	Aha, like there's something stopping you from experiencing things more fully; you feel there's more to come but it can't be reached. You can really sense the dullness but there's something more beyond that.	Here Cath is following Sam in her frame of reference but also helping her to focus on her internal felt sense of the dullness or there being something 'more to me'.
C4.	Exactly, like I want to feel that something more, I know there's more and I just can't seem to get at it, to get a better sense of me ... [Short period of silence for around 30 seconds where Sam seems to have 'gone inside herself'.] I guess there's an upside to this too ... I think it started when I first went to my doctor. God, I was really all over the place then. In fact, the opposite to now.	Sam notices inside that she comes to a different meaning of the flat feelings. Now they become something more; new experience is being symbolised.

T4.	Right, so you feel things have been really different, when they were, you were really feeling a lot of things and in a really up and down kind of way. Is that it?	Cath is accepting Sam here and not attempting to cajole her or push her into any specific direction and simply stays close to her moment by moment expressions. She notices that this apparent change in focus has come following the responses to her last empathic reflection. Sam seems to have made something of a connection by turning inside and getting closer to the 'dullness' and the something more.
C5.	I was really up and down back then and it was frightening to be honest. I didn't feel … I wasn't in control of my feelings and one minute I was going about my day-to-day stuff and that and the next I was rock bottom, crying and not feeling like there was any point to anything.	
T5.	You really were as low as you could get right then, at rock bottom, in those moments … which seemed to just come on so fast and you'd fall so far down into that feeling … of pointlessness. Sounds like it was quite a scary thing for you.	Cath is lowering her tone here to match as Sam seems to be getting in to something potentially quite upsetting as she recalls how she'd been falling in the past. The gentle tone is helping Sam to feel contained and safe in the relationship.
C6.	It was scary, and I was scared of what I might do sometimes.	
T6.	Scared of maybe hurting yourself or harming yourself in some way …?	
C7.	Yup, I knew I never would though and I've never felt suicidal, properly like, but it was scary to go so low so quickly. So that's how it used to be before I started taking the medication, you know. I went to the doctors and they prescribed me these antidepressants that I told you about before.	
T7.	Right, so there were times that you've been so low that you thought about suicide. Then the medication seemed to help you, sort of level your mood, is that it?	

(Continued)

(Continued)

C8.	Well, kind of.	
T8.	Kind of, and kind of not too. You still get so low you feel suicidal?	Cath is checking her core meaning here as she's got a little confused if Sam means she still 'kind of gets suicidal' and she needs to check this out as she is aware of the increased risks associated with antidepressant medication and suicide, and depression and suicide. and doesn't want to gloss over anything really important.
C9.	No, no not suicidal anymore. Mostly kind of stopped the up and down, or at least stopped the down, 'cause after that there were no ups really.	
T9.	Right, so the medication flattened things off; stopped you going down but also kind of put a lid on things too … you feel it's existing on a level but with little variation.	Cath is clearer now that Sam is not referring to a suicide risk and so is able to re-enter the frame of reference more fully. She is staying with the expressions and trying to get the clarity to help Sam understand her experiencing fully and with a greater differentiated form. The feeling has changed from feeling flat, and dull into something else … at C10 below it becomes known as 'feeling stuck' …
C10.	Yeah, no variation at all. I now just feel stuck, like I can't get to my feelings at all. I don't feel like I am going down at all nowadays. Not since we've done the work here in the counselling. I feel much stronger in myself and more able to manage with life. In fact, I feel like I am managing to do most things. Most things except feel properly; I'm just stuck in this rut.	
T11.	Aha, you are feeling in a rut, stuck and not able to get to some of the feelings you really want to; and you're scared of going back to those days where you could like, just drop down really suddenly into a low mood and feel dreadful.	Cath is trying to be specific about the feelings that Sam is experiencing and is acknowledging that there is 'stuckness' as well as fear about what might happen. Like the 'stuckness' is related to the fear.

		Cath is aware in the session that Sam is feeling that she'd like to stop taking the medication at some point. Cath is holding this in her awareness and leaving it to one side for the time being and is staying as close as she possibly can to Sam's immediate experiencing. She doesn't want to direct Sam to talk about the medication and its impact on therapy at this stage because she believes that Sam will introduce the topic when needed. There are no significant side effects present as Sam has been taking the medication for some time. However, Cath is aware that Sam is taking quite a high dose and this hasn't been reviewed by the GP for some time.
C12.	Yes, that's about it. I'm stuck. I know there's more to work on, more for me to do in therapy but I feel stuck and feel it really is to do with how I changed after starting to take the antidepressants and I don't want go back to how I was before but I can't really feel my emotions properly ...	
T12.	Right, so it's like 'here I am stuck with what to do', scared of going backwards but wanting to work more on emotions, but you just can't feel them enough ... something like that ...	Here Cath uses a form of empathy that uses a 'first person reflection' as if she is speaking from Sam's frame. This is a powerful and evocative form of empathic responding.
C13.	Exactly that. There's my dilemma. I feel stuck in moving forward because my feelings seem hard to reach inside myself and I know that I do feel scared of going back to how I was before ... [Short silence again, then] What would you suggest that I do?	

(Continued)

(Continued)

T13.	I can really hear that dilemma and how important it feels for you to get this right for yourself. Like you really want to make a decision here but you're also unsure which way to go … [*Cath pauses for a few seconds.*] You really want me to suggest a way forward for you, and I guess that's kind of a difficult thing for me to do. As I am trying to understand how it is for you I guess I don't think that I can be really certain that I know for sure what is best for you. As you know I'm not a medical doctor, and do not have the experience of being a prescriber and it wouldn't be right for me to tell you what to do about taking antidepressants or not. I do hear you're feeling stuck and you worry about going backwards and these things are really important to you. You want to continue to progress but feel blocked because of feeling dull and flat. You also feel anxious about stopping the antidepressants because of how distressed you once were before. It's like you're not sure you can fully trust your own choices yet, is that it?	Here Cath is being very careful to not immediately and unthinkingly give instruction to Sam as she wants to be clear about her role and her area of expertise and the limits to this. The proposal to discuss any changes to antidepressants with the prescriber is important and an ethical action on Cath's part.
C14.	Yes, that fits for me. Like I want to stop taking the medication because I do feel like it's not helping me, but I don't know if I can really trust that in myself at the moment and to not slip back into those really depressing feelings I used to have.	

T14.	Right, so you feel stuck in making progress in therapy and stuck in whether you can trust your own choices. That's really a difficult position to be in.	In this response Cath doesn't try to force the issue in any specific direction even though she feels that Sam is really opening things up for herself. The unconditionality in Cath's responses are what creates the chance for Sam to take the dialogue in whatever direction she feels would be the right direction for change.
C15.	It is, and at the same time I really think we're getting somewhere, even just opening up and talking about this is helping me *feel* like there are at least some choices for me now. I haven't felt that for a long time and, as we're talking about it here, I really feel like maybe I could one day stop taking the antidepressants.	
T15.	It feels a bit of a relief for you to get this out into the open. There's a sense of more choice for yourself and that feels a little more hopeful.	Cath emphasizes the feeling of relief and hope here, and this is linked to the perception of choice. PCE theory stresses how important it is for the client to perceive there to be choices. Sam is experiencing in her self-concept the feeling of being unable to trust herself, and feelings of being stuck and frightened are starting to become more flexible and fluid and this gives the feeling of relief and of potential. As these feelings are experienced in more specific terms they have more impact on her awareness.
C16.	Hmmm. I guess, now I think about it, I could do lots of things really; I could maybe talk to my GP about how I'm feeling, and I could see what they say. You know like when	

(Continued)

(Continued)

	I went to them before when I was really scared. I do feel ready to make a change and starting to think about life without medication again does make me feel a little bit … excited to be honest … [*Sam expresses this with a little surprise in her voice.*]	
T16.	You feel like something is shifting, like there's more a *feeling* there, you're excited about this and maybe a little surprised to feel that. So, you might follow up with this outside the session.	Cath reflects the feelings that Sam has expressed and also the sense of surprise that Sam has experienced at her ability to experience feelings. Cath expresses the possibility that Sam can speak to her GP although she doesn't want to create a sense of conditionality about this for Sam. If Sam decided not to visit the GP and return next time that would be equally acceptable.
C17.	Yes. I really feel that I will; I want to look at this with my GP. That's my next step.	

Following the session Sam did book an appointment and went to speak to her GP. She has a good relationship with the GP and whilst she hasn't been to see the doctor since she started counselling, the GP recalls just how low Sam had been before taking antidepressants. The GP looked at her notes and reminded Sam that back at the time when she first came to see the GP she hadn't wanted to go to counselling and that the antidepressants had actually been offered as a second line option. The GP really supported Sam's decision to start counselling and said they thought it seemed timely to review the anti-depressant prescription, especially as Sam was now making constructive changes through counselling. The GP acknowledged that the medication couldn't possibly lead to the changes Sam was making in therapy and that she must have been putting a lot into the counselling. Sam and the GP discussed a tapering process where Sam would gradually reduce her dosage during which time she would keep in regular contact with the GP. The GP wrote to Cath and explained the process that had been agreed with Sam. Sam missed the next week's session due to a child care situation and then returned two weeks later having already started to taper her antidepressants with the GP's support. This short interaction below was about five minutes into the next meeting and shows how things unfolded.

Session 10

C1.	Yeah, I'm really glad I went to speak to the doctor about the antidepressants. They were really supportive, and we agreed that I'd gradually start to reduce the dose. Did you get a letter?	
T1.	Yes, thank you, I got the letter, you sound relieved by looking at this with the GP.	
C2.	I do, I think I'd been avoiding facing up to the issue in myself. Like I'd become a bit stuck but mostly that feeling of being stuck was about not feeling confident enough to try things without the medication.	
T2.	Right, so feeling that you were a bit scared of even thinking too much about coming off antidepressants. That trust in yourself needed to find a voice.	
C3.	Yeah, I was scared that I would lose what I've gained in counselling, I think, and I didn't want to go backwards.	
T3.	You worried about going back to that dark place where you would feel very low.	
C4.	Yes, I was but I know now that I won't or if I do, I will know what I can do to help myself. I've really learnt that I'm more aware of my needs than I was before. I learnt this by facing the antidepressant issue … that I can do things even when I'm scared or don't believe in myself.	
T4.	You've really come to trust in yourself more and what you're capable of achieving.	Cath is empathically tracking Sam here as she is clearly expressing how she has internalised the locus of evaluation. Cath is feeling satisfied that her empathic following in the previous meeting was experienced by Sam as without threat to the self-configuration that really didn't trust in herself.
C5.	I have, I'm quite surprised that this is actually me saying these things.	

(Continued)

(Continued)

T5.	Is this really me, do I really believe in myself this much ...?	Cath reflects the new sense of self emerging in Sam again using a first-person empathic response. As personal constructs are revised it is natural for a new, more resilient self-concept to be configured.
C6.	That's right, and I do now. I really feel I can trust in myself and I know what I need much more clearly now. I've learnt to trust my feelings.	
T6.	Right, so now it's like you can feel things more clearly and you are the one that knows yourself and your needs best ...	
C7.	That's right. And I know I can do this. And I can FEEL it [Laughs.]	
T7.	You can FEEL it right now, I can see it too on your face and hear it right here in your voice.	

Following this session Sam continued to work on the self-discrepancies in her self-concept, moving from a person that really experienced a lot of fear and self-doubt to someone that could achieve things in life, and as someone who could really trust in her own feelings and be able to self-direct through the challenges of life. Importantly, in these exchanges Cath never tells Sam what to do or how to approach coming off her antidepressants. For Cath this is important; Cath had her own beliefs about antidepressant use and the effects this can have on therapy. Nevertheless, she realises it could have been unethical in these circumstances to give direct advice on what Sam should do. Instead, Cath was willing and open to engage in discussion about the antidepressants and the meaning of this to Sam. Cath was able to support Sam to explore her thoughts about stopping, which resulted in Sam using her agency to approach the topic with her GP. Cath remained open to any further exploration and for the session to follow whichever direction Sam wanted to take it.

This section has looked at the issue of antidepressants within PCE-CfD. These issues are complex, and therapists really need to appreciate the complexity and be informed about different types of prescribed psychiatric drugs and their effects. Importantly, therapists should also be aware that clients will feel very differently about their use of antidepressants and to avoid making assumptions about how clients will feel. It is important for PCE-CfD therapists to engage in these explorations with the client. As we saw above, even discussing the topic in an accepting environment can sometimes be sufficient for the client to take further action and make constructive decisions in their change process. In PCE-CfD, being able to access emotions and work with these is an important part of the therapeutic process. Antidepressants can be a barrier to this, but not always.

Process-facilitation responses

In this section further consideration will be given to the notion of process-facilitation responses and their place within PCE-CfD. These responses are often taken directly from EFT or the focusing approach. In PCE-CfD, it is recognised that there is a broad scope for the sensitive use of process-facilitation responses. These are, as stated earlier, invitations to clients and are intended to help focus on supporting the process and expression of feelings and for developing greater understanding of self-experiences and their implicit meanings. For this to be maintained within a constructive therapeutic relationship, there needs to be a significant degree of attention paid to ensuring that these process-facilitation responses are conveying the therapeutic attitudes of empathy, positive regard and genuineness.

There are several such responses that are recognised as being part of PCE-CfD. These are clearing a space, systematic evocative unfolding, emotion regulation, processing problematic dialogues between self-configurations, creating meaning, and unfinished business. However, there are also other process-facilitation responses that have been proposed by David Rennie (1998) that are also very helpful in supporting clients process experiences and would be consistent with PCE therapy. For example, Rennie suggests that the therapist can respond to their client by using metaphor and imagery, being transparent, making process identification responses, and through metacommunication. As the PCE-CfD approach continues to develop, these and other response modes will undoubtedly be researched further.

For the remainder of this chapter, process-facilitation responses will be explored as they are offered as an emergent property of the natural flow of the therapeutic dialogue. This will show how their skilled application can go some way to help further develop the empathic understanding and unconditional acceptance for the client. We have already seen in the previous chapters examples of clearing a space, meaning creation and emotion regulation. In the examples below we will focus on process-facilitating responses, including processing unfinished business and systematic evocative unfolding with some further meaning creation work.

Case vignette 2: A return to Habiba and Steph

Unfinished business

Increasingly in everyday therapeutic discourse, having to process feelings and emotions related to unresolved past relationships is referred to as processing 'unfinished business'. It refers to unresolved interpersonal issues which the counsellor will become aware of through empathic engagement with the client. Lingering unresolved feelings such as hurt and resentment relating to a person who was significant but may no longer be present in the client's life are usually indicative of unfinished business. In these instances, the key process-facilitation response is to metaphorically bring the missing third party into the room. This is done by exploring the client's experience of the significant other in the client's imagination. We saw an example of a similar process to this in Chapter 4 when Alan was working with Jill on processing his feelings about his father.

What follows is the process of working with a self-configuration, except that this time it is the absent third party who is engaged in dialogue in the client's imagination. Often, it can simply be a matter of saying what was left unsaid or expressing feelings towards the other person, and on other occasions the client might engage in more complex dialogue with the missing person. It goes without saying that addressing unfinished business head-on can be extremely difficult for the client, and the counsellor must be ready to support the client to regulate their emotions as the work proceeds.

Working with unfinished business can be a creative way of helping clients express long-held resentments. It is worth noting that dialogue with a missing person need not be limited to verbal exchanges, and it is not even necessary for them to be completed in the therapy session. Some clients, especially those who are used to keeping diaries, might find it useful to write a letter to the missing person. It is not necessary to specify a series of stages for resolving or 'finishing' the unfinished business, other than to acknowledge that along the way clients might identify and work with unmet needs, revise their perception of the other, say goodbye or let go of the other (or find an adaptive way of holding them close) and so on. Resolution of unfinished business will almost certainly be signalled by an experiential shift clearly felt by the client when the other person is called to mind.

Earlier the work of Habiba and her counsellor Steph was introduced. This vignette sees a return to this therapeutic dyad. Sessions five to eight saw Habiba gaining in confidence slowly and tentatively. The meaning-creation work also indicated that she had developed a slightly different way of understanding love which left her feeling less than *completely* violated and betrayed by her expectations. Having said that, there are no dramatic breakthroughs. She feels stronger in herself, less beaten up and betrayed and *thinks* about 'stepping outside the front door' – a metaphor she uses to describe getting more involved in a world beyond her children and reconnecting with her friends and community.

She identifies one obstacle to her feeling able to try to 'step out': her sense of shame, humiliation and worthlessness brought about by her husband's actions.

Session 9

C1.	It's his fault, I still think that, deep down. I can't find a way round it. He can't undo what he's done. He doesn't want to and I don't want him to. I hate him for it ... I'm sorry I keep saying that over and over, but it's true. I didn't do anything. He did and he's ... I'm too ashamed to ... I have very bad feelings for him.	Steph realises that not only are the feelings very present for Habiba, but that there might be a need to complete some possibly unfinished business with her husband.
T1.	You blame him, and you feel very strongly that he *is* to blame. When you talk like this, it's almost as if he is in the room here. How would it feel if were like to try something ... to see if you can move past these feelings? Would that be helpful?	Two chairs are not necessary to facilitate this kind of dialogue, especially when a client finds visualisation as easy as Habiba.
C2.	It depends, but you're sort of right about him being here. I can see him clearly, even though it's been years.	Unfinished business can be finished in a number of ways, limited only by the creativity of the client and flexibility of the counsellor. Artwork and writing are commonly used by counsellors with expressive therapy experience. It is important to remember that all chair work actually has its roots in drama therapy.
T2.	OK, so it's not a big leap of your imagination to think what you would like to say to him if he really were here now. What would you say?	
C3.	What, you mean here, now, like standing over there?	
T3.	Yes, if that's what you can imagine. That he's standing there now, what would you say to him?	
C4.	Well, okay. You ... you bastard! I hate you! You lied to me, you have ruined my life and ... I ... want you to know that. To know *how much* ... *how bad* you have been! You should be ashamed of yourself!	

(Continued)

(Continued)

T4.	Okay, wow, that was one barrel of your shot-gun, so to speak. But since you can see him, how about trying something a little more difficult, how about making it really personal and using his name.	It is a risk to see if Habiba can tolerate using Rafiq's name. Steph uses her sensing and moment-to-moment understanding of where Habiba is up to.
C5.	[*Habiba looks at Steph intently for a second, gives a half-smile, takes a deep breath ...*] Rafiq, you bastard, it's you who should be ashamed, not me! *Not me!!*	

Habiba continues to express anger at Rafiq for several minutes, with Steph following closely and supporting her expressions. During this time, she begins to feel stronger in relation to the Rafiq in her imagination and can shift her feeling of shame and humiliation. Subsequently, when the session returns to empathic following she feels stronger in herself. With this increase in confidence she plucks up the courage to 'step outside the front door'. To begin with this is still in the service of her children – she joins the parent–teacher group at their school and helps plan a fundraising event.

The dialogue above is an example of a straightforward process-facilitation response to support the client working with unfinished business. Of course, it is not always this straightforward and sometimes clients will be less inclined to engage in the activity. In these circumstances the PCE-CfD therapist always respects the client's choice and right to self-direction in the sessions. Alternatively, a client might become so distressed that they are not able to engage in the process of dialogue with the other person. The PCE-CfD therapist's task then is to help regulate the client's emotions with them, so they can process their experiences and not become overwhelmed.

A systematic evocative unfolding and meaning creation dialogue

As stated previously within this book, it is not uncommon for people who come to therapy and feel depressed to have previously experienced something traumatic in their life. This is of course also possible in other presentations, such as feeling anxious. However, often distressing events that include instances where people are treated harshly and made to feel worthless can have a lasting negative effect on the self-concept. Repeated attempts to change one's self-perceptions and evaluations through trying to protect others or please them invariably end unsuccessfully, and with feeling increasingly more worthless or powerless to change. These negative self-perceptions require therapists to be sensitive, caring and to create the accepting and empathic environment for deep searching and discovery required to reach a different self-evaluation. Close empathic following of one sort is referred to in PCE therapy as 'systematic evocative unfolding', a term which is taken directly from EFT. This often leads to the uncovering of distressing memories and emotional experiences that can be processed, giving way to finding new meanings and understanding about experiences and the self.

The need to address important aspects within the self-structure became the focus for Habiba in therapy. As Habiba continues making steady progress with Steph for a few more weeks, she begins to focus in on deeper self-experiences. In these sessions Habiba is starting to understand herself in increasingly differentiated terms; she sees that many of her feelings towards herself are really rooted in introjected values about herself taken on from earlier experiences in childhood. Some of these self-perceptions are related to views about herself acquired through experiences at school. We pick up the therapy at session 12 when Habiba is on the verge of disclosing something that has been really troubling her for some time but only now is she starting to symbolise her feelings more clearly.

Session 12

C1.	There's something I keep remembering and … It's hard to say.	Habiba is keen to disclose something important to Steph but Steph has no intention to cajole or convince Habiba that she must say what she's been remembering of late. Steph is working hard to stay close to Habiba's experiencing from her frame of reference and check her understanding of the core meaning.
T1.	It sounds important Habiba … you keep remembering it but you're not sure if you can say … here … or at all? Is that right?	
C2.	Both really … but you've been so helpful … I would never have got this far without your help.	
T2.	You feel I have helped … but you're not sure if you can say this memory … It feels risky to say it to me?	
C3.	Yeah … risky … but oh, I've got to say it to someone.	

(Continued)

(Continued)

T3.	You feel you've got to say it to someone and this place has been ok for you to say many things, is that right?	
C4.	I've felt free here at times … freer than ever.	
T4.	Free, free to say anything?	
C5.	Yes, yes, it's different, really different.	
T5.	That sounds important Habiba, that somehow you may risk saying something but you're unsure how I may receive what you say.	Here Steph really gets the sense that for Habiba the risk is in confronting Steph with what she has to say. She feels that their differences might prevent Steph from truly understanding. However, the groundwork of their relationship has been laid and there is sufficient accepting presence being shown by Steph that Habiba feels secure enough to proceed with sharing her experience.
C6.	Oh … how can you hear it, really, how can you know?	
T6.	You think I can't really hear as how would I know; how could I understand?	
C7.	Yeah well, we're different, you have no idea … it was hell.	
T7.	So powerful a feeling, 'hell', unthinkable and so distressing and I am different, you feel that is a barrier.	
C8.	[*After a pause of about two minutes*] … A teacher should know better.	
T8.	A teacher, someone with power sounds, really scary.	In this passage Steph gently follows Habiba in expressing these distressing thoughts from her past. She rightly empathically understands the issues in the here and now that Habiba is feeling about disclosing her experiences of racism. Steph does not back away from this and uses the words chosen by Habiba to validate her meaning of 'racist teacher'.
C9.	Oh, it's in my dreams … her face, shouting those words, in front of the class … oh, I couldn't tell my parents, they were so proud, so sensitive, if I'd said anything to them, it would have been a nightmare, they'd have made such a fuss …	
T9.	You couldn't tell your parents and it haunts you in your dreams, you can't say but you wish you could and it feels like you are trying to Habiba, it sounds so important.	

C10.	She was a racist; my teacher was a racist and she treated me like dirt, I thought I was nothing, so when I met Rafiq I felt grateful ... I felt grateful ...	Steph is also supporting Habiba in making sense of how the racism left her feeling worthless and also ashamed to tell her parents. Although Habiba doesn't use the word 'shame' to convey her feeling, Steph does this and it fits for Habiba. This helps Habiba develop a greater experiential specificity and emotion focus.
T10.	This sounds so very important to remember Habiba, that someone in power made you feel ... it's ... The racist teacher, as if she made you feel ... unworthy or, powerless?	
	[*Habiba has head down, nods in agreement, slowly.*]	
	And ... is it you fear I won't accept or believe this, that somehow, as a white woman, how can I possibly understand?	
C11.	Hmmm. [*Lifts head to look at Steph in the eye. Then closes her eyes and nods in agreement.*]	
T11.	I am so relieved you have risked telling me Habiba, and understand you felt unsure to let me know ... a racist teacher with so much power all those years at school ... so deeply threatening. You couldn't tell your parents, and it went in so deeply that when you met Rafiq you felt grateful.	
C12.	Yeah. I felt worthless and he just came along, and I felt good, at first. It's always been there though.	
T12.	Something so deep inside in you that's been pushing its way into your awareness all this time.	
C13.	I hate her ... how dare she do that to a child. I was the only girl in the school who looked like me and she made everyone believe I was less than they were.	

(Continued)

(Continued)

T13.	An unbearable and unjust thing to do to anyone Habiba, she exploited her power and treated you so badly. [*Habiba has started trembling.*] I wonder if you can just try and breathe a bit Habiba, just breathe in and slowly let the breath out. [*Habiba breathes a little more consistently and starts softly weeping.*] [*Steph sits quiet for a minute then says*] It's really important for you to let those tears fall. Habiba, thank you for letting me be with you in this. [*Head in hand, H continues to weep … after a few minutes she looks up.*)	Steph is aware that by trembling Habiba is in an intense, and possibly cathartic, process. This is not unusual in PCE-CfD as the organismic impact of an internalised and unexpressed event will inevitably involve some element of embodied reaction. Steph quietly acknowledges the tears and validates Habiba by expressing her unconditional positive regard for Habiba demonstrating her accepting presence. This is particularly important at this point as Habiba had previously made it very clear that she wasn't sure if she could risk sharing this experience of racism with Steph.
C14.	I need to say … to cry to get it out after 30 years of not saying … ever …	
T14.	You've held on for so many years and you don't want that pain any more.	

Throughout this dialogue Steph was continuously and closely empathically tracking Habiba and enabling her to follow her next right step as she unfolds her experiencing. In PCE-CfD, the therapist does not have to make full sense of the client's expressions all the time; many skilled PCE therapists will be able to tolerate significant amounts of uncertainty and confusion within their client's process. Habiba was clear and Steph was able to help her to gain the satisfaction she sought through symbolising and expressing deep emotions from her past. What is noticeable in this passage is how there was an option for Steph to introduce chair work to Habiba but she didn't. At the point where Habiba introduced her feelings towards her teacher who had expressed racist attitudes towards Habiba, it could have been possible to see if there was a need for something more directive. Instead, Steph sensed that Habiba was making her own way and didn't require the additional suggestion and so stayed with the unfolding of this traumatic experience.

Through this systematic unfolding, led by Habiba and facilitated by Steph, a greater clarity of feeling was achieved and Habiba developed new understanding and meaning about her experiences and she began the process of revising her self-concept. Habiba returns in session 13.

Session 13

C1.	I feel so much happier.	Steph is instantly responsive to Habiba's expression. Notice that Steph does not say 'that is good'. To say something is 'good' generates a value judgement which may indicate to a client that their happy feelings are better than others. Steph validates the importance to Habiba of feeling happy.
T1.	You're feeling good and I can see you smiling.	
C2.	I went out last session and then I drove to my mum's. I told her about what happened to me when I was younger at the school, she believed me. We both cried.	
T2.	So much, so much in one day ... you risked speaking your truth and then you broke a silence.	
C3.	Yeah, yeah, it's so different now I feel so different.	
T3.	Something different ... you know you feel different ... is it the happy thing you said, you feel happier and that's so different	Steph continues to track and engage with implicit emotion.
C4.	[*Laughs.*] Yeah, I feel no one can get to me anymore. Really. Everything's changed, but nothing's changed. I still live where I live, I still do what I do, but inside, it's so very different.	
T4.	Something inside no longer hurts?	
C5.	Yeah – I tell you, it's bigger than that, it's like I said last week, I feel free here, but now I feel free outside too.	

In the sessions above the majority of therapist responses are close empathic tracking responses. Another way of being empathic more suited to some client–therapist dyads is for the therapist to engage more evocatively with emotions. Evocative empathy can be a helpful way to support clients who might struggle to touch on emotions because of many years of learning that it didn't help them to do so. Such learning is often had in the context of personal relationships with significant others. Therapy provides an opportunity for a different kind of relational space where the client can express themselves in new ways. As the client becomes more aware of and accurately symbolises previously denied or distorted experiences, the therapist can help the client learn that their experiencing can be trusted once more. As previously stated, clients who seem stuck in processing experience in a depressed manner might find it difficult to express emotional aspects of their experiencing.

Through the sessions that have looked at Habiba and Steph's work together a number of examples of both therapist responses and client processes have been explored. These examples highlight the multi-layered feature of a client who is feeling depressed. Habiba and Steph have shown us how much more complex the experience of being depressed often is and how the focus on 'symptoms' can be a significant block to making therapeutic progress. For example, Habiba has shown how the initial presentation of depressed experiencing was really an expression of many other factors that had come together in her life and left her feeling this way. These included the distress of having been left by her husband and the sense of loss this elicited. However, this was understood in terms of the shattering of a cherished belief and other strong conditions of worth. Then still further into the work she uncovered past upsetting and traumatic experiences of racism that had left their mark and contributed to feelings of worthlessness. The final step in this cycle was for her to make a new meaning and come to understand herself as free and not needing to be loved by Rafiq for ever in order to feel worthy.

Case vignette 3: Alicja and Victor

Finally in this chapter one further case example and vignette is used to show how empathic responses within PCE-CfD can be evocative in their focus and feature a process-facilitation focus. Both these aspects of empathy can help the client to experience more fully their emotions. Alicja is a 60-year-old Polish woman and has lived in the UK for 25 years. Her children and her grandchildren live close by to her and are usually around for her if she needs them. This is Alicja's ninth session out of a potential 20. Alicja came to therapy due to a long-term illness that she feels has contributed to her feeling depressed for some time. Alicja has talked in previous sessions about her sense of isolation, feeling alone and abandoned by her own parents and extended family. Alicja's parents stayed in Poland and she has had little contact with them since moving to the UK, having had a difficult childhood, and experiencing a lot of conflict in the family home. Victor thinks that Alicja has engaged well with the therapy and that whilst she is working on some significant issues in her life, there are further aspects of herself that could become the focus of therapy. However, he is keen to respect Alicja in therapy and does not push her towards anything specific that might be based on his own thoughts about Alicja. The therapeutic relationship is relatively well established and they both feel that the therapy is going well. Despite these positive aspects of the therapy, Victor has often felt and discussed in supervision that Alicja could end therapy quite suddenly and without reaching the full 20-sessions permitted. We pick it up about 20 minutes in, where Alicja is talking about her daughter and granddaughter.

Session 9

C1.	You would think she'd want her Mum with her on her child's birthday.	

T1.	It's difficult to make sense of it. 'Why wouldn't she want me there?'	Here Victor is noticing to Alicja how she is processing her experience.
		Victor is speaking from the client's 'I' perspective and is thus able to express and communicate a deep empathy. In turn, and with his attuned tone in his voice, it helps communicate an accepting presence.
C2.	I know! You'd think she'd want her daughter to be with me, her Nana. [*Close to tears.*]	
T2.	It really hurts that you don't get to be together ... that she doesn't want you to be there.	Here the response is showing two features of empathic understanding. First is the reflection that focuses on the content, and second is the expression of a close attunement to the in-the-moment feeling that uses a slight empathic conjecture that the client is feeling deeply hurt. This is helpful for expressing psychological holding as the therapist is being with the client's vulnerability.
C3.	She knows how hard it has been for me since my partner died, and then I got ill ... [*Tears stop her talking.*]	
T3.	Those feelings just stop you in your tracks. Sadness, loss ... It is hard to hold it all?	Victor is very tuned into how Alicja is experiencing at present. He is empathising with how she experiences the rejection of her daughter as a kind of jolting and being stopped in her tracks; this empathic statement is evocative.
		Victor's response also includes another empathic conjecture identifying the feelings of sadness and loss. As Alicja's tears start to fall he recognises the potential for her to be overwhelmed and ends his statement offering a sense of how hard it is to hold it all. This recognition is also providing a sense of psychological holding.

(Continued)

(Continued)

C4.	It is a big ball of pain ... here in my chest ... that I can't seem to shift ... I can't seem to share ... with her, with any of them.	
T4.	It takes up this space here [*Points to chest.*] ... and it looks like it's hard to even swallow? It is too much to hold but no one else will be with it, with you ...	Victor's response shows he is empathising with Alicja's experience of holding the pain. He tentatively checks how this is being experienced and acknowledges and checks out the sense of overwhelm.
C5.	Yeah, I feel like I must swallow it down.	
T5.	That feels like the only option with these painful feelings, this ball of pain, that it isn't ok to share and leaves you feeling in pain, alone ...	In this response Victor is helping with unpacking the ball of pain by differentiating the experience. He also seems to get the core meaning that there's nobody to share the feelings with, leading to a sense of aloneness.
C6.	If I tried to share how I feel ... it is just turned into more of me not being a good mum.	
T6.	Sharing it, or even just having these feelings, means 'There you go it is just another way I am proving that I am not a good mum'?	Here Victor empathises and shows his understanding of the core meaning – 'I am a bad mum'.
C7.	Yeah, then I can't speak at all, I swallow it down, by myself, and feel terrible.	
T7.	Just feels really terrible, you hide away, and you hide 'it' away, swallowing *it* down but *it* tastes and feels awful.	The response here is attending to how *it* feels to swallow down the experience of feeling like a bad mother. In PCE-CfD the 'it' is the felt sense of something else. When the client works at differentiating the 'it', then they become closer to their experiential process.
C8.	I am just left with this empty feeling then. Even I don't want to be with me.	
T8.	Emptied out, like you don't want to even be with yourself ... feels like it is a stuck place you are used to being in?	Alicja is moving the track here to being alone and Victor continues to track the 'empty' feeling.

C9.	It is, it feels all too familiar. It is like a really dark familiar room, where I go when I am not wanted.	
T9.	Feels familiar, not being wanted. Like the only thing to do is take yourself away. To this place.	Victor responds to Alicja's agency by responding to how she takes herself away. This is showing an understanding of how Alicja regulates her own emotions and is empowering.
C10.	Yeah. I seem to be alone, too much. [*Sort of shivers.*]	
T10.	It is familiar, and it is dark, like it is both safe but also a really cold isolated place to be ...	Victor again empathises with what he sees and offers the conjecture that it is a familiar/safe place but also a cold isolated place. This is really helping Alicja to become more specific about her experiences and the responses facilitate greater expression, elaboration and connection.
C11.	[*Makes a movement like a shiver with her body.*] Yeah, thinking of it now makes me shiver ... I am sick of it though ... sick of putting myself there.	
T11.	Feels like you put yourself there? And you really desperately want to find a different way, a different place to go with these feelings.	Victor empathises with the client's reflexivity and agency where the client is identifying what she does and what she wants to do.
C12.	I start to wonder if I am just being selfish, or over dramatic, no one seems to want to hear it.	
T12.	There are all these feelings ... and there is also this part of yourself, which questions this and starts telling you that 'It is not ok to have these feelings, to burden other people'? So, then you are still left with them and now feel even worse because you aren't supposed to have them or tell anyone about them. It seems like it just builds up and that ball gets bigger. And you have to be alone with it, but that it is horrible being alone so then you just feel this awful emptiness.	Victor's response here is longer than usual. He feels that they are close to something important for Alicja and he wants to convey his deep acceptance and offer a psychologically holding response acknowledging the complexity of the emotions. In doing so he also empathises with the different configurations/conflict splits.

(Continued)

(Continued)

C13.	God, it is just seems to be so impossible, exhausting.	
T13.	So difficult to see a way out of it? There are these painful feelings and there is the feeling not to share them. You sense that you do it to yourself. That this is somehow your own rule.	Victor is actively reflecting back Alicja's autonomy by recognising her agency in this process but also how she is bound by her own psychological structures.
C14.	Yeah, but I can hear myself now wanting to take the feelings away, push them down.	
T14.	You feel it right now? Telling yourself to push them away? There's a forceful feeling of pushing yourself around.	Here it is possible to see how Victor is working with the client's immediate experiential process of pushing her own feelings away.
C15.	It is a strong force, like I am angry about it, impatient, it just isn't ok, like I'm telling myself 'If you were a good mum you wouldn't be having this problem? So you should just stop being so self-pitying about it and get on with it?'	
T15.	On the one hand it feels really difficult and on the other you're feeling really angry and scolding yourself. Sounds really harsh, this voice telling yourself to stop having these feelings. Keep them to yourself.	These empathic responses are helpful for Alicja as they have a clear 'checking' tone to them. This invites Alicja to explore further and develop greater specificity. Victor notices the marker of the critic here but does not stop the flow to invite Alicja to explore that in different ways to how they are working. The empathy is doing fine at supporting Alicja's self-directing through the process.
C16.	Yeah, it is always there, I don't notice it most of the time, but it is always there.	
T16.	Always there being critical, telling you off.	
C17.	It has never been ok to be sad or needy, I was always told I was too needy.	

T17.	And now you're telling yourself all the time 'You are too needy' and the feelings have to be swallowed down ... And you want to do something different, rather than just 'punish'?	Victor really gets the core meaning of the critical voice and reflects that it is like a punishment. He is also hearing that Alicja has had enough of this in her experiencing and senses that she wants to change. This is very supportive of Alicja's autonomy.
C18.	Yeah, punish! That's what it feels like. I was punished for having feelings! As a child! How ridiculous! When I look back I can't believe it really.	

In this dialogue Victor has been empathically following Alicja. The aim here is to show that even when the client has first come to therapy with a strong condition of worth about expressing emotions, it is possible to remain steady and consistent in experiencing an empathic attitude towards the client and that this can, for some clients, be just what they need more than other forms of process-facilitation responses. There were a number of opportunities where Victor might have suggested using a different approach such as a two-chair dialogue. However, he could see that this might have disrupted the flow for Alicja and so he continues in the rich vein of empathic resonance they were immersed in.

In this chapter we have considered several important points for the practice of PCE-CfD. The issue of prescribed psychiatric drugs is one that will continue to evolve as the research develops. In the meantime, PCE-CfD therapists should feel confident that they are able to engage in meaningful discussion and dialogue about antidepressants when it is introduced by their clients and becomes a significant feature in the client's experiencing. PCE-CfD therapists would be advised to inform themselves about the emerging work of the APPG on prescribed drug dependency and specifically read about the use, effects and symptoms of withdrawal from antidepressant medication.

In addition, we have seen how PCE-CfD therapists can support clients to process their emotional responses and facilitate finding new meanings. This might be in connection to past relationships and distressing experiences. Person-centred theory shows us that when clients become more open to their experiences, and can process experiences more fluidly, they are likely to be moving through a change process and towards better functioning. The therapist's use of process-facilitation responses will help clients express themselves, find new meaning in their experiences and ultimately move closer to evaluating their experiences based on the internal organismic valuing process that they have become estranged from.

Competences covered in this chapter

- **B7** – Ability to experience and communicate empathy
- **B8** – Ability to experience and to communicate a fundamentally accepting attitude to clients
- **B9** – Ability to maintain authenticity in the therapeutic relationship
- **B6** – Ability to work with the client to establish a therapeutic aim
- **S1** – Ability to help clients to access and express emotions
- **S2** – Ability to help clients articulate emotions
- **S3** – Ability to help clients reflect on and develop emotional meanings
- **S4** – Ability to help clients make sense of experiences that are confusing and distressing
- **M3** – Working with the whole person
- **M4** – Maintaining a person-centred stance
- **M6** – Maintaining psychological contact
- **M7** – Capacity to balance therapeutic tasks
- **M8** – Integrating the therapist's experience into the therapeutic relationship

(Competences are listed in Appendix 1)

7

Final Phase and Endings

Chapter overview

- Case vignette 1: Joshua and Naomi
- Case vignette 2: Gerald and John
- Measurement, progress, and endings: Sites of contestation
  - Measurement and outcomes in PCE therapy
  - Measurement guided endings

The final phase and endings in particular are an important part of the process of therapy. An ending is often the start of something new for the client: something that follows the conclusion of what has, hopefully, been a successful and constructive period of change in the client's life. The ending of a period of psychotherapeutic work involves the ending of a relationship, one in which much about the client's life is likely to have been shared. For these reasons, and others possibly, at the end of therapy both the client and therapist are likely to experience a range of feelings. These feelings about the ending might indicate significant meanings about the relationship, about the work that has been completed during this period of the client's life, and links to previous life experiences involving endings. However, whilst the ending is the final event, the period leading in to the ending is a crucial phase in the therapeutic process. How this is *approached* is important for both client and therapist.

In the literature, this phase of the therapeutic process has often been referred to as 'termination'. This term is indeed an unfortunate one, which, it has been suggested, might have been adopted into the English language literature due to a poor early translation of one of Freud's writings (Maples & Walker, 2014). The work that gets done within the ending phase of therapy might vary across different therapeutic approaches. For example, in psychoanalysis there has been debate about the 'techniques' used to work towards the ending. One approach might be for the analyst to agree the end date with the analysand and then continue to work on the principles of 'transference and resistance analysis' whilst the analysand would be expected to go through 'regression, reactivation of symptom complexes and a mourning process' (Golland, 1997: 259).

In PCE-CfD, the final phase of therapy will proceed with the client firmly continuing to drive the process and direction of change. The actual ending of therapy might be arrived at when a point of agreement is reached that the work done is sufficient for the client's current needs. Alternatively, when the client has decided to end therapy prior to reaching the conclusion of their allocated sessions, this might result in either a planned or unplanned ending. Another scenario might be if the client's allocation of sessions is reached, but the ending must be imposed by the structures of the service. In each of these situations, in which the ending of therapy takes place, the uniqueness of the client–therapist relationship will also contribute to the experience of this process and the feelings about the ending being faced. All these points suggest that, during the final phase and ending of therapy, there is a lot to consider and much will be going on.

How the PCE-CfD therapist feels personally about the ending of therapy is also likely to be a factor. Personal feelings that are stirred at the final phase of therapy and ending are a factor that will need to be worked with in supervision. Feelings about endings and their relation to the work going on in therapy are important and essential issues in supervision for PCE-CfD even though this is often provided as a time-limited approach. It is important to ensure that the therapist remains congruent in the relationship, and this is something discussed in more detail in the next chapter.

There are two factors here. The first is the important issue thrown up by working in a time-limited way and to the agreed number of sessions that the IAPT services model are designed around. The second relates to the issue that PCE therapy is based on a growth paradigm and, if time and context permit, will likely extend well beyond any period that sees the distress of depression diminish. This contrasts with the many therapies that are premised on or practised as a deficit model (such as those associated with medical model approaches). Such therapies will consider the end of therapy to have been reached when the client no longer reports significant levels of the 'symptoms' of the diagnosed condition for which they have been referred to therapy. Under such medical model approaches, the client might well even be considered 'cured' (or at least symptom free) and ready for 'discharge' from the service. For PCE therapists, this logic doesn't fit. Even though many clients might initially attend PCE-CfD because a professional has diagnosed them with depression, PCE-CfD therapists do not set about the therapy by targeting the specific symptoms or processes associated with the diagnostic criteria. Rogers was clear on this point; the person-centred approach does not see clients as sick or in need of diagnosis. This remains a very fundamental difference between PCE-CfD therapy and other approaches. Indeed, Rogers said on the concept of diagnosis that therapy itself is a kind of diagnosis. So it happens naturally and it might well be that the ending of therapy is marked by the client's own highly differentiated and articulate exposition of their understanding of themselves and their reasons for coming to therapy.

One important issue related to endings in the context of PCE-CfD is that of outcome measurement. In the context of payment by results, now in place in many IAPT services, the pressure of ending can be felt keenly, and the use of measures to drive this phase and process of therapy is evident. This issue and the conflict of values and ethics for PCE-CfD therapists in IAPT contexts have been discussed by Proctor and Hayes (2017) and some of these issues are addressed in more detail below.

The focus of this chapter is to consider the issues mentioned above that relate to the final phase and ending in PCE-CfD. As with the other chapters on the process of PCE-CfD, case examples and vignettes have been developed to highlight the practice and address some of the issues the therapist might face.

First, the ending of therapy is considered by exploring one client's experience of reconnecting to the organismic valuing process (OVP). As we have seen throughout this book, clients will often be depressed and distressed because of introjected values that lead to conditions of worth. As therapy takes place, the client rediscovers their capacity for valuing experiences based on the internal valuing system that is intrinsic to their personal being.

Second, the issue of working in a statutory health service setting is considered. The IAPT version of the PCE-CfD specifies up to 20 sessions for more severely distressed clients; some clients will need to end therapy having reached that point, regardless of whether they feel their work is complete. Some might end before this point, and some services might offer fewer than the recommended 20-session guideline. Such a scenario is worked out in a case example.

Third, the issue of measurement and outcomes in PCE-CfD and how this is linked to the ending of therapy is explored. This is closely related to when, in statutory health services in the UK, outcome and therapy progress are routinely monitored and are factors in the funding and case management of therapists. Here the potential impact on the ending of therapy will be considered, but also measurement is explored to see how therapists can consider using a broader range of measures to help them in the collaborative decision making with their clients and possibly have greater influence over their service managers and commissioners.

Case vignette 1: Joshua and Naomi

Ending in PCE therapy will often come at a time when the client has shifted from relying on an introjected valuing system and returns to the internal and OVP system. In this case example and vignette, the work with a client Joshua, and the therapist Naomi, is developed to show an example of ending the counselling

(Continued)

(Continued)

process. Towards the end of therapy, the client's conditions of worth are a less potent factor in guiding his actions and he becomes more fully in touch with his own OVP. He subsequently feels less distress through incongruence and is ready to end.

Joshua is a 23-year-old, white, Welsh male client living in England. This was his 19th session out of a possible 20 available in the service. Joshua had left school when he was 16 with just three GCSEs. He had tried to go to college for the sixth form but dropped out. During that time, he had been suspended from college twice for his behaviour that was considered inappropriate or unacceptable by the college principal. The 'bad boy' image that Joshua had developed was both a blessing and a curse. It certainly gave him an identity that got some positive attention from peers. However, it also became more of a vicious cycle in that he constantly felt as though he needed to live up to his 'reputation'. When he first attended therapy, he said that he had felt anxious for as long as he could remember. He said that having always felt anxious had led to him feeling very down and low in mood as he felt he'd never be able to change himself. Prior to starting therapy, and after some considerable time of feeling low, he had started taking ketamine with friends to block out his negative feelings about himself. Subsequently, family relationships started to deteriorate. That was the point he entered therapy. Therapy had progressed really well. Over the course of several months he'd had 19 sessions and had managed to get himself a job at a local supermarket and had started volunteering as a football coach for a local charity that works with young children from disadvantaged backgrounds.

Session 19

C1.	I feel more centred; things are smoother … I seem to be able to handle situations that left me churned up in the past.	
T1.	You feel you are reviewing where you are at now and finding that you feel calmer? More capable.	Naomi simply but accurately identifies the process and agency in recognising that Joshua is reviewing his new capacity for emotion processing. At the same time, she is also checking her understanding of the client's focus and meaning.
C2.	Yeah. Like I had this family get together, which I would normally fret about for ages in advance, and then it came and went, and I even enjoyed it! Even my eldest brother didn't seem so bad.	

T2.	You feel surprised, pleased with yourself even. It's like you hadn't expected that enjoyment was possible for you with your family.	
C3.	Yeah! I suppose I am surprised, yeah, pleasantly actually. I don't think it is true that there isn't fear still; I just don't end up catastrophising, or getting down and then avoiding going out. It doesn't run away with me. I deal with it differently	
T3.	The anxiety can be there and err, it is ok knowing you have different ways of coping with it. It's like a different relationship with it, it's no longer the 'boss' of you ...?	Here Naomi is checking her understanding by tentatively empathically reflecting her understanding. This is apparent in the tone and slight intonation of an implicit question in her checking statement. This is a close tracking of the client.
C4.	Ha! Yeah it doesn't rule me, where I end up in that spiral of feeling stuck. It comes, and I feel, more confident that it will pass. I have lots of other things to think about, there is so much more going on for me now. The fear never gave me a moment's peace before, I was a slave to it. Bizarrely even though I felt it controlled me I think I was a bit addicted to it, or I'd get preoccupied by it ... er ...	
T4.	So, it is like when it comes you can say hello, acknowledge it but it takes up so much less attention and space. It must exist with positive stuff, other stuff you've got going on. You feel like you don't get overwhelmed by it? And here you are sitting ... now asking different questions of it, like if it served some purpose ... just by taking up space and being the centre of your focus.	It is clear that Naomi has a good understanding of Joshua now and is empathising with his idiosyncratic experiential process and reflecting a resolution of the conflict split, recognising the client's capacity to regulate his emotions and she is also with the client's leading edge.

(Continued)

(Continued)

At this point Naomi and Joshua have developed a very good relationship. Joshua has made significant progress in terms of his feelings and experiences of depression. He is active in life again, feels able to go out and meet family and friends and, in doing so, is aware of how much better he feels about himself as a result. As he has just one more session available at the service where Naomi works, this is looking like a good place for therapy to have reached. However, it is not uncommon for clients who have come to therapy because they feel depressed to feel concerned about maintaining the changes they have made. It can be the case that clients might be worried that they can slide back into a more depressive process and they fear a return to the distress of the recent past.

In PCE-CfD, we might think about changes in the distress of depression as changes in behaviours, changes in feeling and changes in perceptions. Each of these is changed due to the shift in the locus of evaluation. As the client becomes reconnected with the internal valuing system they are more likely to act in ways that will support the development and maintenance of their self-concept in a way that is consistent with their experiencing. This is consistent with Rogers' (1964) theory of the OVP. This notion is also supported by research. Sheldon, Arndt and Houser-Marko (2003) conducted a study that looked at people's behaviours and how these were motivated more by intrinsically satisfying than extrinsic factors. The findings suggested this was true regardless of other variables such as social desirability, different underlying motives for goal content, or personal value preferences. They concluded that this was suggestive of an intrinsic tendency towards moving in the direction of behaviours beneficial to the development of the organism. So, as Joshua develops the connection to his OVP, his behaviours will also change, and he will perceive experiences in more realistic terms.

In a second and more recent study, Murphy, Demetriou and Joseph (2015) looked at the mediating effect of intrinsic motivations on people's conditions of worth and personal growth following a traumatic event. This research suggested that when people followed their intrinsic motivations more, they were also more likely to have shown lower conditions of worth and more post-traumatic growth. What we can conclude from this is that a shift in the client's valuing from external to internal is a key point in the therapeutic process.

In the dialogue below, Joshua shows how this internal valuing can form part of consolidating change as the work moves through the final phase further towards the ending of therapy.

C5.	Yeah, I felt that I was watching my life just wash away, I couldn't work, I didn't get out, I would stay awake all night, play video games. Then, if I could, I would score some Special K. Zonk out for a couple of days, supposedly hanging out with mates, but it's just a grim room with lots of other zombies, and it was just so empty, but it stopped the depression for a bit ... But now I think it didn't, not really, it just put me in a hole, a deep pit and at least it was, I was numb ... God! Thank God I got out of that!	
T5.	It's a real and deeply felt relief to be out of that, that dark place. Like you have Got out by the skin of your teeth ...	
C6.	[*Slumps, blows air out of his mouth.*] Yeah, God it was hell really, and I'd hate to go back.	
T6.	As you're looking at that and feeling some of that hell right now? Along with the relief? [*Naomi breathes out reflecting the relief.*] There was something scary about that er, way of dealing with the, it? You didn't feel equipped to get out? Is that right?	Naomi stays grounded with the client's connection to a difficult experience and does not try to move him on from it before he has finished processing the experience. Naomi is psychologically holding all the elements; she does this by tentatively reflecting that hellish feeling and the relief are both present. By also acknowledging the fear that is/was there about the lack of power or the responsibility is further example of psychologically holding all elements equally and is thus able to convey the experience of unconditional positive regard of Joshua.

(Continued)

(Continued)

C7.	It scares me now when I look back. [*Shudders.*] God, I don't even think that I was scared about it, about that, then. Not in a worried about my health kind of way. I was just in a total panic or I was numb. It's what everyone does who I know or knew. I mean there is eff all to do around here, that's what drags you down, or did, I just found ways to numb, to fill up the space where my life should have been.	
T7.	You look back and it makes you shiver, to see how little you, er, 'cared for yourself' then? You do wonder and feel some sadness thinking about how empty it was for you and is for others.	Here Naomi tracks Joshua and again communicates the unconditionally accepting attitude she feels towards him. She is psychologically holding all the self-experiences equally.
C8.	Yeah it does make me sad thinking about it, how lost I was. I was just trying to fit in with all my mates, just so worried about being acceptable to the lads and that … I am just so pleased to not always be the problem anymore. Being a constant worry for others and in a constant low mood about myself. It was like a constant hum droning on in my head, it's there sometimes but I feel like I can hear other stuff now. Like I'm able to listen to myself more and let that be my guide. I really think I am getting somewhere now. One more session then, seems like we're nearly done then …	

Earlier in this book (see Chapter 2) the process of change was presented, and looked at how the client moves from fixed and rigid to more fluid and flexible ways of perceiving. In the dialogue above we can see how the therapist, Naomi, is closely tracking and empathically responding to Joshua in a way that conveys her unconditional positive regard(UPR) of him. This is important because as Joshua experiences the UPR of the therapist, he can permit more and more of his experience in awareness. As he does this, he is being more congruent and can unconditionally accept more of his experiences and for these to be accurately symbolised in awareness. The nature of change regarding UPR is that the client comes to accept themselves more as a direct response to their perceptions of the therapist's experiencing of UPR towards the client's self-experiences. Bozarth (1984/2001: 173) has stated that the therapist's UPR is the primary change agent within the theory of the necessary and sufficient conditions. In his reformulation of Rogers's (1957) statement of the six necessary and sufficient conditions, Bozarth (p. 173) states that 'genuineness and empathic understanding are viewed as two contextual attitudes for the primary condition for change; i.e. unconditional positive regard.' Rogers (1959) also stated that the outcomes of therapy include the client being a) more congruent and open to experience, b) more realistic and objective in perceptions and c) more effective in problem solving; this suggests more enhanced psychological adjustment, increased degree of positive self-regard, more acceptance of others, and behaviour being perceived as more social and mature by others. For Rogers, these outcomes are achieved by the client being able to tolerate more of the threat of incongruence and by reacting to experience less by way of conditions of worth and more by way of the OVP. As we consider the dialogue above, it is possible to see how Joshua is showing that he can tolerate his incongruence and feel the anxiety this creates. He can see and accept himself and his actions in the past without trying to explain them away and instead accepts them as an aspect of himself. Joshua is close to a point that might indicate he is ready to end therapy based on this connection to his internal and OVP, notwithstanding that he must anyway due to the number of sessions being available.

Reaching the ending of therapy can come at a point which might be a surprise to the therapist, especially if this is before the client has reached the number of available sessions. In this regard the client is ending before completing. However, in PCE-CfD, the therapist is always respectful of the client's decision to end at the point that feels right for the client. It could be said that an overarching aim of any PCE therapy is to support the development of the client's self-determination (Grant, 1990). In this sense, when the client feels they are ready to end, the therapist needs to respect that decision. That's not to say the therapist will always agree with the client, but respecting their sovereignty as a person is essential. The actual number of sessions a client needs is ideally always determined by the client. However, many therapists now work in settings where the number of sessions will be determined by the service. This is likely to be due to the contract and basis upon which the service has been commissioned or funded. It is rare for people who don't have access to a lot of money to be able to engage in open-ended therapy. This notion of going on infinitely in therapy takes us back to earlier in this chapter when discussing the meaning of the final phase and ending of therapy in regard to the concept of termination. It is suggested that Freud's seminal text *Die endliche und Die Unendliche Analyze*, which was originally translated as 'Analysis terminable and interminable' would have been more accurately translated as 'Analysis finite and infinite'; this would have been preferable as there are no roots to the word 'termination' in German (Leupold-Löwenthall, 1988) and would have removed the somewhat negative connotation of the idea of 'termination' of therapy.

Case vignette 2: Gerald and John

Gerald, a 58-year-old white male client, came to counselling having experienced a persistent low mood for several months. Visiting his doctor for physical symptoms including aching muscles and joints and feeling very fatigued most of the time but particularly getting worse as the day wore on, the doctor suggested that he try to talk to someone about his low mood. At first Gerald was very sceptical about counselling; never having tried it before, he had always felt that counselling was suitable for other people. After discussing these concerns with his doctor, he agreed that it might be something that could help and that there was nothing to lose in giving it a go. Gerald was referred to see John, also a white male in his fifties. John had previously worked as a firefighter before training to become a counsellor. He and Gerald struck up a good relationship and Gerald found it easier to talk to John than he had anticipated.

The therapy took place within the NHS provision and was therefore under the IAPT arrangement in Gerald's local area. The provider was a third-sector organisation commissioned by the Clinical Commissioning Group. The service was able to provide clients with up to 20 sessions of PCE-CfD. We pick up the dialogue in session 10, following a short break where John had taken some annual leave for two weeks. Prior to this Gerald had been making steady progress, although John had been a little concerned about the impact of the break on Gerald's momentum toward change. The aim of this extract is to show that clients often reach a point in therapy where they personally feel ready to end, and that this might come well before the number of sessions available has been reached.

Session 10

T1.	Thank you for completing the measures Gerald. Where would you like to start today?	
C1.	Thanks, John. Yes, it is good to see you. It feels good to be back here.	
T2.	It feels good to be back and to begin therapy again after this short break.	
C2.	Yeah, it feels good, I think maybe because I no longer feel that dread that I used to get ...	
T3.	The dread ... the dread of being in therapy?	

C3.	Yeah, and the rest!	
T4.	So, something has shifted … during the break, is that right? No more dread about coming to therapy and talking about things.	
C4.	Yeah really shifted. I was worried when you were going away, that in some way I'd retreat again into feeling despair.	
T5.	That really was a worry for you and was something you wondered about as we approached the short break.	
C5.	Yes, and that was really very useful actually; not hiding from the fear I had about it. Talking about it, and you know – well, it didn't happen.	
T6.	There was no retreat into despair and you've found the talking about and being open to your feelings a really helpful thing to do.	
C6.	Yeah, exactly, there was no retreat into despair and I feel like this is the end now. I've learned about how important that is, to talk about my feelings. I didn't want to cancel our session today as I wanted to say goodbye, but I really feel I don't need this anymore.	
T7.	You feel ready to end. That you don't need the space for therapy anymore. Something has happened that you have learned and feel that's enough for you.	John is a little surprised to hear Gerald to say that he wants to end therapy. He is a bit concerned that it might be because he was away and needs to check himself inside as this could become the focus of the session if John is not congruent. John doesn't want to mistrust Gerald's sense of the right time for him to end therapy.
C7.	Yeah, and honestly, I didn't imagine back in August I'd be anywhere near to this.	
T8.	It seemed impossible to imagine you'd feel ready to stop by now and even though we've plenty of time left together this feels the right time to end.	John stays empathically close to Gerald in these exchanges and does not sense any hint that Gerald is not being authentic.

(Continued)

(Continued)

C8.	Don't get me wrong, it's been really hard to come to this, to these sessions and to talk, but now I know what I feel is relevant. And I can feel low sometimes and accept it's ok to feel that way and not feel guilty about feeling it and that it doesn't mean I'm not going to be able to do other things that day, or that the next day won't be a bit better. I've really got more belief in myself and accept that things change quite a bit through life and that I can cope better with life now.	
T9.	You feel you can still be low sometimes but somehow you no longer need the guilt about the feelings and you can accept these feelings more readily.	
C9.	Completely … and there was a moment when you were away where I had a difficult day. I remembered stuff that we'd spoken about, you know, but I found myself sort of offering myself some understanding – like, of course I'm going to feel these feelings, that was a rubbish time and I can't undo those experiences, and now I can accept the feelings I have are ok and not too scary.	
T10.	It sounds as though you can allow yourself a wider range of feelings now and know you will still be okay?	John is sensing and reflecting this increase in openness to experience that Gerald seems to be describing.
C10.	Oh yes, I am able to recognise and understand much of what was behind my low mood. It was a … a real loss of confidence and I'm beginning to really have moments where I feel ok now and that's good for me.	
T11.	You feel as though you really believe you can end our sessions and have this belief in yourself?	
C11.	Yes, I do. It's been interesting to experience this, being listened to. I've noticed I am also listening to others, and it makes a difference because if I really listen then I don't make up in my head what I think the other person is saying. It's great.	

T12.	You feel really different and your perceptions of how others might think or feel about you have changed too.	
C12.	Hmm – I guess yeah, yeah there's a freedom, a way of knowing, I can have emotions now; they may still feel a bit 'unclear' at times to me at the moment but what makes them worse is not letting them out in the open.	
T13.	You really feel more open to your own feelings and not denying them expression.	
C13.	Yeah, they don't have to be wrong, I can just accept the feelings and eventually it's like, they lessen and something else happens or comes along. Being open, as you say, seems to help things change. I used to try and stay fixed on things but that didn't work so well. I can see that now.	
T14.	Something happens when you're open to your feelings and you can trust this process inside you now.	

The remainder of the session was used to consider what Gerald might do to support himself if he began to feel depressed again and how and when he might be able to get further help if required. This consolidation work as the ending approaches is an important feature of the final phase of therapy. In instances such as the above, it is not uncommon for the therapist to be concerned that the client is ending therapy too soon. They may have their own ideas about what the client needs or think that they might benefit from having more sessions. As we have stated above, the ending of therapy in PCE-CfD is always, wherever possible, determined by the client. PCE therapists strive to trust the client to know what is right for them and if the therapy is achieving the aim of supporting the client's autonomy, then therapists can trust the client's decision to end sessions when that feels right for the client. However, that is not say that some clients, some of the time, might leave therapy prematurely. Therefore, if this is a persisting feeling that the therapist has towards the client, it will be important to discuss this with the client in a transparent way. Doing this in a way that conveys the therapist's UPR for the client's decision to end is likely to leave the client feeling that they can continue or come back in the future if required. If the client feels judged by the therapist, then the chances are they may well feel embarrassed or ashamed and will avoid returning to therapy. Mearns and Thorne (2013) suggest that in addition to attending to and

(Continued)

(Continued)

reviewing the counselling process at ending, the therapist and client might also pay attention to their relationship and whether there is any unfinished business between them. In the example above, for instance, time could also be spent exploring the impact of the break that had intervened between their previous session and the last session in which Gerald has decided he's gone far enough for now. Issues related to whether Gerald had felt abandoned or was angry with John for taking a planned holiday during their sessions might also be worthy of exploration, but these decisions must be made by the therapist based on their unique relationship with the client and should not be forced on to the relationship by the therapist.

Measurement, progress and endings: sites of contestation

There is much to say about the use of outcome measures in counselling and psychotherapy in contemporary contexts, and in the last two decades particularly. Some might argue, as Totton (1997) has, that to go along with the therapy world's obsession with outcome monitoring is in a way to be complicit with the medical model view of therapy. There is no doubt that the way that measurement of therapy effectiveness has been used in some sections of the profession has been heavily influenced by the medical model. For example, the routine session-by-session monitoring of clients accessing therapy in primary care settings such as the IAPT programmes available in the UK are extreme. However, Totton (p. 131) also notes that working within the system to make some therapy available that otherwise wouldn't be, is a kind of 'guerrilla tactic'. He argues that taking therapy into settings where it becomes more widely available to those who cannot afford private fees is an effort on the part of some to change the system from within. Some might go as far to suggest that this might even be an opportunity to change and dismantle the medical model from the inside. This is certainly something that others have argued in the development of person-centred counselling in the NHS (House, 1996; Pearce, 2014). Engaging in this 'guerrilla tactic' can be challenging for the people involved, and it is a familiar story to hear that therapists who once entered the healthcare system as practising PCE therapists are, after several years, ground down by the medical model system and will often adopt the values, language and prescriptions of this world view without even noticing. Often, as we will see in the next chapter, when accessing training for PCE-CfD, trainees report that they are re-awakened through the process of training in the PCE-CfD approach. It's like 'coming home', they will often say. Certainly, something to bear in mind with this issue, and in the remainder of this section, is the plea made by Totton (1997) about the philosopher Michel Foucault: that we should all strive to make the places where these issues are being addressed, whether that be in NHS service settings or any other setting, 'sites of contestation' wherein we can challenge the hierarchies and the power structures in place and make the best of such circumstances.

With all of this in mind, the remainder of this chapter will consider and engage critically with some of the issues that are relevant to practice in contemporary contexts in regard to the use of measurement and outcome monitoring. After all, outcome monitoring is now an integral aspect of providing therapy within the NHS and statutory health care settings. Importantly, for many therapists, being able to speak the language of their 'employers and funders' will enable them to engage more effectively when defending and ensuring the place of PCE therapy within various settings. For PCE therapists specifically, it is essential to understand what they are measuring and how this differs from people's actual experiences. Remembering that the measures and scales used in both research and routine outcome monitoring are always approximations of the experiences of clients, and we must never fall into the trap of taking the data collected through the measurement tools as a replacement for the actual experiences of clients.

PCE-CfD therapists must also consider the constructs that different measurement scales are attempting to represent. For example, the National Minimum Data Set (NMDS) – the collection of scales used within the vast majority of IAPT services in the UK – is a set of measures focused on medical model constructs. For example, both the GAD-7 and the PHQ-9 are measurement scales that attempt to represent people's symptoms of anxiety and depression respectively. These scales are widely and freely available for use. Originally, they were developed by Spitzer et al. (1994) for use in clinical trials for antidepressant and other prescribed psychiatric drugs. They are available through Pfizer online (www.phqscreeners.com/) and the PHQ-9 is reproduced here for use in training courses (see Appendix 4). We must question the utility of these scales for evaluating the effects of the PCE-CfD approach because the approach is not based on the medical model ideology.

Measuring outcome in PCE-CfD therapy

The field of PCE therapy has a long history in the humanistic school of psychology. Since the 1950s, the humanistic psychology approach has been concerned with the concepts of optimal or full functioning. Rogers' theory of personality is not merely a theory of psychopathology but is also a theory of optimal human functioning. In PCE theory, wellbeing and health are not simply associated with or can be reduced to the absence of distressing experiences, such as those associated with depression. Take for example the PHQ-9 scale mentioned above. The scale itself measures the presence of experiences that are considered to represent the phenomenon of depression. However, the scale itself assumes that depression is a unipolar construct and therefore could be argued that it deals only with one end of a continuum: that is, when functioning has dipped beneath the midpoint (zero) and being symptom free. Joseph and Lewis (1998) and later Joseph, Linley, Harwood, Lewis and

McCollam (2004) have argued that whilst people scoring highly on some measures of depression might well represent the presence of depression, scoring very low on a measure does nothing to tell us about the presence of wellbeing or happiness, which could be considered to exist at the opposite end of a continuum of depression. Likewise, the absence of happiness does nothing to tell us about the presence of depression. What is required is a more nuanced understanding of the complex nature of emotions and cognitions that accompany our ever-changing experiential states as we move in one direction or another along the continuum of depression–happiness.

One way of appreciating the complexity of the wider range of experiences people have is to consider depression and happiness as opposite ends of a bipolar construct. This idea has received much support in the literature (Russell & Feldman Barrett, 1999; Watson, Wiese, Vaidya & Tellegen, 1999; Yik, Russell & Feldman Barrett, 1999). PCE-CfD therapists could, for example, consider using the depression–happiness scale (or the shorter version: see Appendix 4) to determine the impact of therapy on more than simply the absence of a set of symptoms of depression. Measuring depression–happiness as a bipolar construct is far more in keeping with the PCE theory than the reductionist versions that only see depression as a unipolar construct. Whilst there are many scales available that can measure depression, the depression–happiness scale is one of the first to attempt to intentionally use the depression–happiness construct.

There are many issues for PCE-CfD therapists to consider when it comes to thinking about measurement. When PCE-CfD therapists are required to collect outcome data or monitor the effectiveness of their services for funding purposes, they could consider using PCE theory consistent measures rather than rely solely on measures of symptoms of diagnostic categories. These measures would perhaps be more likely to assess changes in functioning using constructs reflected in the theory and could, for example, relate to actualisation processes. One such scale by Wood, Linley, Maltby, Baliousis and Joseph (2008) is the Authenticity Scale (see Appendix 4). This short self-report questionnaire is a measure of personal authenticity. Within the scale, authenticity is conceptualised as a measure of personality functioning that is consistent with Rogers' (1959) description of congruence. The scale consists of three sub-scales, which include items measuring self-alienation, authentic living and accepting external influence. The scale has good psychometric properties and has been used widely in a range of psychological studies, focusing mainly on general population samples in the study of correlates of authenticity in other personality variables. Further research is needed to look at the clinical utility of the Authenticity Scale to develop the necessary normative and clinical data for computing cut-off scores, allowing for comparison with other scales that focus more on symptoms of diagnostic categories.

In the PCE theory of depression in Chapter 3, it was proposed that depression can be understood as a particular form of discrepancy between self and experience. We also said that as the self-concept becomes differentiated from experience, and values from significant others are introjected, we start to act on those introjected values as if they were our own values. Once this is the case, then we have developed conditions of worth. Conditions of worth can lead to a rigidity in the self-structure and this is associated with the experience of depression. Through PCE therapy, it is reasonable that we might expect to see changes in the conditions of worth that clients seem to have. Or at least we might expect to see the client become more able to act in accord with their OVP. When clients do this, it is because they are being more self-accepting and able to experience more positive self-regard and rely less on the positive regard from others.

The concept of positive self-regard is central to Rogers's (1959) theory of personality development. Patterson and Joseph (2006) developed a self-report scale that attempts to measure this construct and called it the unconditional positive self-regard scale (UPSR). The scale consists of two separate subscales, one to represent the level of positive self-regard and the other to represent the level of unconditionality of self-regard. This breakdown of the construct into the two subscales reflects the Barrett-Lennard relationship inventory (Barrett-Lennard, 1962) subscale for UPR in relationships. The UPSR scale showed good psychometric properties and the self-regard subscale correlated statistically significantly in a negative direction, with depression using the depression subscale of hospital anxiety and depression scale (Dagnan, Trower & Chadwock, 2000). The scale has been used in a small but growing number of studies in relation to the field of PCE therapy, with two recent studies examining the role of UPSR in post-traumatic growth (Flanagan, Patterson & Joseph, 2015; Murphy, Demetriou & Joseph, 2015). The concept of UPSR has also been shown to be related to intrinsic aspiration, suggesting that people with lower conditions of worth might also follow their intrinsic aspirations more than those with higher conditions of worth (Murphy, Joseph, Demetriou & Karimi-Mofrad, 2017). Overall this measure shows promise as a scale that could be used to collect data with clients in therapy, with further research being required to confirm the clinical utility.

There are two further measures that might be considered for use within PCE therapy. The first is the Strathclyde Inventory (Freire, 2007) (see Appendix 4). The Strathclyde Inventory is a measure of congruence that has been used in the clinic setting by researchers in the Strathclyde University Research Clinic. The scale was validated (Freire, Elliott & Cooper, 2007) for use in a clinical population and has since been translated into French (Zech, Brison, Elliott, Rodgers & Cornelius-White, 2018). The scale was designed to measure the changes in personality and moving towards fully functioning that might occur within PCE-CfD therapy, and goes beyond merely measuring changes in symptoms. It is quite likely that changes in the Strathclyde Inventory would be observed in clients who are also changing in the level of depression feelings.

The final scale to be considered here is the personal questionnaire (PQ) (see Appendix 4). The scale was first developed by Shapiro (1961) and has been further developed recently by Elliott, Wagner, Sales, Rodgers, Alves and Café (2016). The PQ is a client-generated individualised outcome measure. Clients are supported by therapists during the assessment stage of therapy to identify a range of problems that are causing them distress. The therapist and client then construct the list of personal problems into a scale which the client can rate their personal problems on a 7-point Likert type scale. The client can consider their progress in therapy based on the very personalised list of items. The scale has shown good convergent validity with a range of other measures commonly used in therapy outcome measurement (e.g. CORE, see Evans et al., 2002). The PQ aims to recognise that each client who comes to therapy is bringing their own version of distress. Even when this might involve having been diagnosed with depression by their GP or a psychiatrist, the client inevitably has their own personal experience and account of what that means for them. How this is manifest in their life, and how they are able to describe the phenomenon in terms of their emotions, thoughts and behaviours, can be recorded on the PQ form. The PQ is an easy to use, idiographic outcome scale that gets very close to representing the changes clients make in regard to their personal difficulties.

Having now considered, in some detail, the range of potential measures that PCE therapists might use if required to demonstrate their effects, it is important to end this section by reminding ourselves that we must always question the purpose and motivations for using such scales. Some might argue that if using the scales, this should (and can) produce some therapeutic advantages (see Lambert, 2013a for a fuller discussion). Many services are using and collecting outcome data for the purposes of funding. This is a complex issue and one that is rightly political in terms of the issues at stake. Asking clients to complete the measures should always have some demonstrable benefit, be it directly to the client themselves or to the service as a whole, in securing the future funding for more people to gain access. One thing is quite certain; if PCE therapists want to work in the public sector, such as in IAPT services and the NHS, then it is extremely likely that, for the foreseeable future, they will be required to use outcome measures. Whilst many will not feel at ease with this, it might be more worthwhile expending energy and effort into changing the range of measures that are used, rather than simply protesting about the presence of any measures at all. It might prove more fruitful to work at steering the measures used away from being exclusively diagnostically oriented scales, to ones that can demonstrate personal growth and wellbeing. This act itself could be considered a political one, and engaging with commissioners and others on ideological grounds, to record and demonstrate change in PCE therapy that goes beyond symptom reduction, would inevitably call on other therapies to also demonstrate their capacity to do this. This could be one area where PCE-CfD is at an advantage to other therapies also available in the healthcare setting.

Measurement to guide an ending

Following from the section above, it is commonplace for many PCE-CfD therapists to work in settings where they are managed by results. What this means is that services might be commissioned based on the level of distress clients indicate on a specific measure. It is not uncommon for therapists to find they are asked by their managers to present their clients in terms of the data. Some systems now use a 'traffic light' system to highlight how a client is moving through the range of scores on a given scale. 'Are you getting this client close to recovery?' they might say. Or 'We would expect this client to be reaching recovery by now' is another commonly stated claim. The manager in these situations might be acting on the pressure they feel from their managers and so on. The IAPT manual (NCCMH, 2018) places targets on services for both access and recovery rates.

An important factor to understand in the realm of measurement is the idea of 'recovery'. From within the growth paradigm, this concept itself is redundant. However, if you work in a medical model setting (such as the NHS mental health service and IAPT context), then the term is part of the vernacular. Recovery, in the terms intended there, refers to the amount of change a client makes and whether that change carries them over a specific point in the scoring system for the scale. What this means is that people who indicate their distress is above a certain level on the scale can be considered to be in the clinical range. The clinical range will be above a point on the scale referred to as the 'cut-off' point. All scores at or above the cut-off point are in the clinical range. Scores that fall below the clinical cut-off are in the healthy range. The process for determining exactly where the cut-off point falls on a scale are derived through statistical procedures. A useful source for understanding this is Jacobson, Follette and Ravenstorf (1984) or Jacobson and Truax (1991). However, most PCE therapists will be using scales where the cut-off points have already been set and will not need to know the statistics underpinning the rationale. But it is important to understand what is being referred to when the term 'recovery' is being used.

Services, including those in IAPT contexts, use the patient health questionnaire (PHQ-9) as a screening and outcome measure for depression. The scale has 9-items that can be scored using 0, 1, 2 and 3, to the response categories of: not at all, several days, more than half the days, and nearly every day, respectively. This means that the scale will produce a score of between 0 to 27 assuming all items are answered. The PHQ-9 has identified the cut-points of 5, 10, 15 and 20 to represent the categories of mild, moderate, moderately severe and severe depression respectively. This means that a score that falls at or above 5 is somewhere inside the clinical range. A healthy range of 0 to 4 is the conclusion, and 'recovery' ought then to be recognised as a score that falls below the cut-off point. However, it is acknowledged by the developers of the PHQ-9 that scores between 5 to 9 may not require any response and that a period of 'watchful waiting' might be all that is required for recovery to be achieved. PCE therapists will see the inherent difficulties involved in using such scales in isolation as a guide to providing access to or leaving therapy.

To conclude this section on measurement and endings it is worth noting some of the literature that might also be used to underpin and provide a logic for setting the number of therapy sessions within a service. Many services within IAPT are commissioned on the basis that they will provide around six to eight sessions for clients. Payments by results are fixed and progress from a payment made at 'assessment plus two sessions' and 'completed', which essentially means that the client has attended assessment plus anything up to six to eight further sessions. Services that could go beyond this number of sessions have no real financial incentive to do so, other than hope that if they can help the client enough they avoid the revolving-door scenario where the client simply returns a month or two later having ended prematurely.

There has been some research into the number of sessions people attend in therapy and the changes they are likely to make in that time. For example, Kadera, Lambert and Andrews (1996) proposed that after attending for about 20 sessions, at least two-thirds of clients will have managed to reach a significant amount of improvement. Note here that this is referring to 'reliable' change and not necessarily clinical change, in that the client might still be above the clinical cut-off point having made statistically reliable change. However, many clients leave well before this number of sessions, and some may not even have the option of attending this number of sessions. In Lambert's (2013b) report, using the slightly stricter criteria of change that requires clients to be above the clinical cut-off point and to still make a reliable amount of change, that about 21 sessions are required for approximately 50% of clients to reach this point. That means, after 21-sessions of therapy half of clients will not have reached clinically reliable change. Lambert (2013b) also reports that almost double the number of sessions is required for 75% of clients to reach this point. What is also of interest is the rate at which change might take place in therapy contexts where there are more rather than fewer sessions available. According to Baldwin, Berkeljon, Atkins, Olsen and Nielson (2009), longer periods of therapy tend to produce slower rates of change, suggesting that, in studies where change is measured when therapy is only available for ten sessions, the rate of change will be faster compared with studies in which therapy is available for 40 sessions.

Is using measurement of clinical and reliable change even a helpful way of determining change and indicating the ending points of therapy? Or is a different approach required? It is quite likely, as we have seen above in the case of Gerald, that we will have clients who can end therapy quite suddenly or at least before their allocated number of sessions has been reached. One way of understanding this is that the client has reached a more satisfying sense of being in the world, particularly in relation to their reasons for entering therapy. This may or may not be reflected in their outcome measures. Barkham et al. (2006) and Stiles, Barkham, Connell and Mellor-Clark (2008) have proposed what they call the 'good enough level' of change. This is when the client has determined that they have taken what they needed from therapy and that regardless of their scores on the measurement scale, they have reached a level that feels right for them.

To summarise the chapter, it is reasonable to say that when successful PCE therapy occurs, clients will end when they have made a change in the locus of evaluation: that is, when the client is acting more in accord with their OVP than the introjected values and conditions of worth than when they started therapy. When this is the case, they may have become more open to experience, they may have adapted emotion schemes and loosened personal constructs. In essence, they are likely to have moved closer towards fully functioning. When and in what way this change is captured will depend largely on the service setting and context and the motivations of the service and the therapist in the measures they are selecting for use. Having read this chapter, it should be clearer as to the separate ways in which clients will end therapy and how PCE-CfD therapists and services can use measurement to support their practices.

Competences covered in this chapter

- **B10** – Ability to conclude the therapeutic relationship
- **G12** – Ability to use measures to guide therapy and to monitor outcomes
- **M1** – Capacity to implement CfD in a flexible but coherent manner
- **M2** – Capacity to adapt interventions in response to client feedback
- **M4.1** – Ability to balance any tensions between the maintenance of the therapeutic relationship and the achievement of therapeutic tasks
- **M4.2** – Ability to maintain a balance between directive and non-directive dimensions of the therapeutic process

8

Training, Supervision and Research

Chapter overview

- PCE-CfD training
- Supervision
- Personal experiences of PCE-CfD therapists and supervisors
- Research

This chapter[1] will focus on several aspects related to training and supervision in PCE-CfD. First, some issues of training in PCE therapy will be touched upon to provide background knowledge for those that might be relatively new to the PCE approach. It will help to establish how important it is for those training in PCE-CfD to be already grounded in PCE theory, have commitment to personal development and to have gained clinical practice experience as a PCE therapist. The chapter also looks at the requirements for working in the field offering PCE-CfD in the IAPT context. Following this is a section about supervision for PCE-CfD therapists, addressing both general issues and those specific to PCE-CfD. Finally, there is a section on the research evidence for PCE-CfD, including the emerging evidence from researchers based at the University of Sheffield generated through the PRaCTICED trial.

---

[1]This chapter is an updated and edited version of the Training, Supervision and Research chapter in the first edition.

PCE-CfD training

In the field of evidence-based practice (EBP) there is perhaps too much emphasis placed on the question of which type of therapy is the most effective, at the expense of considering other aspects of therapy delivery. The process of making psychological therapies available can be viewed as a system containing a number of important elements additional to the therapeutic approach taken:

- opportunities for the client to access the therapy
- what the client brings in terms of motivation and personal resources
- the skills and personal qualities of the therapist
- opportunities for the therapist to access high-quality training
- the quality of supervision provided to the therapist
- research into the practice and outcomes of therapy

All of these have a bearing on the impact and outcomes of psychological services and, while all are important, the latter three form the focus of the remainder of this chapter.

As depression is the most common single form of psychological distress in the UK and with PCE-CfD available within IAPT, it follows that counsellors working and training within the PCE tradition should have widespread opportunities to train in PCE-CfD. Training in PCE-CfD is ideally available both to those undergoing initial counsellor training as well as to qualified and experienced practitioners. In both cases considerable underpinning skill and knowledge is required for the PCE-CfD competences to be mastered and practised effectively. Therefore, where a PCE-CfD module forms part of an initial training programme, it is important for it to be scheduled towards the end of the programme of study to allow for the prior acquisition of the necessary skill and understanding. Similarly, where PCE-CfD training is offered as continuing professional development (CPD) to qualified and experienced counsellors, it is essential to ensure that those entering the programme have the appropriate foundational theoretical knowledge and skill to be successful and benefit from the training. Nevertheless, even for those therapists that have initially trained in the PCE approach, the impact on practice of working in IAPT for a period of time can be significant. For example, Proctor and Hayes (2017: 4), two experienced PCE-CfD trainers, reported that 'Regardless of initial qualification, most therapists attending the training have been influenced heavily by a solution focused, outcome driven, toolbox-based approach to therapy.' The consequence of this is that training must also focus on allowing trainees to reorient themselves back towards a PCE stance and affiliation with the attitudes associated with the approach.

The elements of knowledge and skill fall into a number of general areas. Training in PCE-CfD builds on core professional competence, requiring proficiency in a number of areas (see competency framework in Appendix 1): knowledge of common mental health problems; ability to work ethically within professional guidelines; ability to work effectively with individuals from a diverse range of backgrounds; ability to undertake a generic assessment;

ability to assess and manage risk of suicide and self-harm; ability to use measures within therapy and to monitor outcomes; ability to make use of supervision.

Theoretical knowledge of the PCE approach is likewise very important, as a solid grounding in this theoretical perspective supports the learning of the more novel aspects of PCE-CfD. Along with theoretical knowledge, the ability to implement the person-centred relational stance grounded in the therapeutic conditions (Rogers, 1957b) is central to learning the PCE-CfD approach. Since training in PCE-CfD rests upon these areas of skill and knowledge, experienced practitioners trained in the person-centred approach, and trainees on dedicated person-centred training, or integrative training based around PCT, are best placed to deliver PCE-CfD. This element of holding a PCE stance is tested at the point of application into existing training programmes in the UK by submission of a written case example of approaching work with a client who is depressed. Describing practice in these terms is very revealing of the therapist's stance and provides a good baseline test for existing theoretical knowledge. Where writing is not possible, then this could be replaced by submitting a short audio recording of a therapist listening and responding to a client whilst maintaining the PCE approach.

A training curriculum (Hill, 2011) for PCE-CfD has been developed and is likely to be of interest to trainers, trainee counsellors and counsellors considering taking up the training. It is illustrative rather than prescriptive and the content of this book maps relatively closely onto the subject areas covered in the curriculum. Assessment of trainee competence on the training programme focuses on practice with clients. As the PCE-CfD competence framework provides the link to evidence of effective practice, as set out in the research literature, it follows that the assessment of trainees should be based on how far they implement the competences with real clients in therapy sessions. This is achieved by trainees submitting a number of audio recordings of sessions and implementation of the competence framework measured by use of a standardised tool, the Person-Centred and Experiential Psychotherapy Scale (PCEPS) developed at Strathclyde University (Freire, Elliott & Westwell, 2014). As competence necessitates not only knowledge but also the application of this to complex real-life situations, counsellor competence can only be truly assessed using real sessions with clients as opposed to role-plays, written case studies or essays. Hence the importance of the PCEPS and the opportunity it provides to assess either live or recorded therapy sessions.

The use of scales such as the PCEPS to assess the effectiveness of therapeutic practice is not a new idea in PCT. Out of concerns that therapeutic practice was not always effective and that the training of therapists was often too academic and theoretical, Truax and Carkhuff (1967) sought to identify from the research and theoretical literature the effective components common to all forms of psychotherapy, develop operational descriptions of these and produce scales which could then be applied to both live and audio-recorded therapy sessions to determine the effectiveness of the therapist. This, they argued, would improve training programmes and the overall standard of therapeutic practice. Empathy, non-possessive warmth and genuineness were identified as being the effective common factors (thereafter often referred to as the 'core conditions') and a rating scale was developed for each, based on grade descriptions denoting levels of each condition. Over the last 40 years these scales, and similar adapted versions of them, have been widely used in person-centred training and many counsellors will have used them to hone their ability to implement the core conditions.

There are parallels between Truax and Carkhuff's work and the development of PCE-CfD and the PCEPS scale. The PCE-CfD project has provided an opportunity to show, through the research literature, how what were often thought to be disparate aspects of therapy assigned to either person-centred *or* experiential approaches are convergent with one another. This has also enabled us to identify and describe effective process-facilitative responses and translate these into practice through training. Like the core condition rating scales, the PCEPS aims to promote effective practice by providing an objective method to assess how successfully therapists are implementing the main principles of the PCE approach.

The development of the PCEPS was led by Beth Freire, Robert Elliott and Graham Westwell at Strathclyde University and supported by seed-corn research funding from the BACP. The driving force behind the project was the challenge to PCE counselling presented by the evidence-based paradigm and the need for a measure which could be used to assess the competence of therapists in RCTs of PCE therapy. RCT methodology requires a demonstration that the psychological therapy being tested in trials is delivered in a way that is faithful to the therapeutic approach it claims to be, often referred to as 'fidelity'. The first part of the process of developing the measure involved constructing a set of high-order competences that capture the essence of the therapeutic approach, using archived audio recordings of therapy to assess the validity of the competences. Once the items on the scale were agreed, teams of raters used the scale with a standard set of recorded therapy sessions to determine whether different raters came up with similar scores, thus testing the reliability of the measure. An initial version of the scale consisted of 15 items with two hypothesised subscales: a person-centred process and an experiential process. These two subscales represented the division between non-directive PCT and a more experiential approach derived from EFT. Long-held theoretical understanding depicted these areas of practice as distinct and so it was originally planned that the measure would need to differentiate between the two. Items on the person-centred subscale included 'client frame of reference/track', 'core meaning', 'client flow', 'warmth', 'accepting presence' and 'genuineness', and items on the experiential subscale included 'collaboration', 'experiential specificity', 'emotion focus', 'client self-development' and 'emotion regulation sensitivity'.

Testing the reliability and validity of the measure was carried out using 120 audio-recorded segments of therapy sessions, systematically selected from 20 clients seen by 10 therapists, three of whom were EFT practitioners and the other seven person-centred. The audio recordings were rated independently by six raters, divided into two teams of three raters each. All raters were person-centred counsellors, three being qualified and experienced and the other three trainees. Each rater scored 60 audio-recorded segments and results were compared across the group. Results indicated that the PCEPS had good internal consistency and reliability. Interestingly, an exploratory factor analysis did not support the distinction between person-centred and experiential practices which had been hypothesised by the authors of the measure (Freire et al., 2014). This meant that items in both the person-centred and experiential subscales were equally applicable across both person-centred and EFT practitioners. It was also felt that the scale was too long and could usefully be abridged. As a result of these findings the scale was reduced to ten items and the subscales taken out (see Figure 8.1).

Several conclusions can be drawn from the fact that the subscales were not found to be valid in their original form. It suggests that person-centred practitioners implement experiential interventions as a natural part of their practice, in the same way that 'some' EFT practitioners naturally adopt a largely person-centred stance in their way of working. This might be the case for the EFT practitioners that formed the sample for the research study. The two areas are much more convergent in practice generally (i.e. independent of the effect of the practitioners in the validation study) than they appear when conceptualised theoretically, and person-centred and experiential competences can be grouped together to form a coherent continuum of practice; hence the evolved term PCE as a single approach to therapy. This is a principle central to the development of PCE-CfD.

PERSON–CENTRED & EXPERIENTIAL PSYCHOTHERAPY SCALE-10 (v. 1.2, 12/12/12)

© 2011, 2012, Robert Elliott & Graham Westwell. (Permission is granted to reproduce this form for educational, training, or supervision purposes, on the condition that it is not changed or sold).

Rate the items according to how well each activity occurred during the therapy segment you've just listened to. It is important to attend to your overall sense of the therapist's immediate experiencing of the client. Try to avoid forming a 'global impression' of the therapist early on in the session.

1.　CLIENT FRAME OF REFERENCE/TRACK:

How much do the therapist's responses convey an understanding of the client's experiences as the client themselves understands or perceives it? To what extent is the therapist following the client's track?

Do the therapist's responses convey an understanding of the client's inner experience or point of view immediately expressed by the client? Or conversely, do therapist's responses add meaning based on the therapist's own frame of reference?

Are the therapist's responses right on client's track? Conversely, are the therapist's responses a diversion from the client's own train of thoughts/feelings?

1 **No tracking**: Therapist's responses convey no understanding of the client's frame of reference; or therapist adds meaning based completely on their own frame of reference.

2 **Minimal tracking**: Therapist's responses convey a poor understanding of the client's frame of reference; or therapist adds meaning partially based on their own frame of reference rather than the client's.

3 **Slightly tracking**: Therapist's responses come close but don't quite reach an adequate understanding of the client's frame of reference; therapist's responses are slight "off" of the client's frame or reference.

4 **Adequate tracking**: Therapist's responses convey an adequate understanding of the client's frame of reference.

5 **Good tracking**: Therapist's responses convey a good understanding of the client's frame of reference.

6 **Excellent tracking**: Therapists' responses convey an accurate understanding of the client's frame of reference and therapist adds no meaning from their own frame of reference.

2. PSYCHOLOGICAL HOLDING:

How well does the therapist metaphorically hold the client when they are experiencing painful, scary, or overwhelming experiences, or when they are connecting with their vulnerabilities?

High scores refer to therapist maintaining a solid, emotional and empathic connection even when the client is in pain or overwhelmed.

Low scores refer to situations in which the therapist avoids responding or acknowledging painful, frightening or overwhelming experiences of the client.

1 **No holding**: Therapist oblivious to client's need to be psychologically held: avoids responding, acknowledging or addressing client's experience/feelings.

2 **Minimal holding**: Therapist seems to be aware of the client's need to be psychologically held but is anxious or insecure when responding to client and diverts or distracts client from their vulnerability.

3 **Slight holding**: Therapist conveys a bit of psychological holding, but not enough and with some insecurity.

4 **Adequate holding**: Therapist manages to hold sufficiently the client's experience.

5 **Good holding**: Therapist calmly and solidly holds the client's experience.

6 **Excellent holding**: Therapist securely holds client's experience with trust, groundedness and acceptance, even when the client is experiencing, for example, pain, fear or overwhelmedness.

(Continued)

Figure 8.1 (Continued)

---

3. EXPERIENTIAL SPECIFICITY:

How much does the therapist appropriately and skilfully work to help the client focus on, elaborate or differentiate specific, idiosyncratic or personal experiences or memories, as opposed to abstractions or generalities?

> *E.g., By reflecting specific client experiences using crisp, precise, differentiated and appropriately empathic reflections; (or asking) for examples or to specify feelings, meanings, memories or other personal experiences.*

1 **No specificity**: therapist consistently responds in a highly abstract, vague or intellectual manner.

2 **Minimal specificity**: therapist seems to have a concept of specificity but doesn't implement adequately, consistently or well; therapist is either somewhat vague or abstract or generally fails to encourage experiential specificity where appropriate.

3 **Slight specificity**: therapist is often or repeatedly vague or abstract; therapist only slightly or occasionally encourages experiential specificity; sometimes responds in a way that points to experiential specificity, at times they fail to do so, or do so in an awkward manner.

4 **Adequate specificity**: where appropriate, therapist generally encourages client experiential specificity, with only minor, temporary lapses or slight awkwardness.

5 **Good specificity**: therapist does enough of this and does it skilfully, where appropriate trying to help the client to elaborate and specify particular experiences.

6 **Excellent specificity**: therapist does this consistently, skilfully, and even creatively, where appropriate, offering the client crisp, precise reflections or questions.

---

4. ACCEPTING PRESENCE:

How well does the therapist's attitude convey an unconditional acceptance of whatever the client brings?

> *Does the therapist's responses convey a grounded, centred, and acceptant presence?*

1 **Explicit nonacceptance**: Therapist explicitly communicates disapproval or criticism of client's experience/meaning/feelings.

2 **Implicit nonacceptance**: Therapist implicitly or indirectly communicates disapproval or criticism of client experience/meaning/feelings.

3 **Incongruent/inconsistent nonacceptance**: Therapist conveys anxiety, worry or defensiveness instead of acceptance; or therapist is not consistent in the communication of acceptance.

4 **Adequate acceptance**: Therapist demonstrates calm and groundedness, with at least some degree of acceptance of the client's experience.

5 **Good acceptance**: Therapist conveys clear, grounded acceptance of the client's experience; therapist does not demonstrate any kind of judgment towards client's experience/behaviour

6 **Excellent acceptance**: Therapist skilfully conveys unconditional acceptance while being clearly grounded and centred in themselves, even in face of intense client vulnerability.

5.   CONTENT DIRECTIVENESS:

How much do the therapist's responses intend to direct the client's content?

Do the therapists' responses introduce explicit new content? e.g., do the therapist's responses convey explanation, interpretation, guidance, teaching, advice, reassurance or confrontation?

1	**"Expert" directiveness**: Therapist overtly and consistently assumes the role of expert in directing the content of the session
2	**Overt directiveness**: Therapist's responses direct client overtly towards a new content.
3	**Slight directiveness**: Therapist's responses direct client clearly but tentatively towards a new content.
4	**Adequate nondirectiveness**: Therapist is generally nondirective of content, with only minor, temporary lapses or slight content direction.
5	**Good nondirectiveness**: Therapist consistently follows the client's lead when responding to content.
6	**Excellent nondirectiveness**: Therapist clearly and consistently follows the client's lead when responding to content in a natural, inviting and unforced manner, with a high level of skill.

6.   EMOTION FOCUS:

How much does the therapist actively work to help the client focus on and actively articulate their emotional experiences and meanings, both explicit and implicit?

E.g., By helping clients focus their attention inwards; by focusing the client's attention on bodily sensations; by reflecting toward emotionally poignant content, by inquiring about client feelings, helping client intensify, heighten or deepen their emotions, by helping clients find ways of describing emotions; or by making empathic conjectures about feelings that have not yet been expressed. Lower scores reflect ignoring implicit or explicit emotions; staying with non-emotional content; focusing on or reflecting generalized emotional states ("feeling bad") or minimizing emotional states (e.g., reflecting "angry" as "annoyed").

1	**No emotion focus**: therapist consistently ignores emotions or responds instead in a highly intellectual manner while focusing entirely on non-emotional content. When the client expresses emotions, the therapist consistently deflects the client away from them.
2	**Minimal emotion focus**: therapist seems to have a concept of emotion focus but doesn't implement adequately, consistently or well; therapist may generally stay with non-emotional content; sometimes deflects client way from their emotion; reflects only general emotional states ("bad") or minimizes client emotion.
3	**Slight emotion focus**: therapist often or repeatedly ignores or deflects client away from emotion; therapist only slightly or occasionally helps client to focus on emotion; while they sometimes respond in a way that points to client emotions, at times they fail to do so, or do so in an awkward manner.

(Continued)

Figure 8.1 (Continued)

4	**Adequate emotion focus**: where appropriate, therapist generally encourages client focus on emotions (by either reflections or other responses), with only minor, temporary lapses or slight awkwardness.
5	**Good emotion focus**: therapist does enough of this and does it skilfully, where appropriate trying to help the client to evoke, deepen and express particular emotions.
6	**Excellent emotion focus**: therapist does this consistently, skilfully, and even creatively, where appropriate, offering the client powerful, evocative reflections or questions, while at the same time enabling the client to feel safe while doing so.

7. DOMINANT OR OVERPOWERING PRESENCE:

To what extent does the therapist project a sense of dominance or authority in the session with the client?

Low scores refer to situations in which the therapist is taking charge of the process of the session; acts in a self-indulgent manner or takes over attention or focus for themselves; interrupting, talking over, silence or controlling the process; or acting in a definite, lecturing, or expert manner.

High scores refer to situations in which the therapist offers the client choice or autonomy in the session, allows the client space to develop their own experience, waits for the client finish their thoughts, is patient with the client, or encourages client empowerment in the session.

1	**Overpowering presence**: Therapist overpowers the client by strongly dominating the interaction, controlling what the client talks about or does in the session; clearly making themselves the centre of attention; or being patronizing toward the client.
2	**Controlling presence**: Therapist clearly controls the client's process of the session, acting in an expert, or dominant manner.
3	**Subtle control**: Therapist subtly, implicitly or indirectly controls what and how the client is in the session.
4	**Noncontrolling presence**: Therapist generally respects client autonomy in the session; therapist does not try to control client's process.
5	**Respectful presence**: Therapist consistently respects client autonomy in the session.
6	**Empowering presence**: Therapist clearly and consistently promotes or validates the client's freedom or choice, allowing client space as they desire.

8. CLARITY OF LANGUAGE:

How well does the therapist use language that communicates simply and clearly to the client?

E.g., therapist's responses are not too wordy, rambling, unnecessarily long; therapist does not use language that is too academic or too abstract; therapist's responses do not get in the client's way.

1	**No clarity**: Therapist's responses are long-winded, tangled, and *confusing*.
2	**Minimal clarity**: Therapist's responses are wordy, rambling or *unfocused*.
3	**Slight clarity**: Therapist's responses are *somewhat clear*, but a bit too abstract or long.
4	**Adequate clarity**: Therapist's responses are *clear but a bit too long*.
5	**Good clarity**: Therapist's responses are *clear and concise*.
6	**Excellent clarity**: Therapist's responses are very clear and concise, even *elegantly* capturing *subtle* client experiences in a few choice words.

9. CORE MEANING:

How well do the therapist's responses reflect the core, or essence, of what the client is communicating or experiencing in the moment?

Responses are not just a reflection of surface content but show an understanding of the client's central/core experience or meaning that is being communicated either implicitly or explicitly in the moment; responses do not take away from the core meaning of client's communication.

1	**No core meaning**: Therapist's responses address **only** the cognitive content or stay **exclusively** in the superficial narrative.
2	**Minimal core meaning**: Therapist's responses address **mainly** the cognitive content or the superficial narrative but bring occasional **glimpses** into the underlying core feeling/experience/meaning.
3	**Slight core meaning**: Therapist's responses **partially but incompletely** address the core meaning/feeling/experience that underlies the client's expressed content.
4	**Adequate core meaning**: Therapist's responses were **close** to the **core** meaning/feeling/experience that underlies the client's expressed content, but do not quite reach it.
5	**Good core meaning**: Therapists' responses accurately address the **core** meaning/feeling/experience that underlies the client's expressed content.
6	**Excellent core meaning**: Therapists' responses address with a high degree of accuracy the **core** meaning/feeling/experience that underlies the client's expressed content.

10. EMOTION REGULATION SENSITIVITY:

How much does the therapist actively work to help the client adjust and maintain their level of emotional arousal for productive self-exploration?

Client agency is central; this is not imposed by the therapist. There are three possible situations:

(a) If the client is overwhelmed by feelings and wants help in moderating them, does the therapist try to help the client to manage these emotions? E.g., By offering a calming and holding presence; by using containing imagery; or by helping the client self-soothe vs. allowing the client to continue to panic or feel overwhelmed or unsafe.

(Continued)

Figure 8.1   (Continued)

> (b)   *If the client is out of touch with their feelings and wants help in accessing them, does the therapist try to help them appropriately increase emotional contact? E.g., by helping them review current concerns and focus on the most important or poignant; by helping them remember and explore memories of emotional experiences; by using vivid imagery or language to promote feelings vs. enhancing distance from emotions.*
>
> (c)   *If the client is at an optimal level of emotional arousal for exploration, does the therapist try to help them continue working at this level, rather than deepening or flattening their emotions?*
>
> 1   **No facilitation**: therapist consistently ignores issues of client emotional regulation, or generally works against client emotional regulation, i.e., allowing client to continue feel overwhelmed or distanced.
>
> 2   **Minimal facilitation**: therapist seems to have a concept of facilitating client emotional regulation but doesn't implement adequately, consistently or well; therapist either generally ignores the client's desire to contain overwhelmed emotion or to approach distanced emotion; sometimes they misdirect the client out of a productive, optimal level of emotional arousal, into either stuck or overwhelmed emotion or emotional distance or avoidance.
>
> 3   **Slight facilitation**: therapist often or repeatedly ignores or deflects client away from their desired level of emotional regulation productive for self-exploration; therapist only slightly facilitates productive self-exploration. While they sometimes respond in a way that facilitates client productive emotional regulation, at times they fail to do so, or do so in an awkward manner.
>
> 4   **Adequate facilitation**: Where appropriate, therapist generally encourages client emotional regulation (e.g., by helping them approach difficult emotions or contain excessive emotional distress as desired by client), with only minor, temporary lapses or slight awkwardness.
>
> 5   **Good facilitation**: therapist does enough emotional regulation facilitation and does it skilfully and in accordance with client's desires, where appropriate trying to help the client to maintain a productive level of emotional arousal.
>
> 6   **Excellent facilitation**: therapist does this consistently, skilfully, and even creatively, where desired, offering the client evocative or focusing responses to help the client approach difficult emotions when they are too distant and to contain overwhelming emotions, all within a safe, holding environment.

Figure 8.1   Person-centred and experiential psychotherapy scale – 10 (v. 1.2, 12/12/12)

Further research continues to be carried out on developing the PCEPS. Westwell (2018) has conducted research looking into the process of training people to use the PCEPS as a valid and reliable rating scale. Westwell designed a study to replicate the reliability and validity studies conducted on the 15-item scale using the new revised 10-item scale, now with a single factor structure at the heart of the scale. In this study, raters were trained to use the measure to try to increase the sensitivity for identifying the competences in real practice settings. Listening to recordings of therapy sessions conducted at the Strathclyde Research Clinic, the new 10-item scale was used by a group of novice raters. Listening to recordings of therapy often provokes strong emotional responses in raters. These emotional responses became an important feature of the research.

Initial ratings using the 10-item version showed low reliability and so Westwell and his team engaged in a process of unpacking the rating process. Because of this research he discovered that raters were sometimes scoring therapy sessions based on reasons other than the presence of the competences. This is a crucially important finding and one that demonstrates the limitations of using rating scales for assessing competency without appropriate or adequate training. To help train raters in using the PCEPS, Westwell provided a series of supervision sessions to create a forum for in-depth reflection on the process. He developed a recording sheet (see Appendix 2 for a copy of the PCEPS therapist self-report form and the emotion reaction form and notation system) for raters to record their emotional reactions to therapists in the recordings. This helped the raters to understand that their initial responses to therapy sessions were often biased by their own emotional reactions to the therapists' style. By going back to listen again to the recording before making a final assessment, the raters' bias was removed. Going through this process several times was developmental for the raters and they reported being much more aware of their own rating processes. Returning to check the reliability of ratings following the training course, Westwell found that these were much improved and thus highlighted the importance for all raters to be thoroughly trained in the use of the PCEPS prior to using it.

The PCEPS measures have the potential to be extremely useful in training and research. As Murphy (2017) and others (Lietaer, 1990) have argued previously, these field trials of the PCEPS support the notion that distinctions between person-centred *and* experiential approaches are far more ideologically driven than theoretically and rooted in actual therapeutic practice. It is now commonplace to see the therapy referred to as PCE therapy by those who recognise the inherent experiential feature of PCT, whilst limiting the extent to which the approach follows the more directive EFT strategies for high-level process direction (Murphy, 2017; Saxon et al., 2017).

To date, several hundred counsellors have undergone training in PCE-CfD in the UK and have completed training using the PCEPS as both a guide and assessment tool. In the interest of improving the training programmes and developing a better understanding of trainees' perspectives, a formal evaluation of the initial roll-out of the training was conducted (Pearce et al., 2012). The training is delivered by a network of accredited providers across England and was intended to be a CPD training, aimed at experienced counsellors who already hold an initial qualification in person-centred or humanistic counselling/psychotherapy. The training consisted of a five-day taught programme followed by 80 hours of supervised and assessed counselling practice (see Hill, 2011). Trainees who had completed both the five-day programme and the 80 hours of practice were invited to participate in the evaluation, which aimed to assess their responses both to the training programme and the competence framework. The evaluation consisted of a survey by questionnaire and follow-up telephone interviews with six participants who had taken part in the survey. The questionnaire asked about sense of self as practitioner pre-training, expectations of the PCE-CfD training, experience of the five-day taught PCE-CfD training programme, attitudes to the PCE-CfD competence framework, experience of supervised practice, experience of the assessment of counselling practice and the impact of the PCE-CfD training on their practice. Of the 60 counsellors contacted to take part in the evaluation, 30 completed the questionnaire online. The majority worked as high-intensity therapists in IAPT services, often in part-time roles.

The survey found that most respondents felt that they had a good understanding of person-centred theory and practice pre-training. Very few felt that they had equal status to therapists from other modalities, particularly CBT, in their service context. Accessing the PCE-CfD training was generally seen as a way to address this and gain enhanced status. The use of the competence framework, together with the PCEPS, as a basis for training and practice were viewed positively and there was broad agreement that the PCE-CfD competence framework accurately described both the person-centred and experiential approach and how to work effectively with depressed clients. Most participants valued the role that supervision played throughout the assessed practice period in helping them align their practice with the PCE-CfD competence framework. Opinion was, however, more divided about participants' experience of having their practice assessed, which some trainees found stressful. However, many trainees agreed that feedback from tutors on assessed practice was clear and supported their development as PCE-CfD therapists.

In terms of the impact of the training programme, the majority of respondents reported being more confident in working with depressed people and approximately half of respondents felt that participating in PCE-CfD training had enhanced their status as therapists. For many participants, the training changed how they practised and had deepened their understanding of how to work with depressed clients. Data from the qualitative interviews tended to support the findings of the survey: 'This training has empowered me. And in the setting of our Trust, I'm now respected more.' There was also an interest in learning the more experiential competences derived from EFT, which for many trainees represented a developing edge to their practice. There was, however, some frustration among trainees at not being able to implement what they had learned on the training programme when they returned to practise in their services: 'The minute the course was finished, it was back to normal, back to try and get clients, you know, patched up in four or five sessions ... I didn't really get a chance to ... really engage in what I'd learnt.' The problem here seemed to be that some services were restricting the number of counselling sessions to a maximum of six, even though on the PCE-CfD programme counsellors had trained in a high-intensity intervention recommended for up to 20 sessions.

On a more positive note, a number of trainees experienced the training as helping them to reconnect with the person-centred and experiential approach and, interestingly, as equipping them to work with clients in greater emotional and relational depth: 'It was going home to a way of working that I had somewhat, not strayed from, but somehow, because of working in a very pressurised

environment, I'd actually lost some of ... the spirit of it.' For experienced practitioners, who had developed a number of different ways of working, the
training seemed to help them realign their practice with the main principles
of the PCE approach.

Since the initial training took place for NHS and other IAPT therapists,
many courses have been provided over the last few years which instigated
another study that was conducted by Drewitt, Pybis, Murphy and Barkham
(2017) to understand the effects of implementing the approach within the
workplace. This was a partial replication of the Pearce et al, (2012) study by
using both a survey and small-scale qualitative interview study. Participants
included were 18 qualified PCE-CfD therapists working within the approach.
In responding to the survey, most participants said they had a very positive
experience of the training programme and that, for many, training had provided some challenges, although nearly all of them (16 out of 18) said that
the training had an impact on their practice, with over half (10 out of 18)
suggesting the course had enhanced their skills. The qualitative interviews
were used to dig deeper into the survey and some interesting findings were
uncovered. For example, the interviews showed there are many challenges
for PCE-CfD therapists working in IAPT settings, most of which relate to the
provision of supervision and the capacity to access qualified PCE-CfD supervisors in the workplace.

PRaCTICED trial training

In the UK, the BACP Research Foundation funded the PRaCTICED trial,
which was designed and run by researchers at the University of Sheffield and
led by Professor Michael Barkham. The PRaCTICED trial is a pragmatic
non-inferiority randomised controlled trial of PCE-CfD compared to CBT for
depression. This trial aims to show that PCE-CfD as it is practised within the
IAPT context will not be significantly inferior in terms of effectiveness to CBT
for moderate and severe depression. The trial will also consider the cost-
effectiveness of each therapy and make a comparison of the costs of providing
the therapy and in supporting clients to recovery. This trial is a landmark
study as it is the first trial to compare PCE-CfD with any other therapy. The
implications of this study are significant and could lead to the sustainability of
availability of PCE-CfD within IAPT services. The trial findings are due to
report in early 2019, slightly after the submission of this manuscript.

Recently, a qualitative study has been published that outlines the findings
of training PCE-CfD therapists that participated in the PRaCTICED trial. Many
of the findings reported are similar to those in the Pearce et al. (2012) and the
Drewitt et al. (2017) studies. This study, by Nye, Connell, Haake and Barkham
(2019), was conducted by researchers and practitioners working on the trial to
investigate this unique experience of training in PCE-CfD, specifically for the
purposes of taking part in the trial. The PRaCTICED trial has adopted the
position of PCE-CfD set out in this book, in recognising that the approach is
based on the latest development of the PCE paradigm. The study involved ten

participants who agreed to take part in an interview. Framework analysis was used, which is a form of thematic analysis, to allow for within-cases and between-cases comparisons of themes. There were a range of findings that highlighted several issues. First, therapists felt 'obliged' to undertake training, which seemed to have an impact on the likelihood of completion. There was also clearly evidence that therapists were very committed to the training. For some, this was concerned with taking an opportunity to develop their skills and also to be part of an opportunity to contribute to an evidence base and develop the PCE-CfD approach. This seemed to be motivated by a concern that the profession of counselling had been neglected because of a focus on CBT. Therapists wanted to use the opportunity of the trial and the training to have a voice within the IAPT setting. The therapists also seemed to have found the training process to be a mutually supportive experience, although there were some anxieties, mainly around the vulnerability of having one's practice exposed. The supportive element might have been due to the trainers, as participants were very satisfied with the quality and availability of the training received. Much like the previous two survey studies, Nye et al. (2019) also reported on therapists' difficulties in the translation of the training when returning to the practice setting. In addition to concerns about recording themselves, participants also reported on the important role of the PCE-CfD supervisor. Where participants struggled the most in this training was in relation to their understanding of PCE-CfD and its fit with their own core theoretical model. This finding is unsurprising as, like many 'schools' of therapy, the person-centred and experiential approach has gone through many years of evolution. This means that drawing together people from either end of a spectrum under an evolving construction of the approach is understandably going to pose challenges, especially for some people who might be firmly rooted to either end of the spectrum. However, the study suggested that people who struggled the most might be those from outside the PCE approach, such as those trained as psychodynamic therapists. Some of the issues arising from this study reflect the earlier experiences, such as working out the balance between the traditional person-centred foundation and working on process-facilitation responses that might be designed to focus more on emotion processes. Finally, these issues and others meant that therapists often felt deskilled for a while before recovering a sense of mastery and skill once more.

Supervision

There are a range of functions of supervision within PCE therapy. A useful resource on supervision, especially for trainees just starting out in becoming a PCE therapist, is the text by Tudor and Worrall (2004). Tudor and Worrall provide a helpful overview of the various models of supervision and offer an informed critique of each of these from the PCE perspective. For qualified therapists and more experienced trainees, primarily, the role of supervision is to support ethical and effective practice. However, Tudor and Worrall suggest that regardless of the level of experience, within the PCE therapy field supervision is about bringing into focus issues, questions and dilemmas. *Issues* are where we most often start and can begin, where we are aware of simply vague or fuzzy feelings about a piece of work or a situation related to the therapy. *Questions* often become clearer after beginning with an issue but might equally be known immediately. And *dilemmas* are a sort of argument, in that the supervisee is in a position and sees they have to move in either one direction or another towards a different outcome. Each of the issues, questions or dilemmas can then be explored using the knowledge and frameworks that might be applied through different domains that frame practice. These might be the workplace, legislation, cultural and so on. The seven domains of supervision are:

1. Clinical
2. Professional
3. Ethical
4. Personal
5. Legal
6. Social
7. Cultural

Whilst the model proposed by Tudor and Worrall (2004) is not adopted by all supervisors in the PCE field, it can certainly help as a framework for practice. Supervision in PCE-CfD can be broken down into two main areas: first, PCE-CfD supervision during the training process; and second, when PCE-CfD therapists have qualified and want to maintain the integrity of their practice within the IAPT context. Access to the former is a standard feature of training; however, access in the second situation is much more challenging due to a lack of qualified PCE-CfD supervisors in IAPT settings. In relation to the model proposed by Tudor and Worrall, PCE-CfD supervision is largely focused on the 'clinical' domain for the purposes of training. Whilst this will remain an important domain once qualified, the other domains will become more evenly presented. It should be noted that during the training period for PCE-CfD, the supervision provided by the course is solely for the purposes of developing the clinical skills and all other questions, issues and dilemmas should be dealt with in the trainee's own ongoing clinical supervisory relationship. The issues as they relate to PCE-CfD supervision are discussed further in the section below.

Supervision in PCE-CfD

For those that are undertaking training in PCE-CfD, an important feature of the supervisory process is to help therapists to align practice with the competence framework, as this provides a link to evidence of effectiveness. This can be viewed as part of the normative function of supervision. The PCE-CfD supervisor, when working with trainees, needs to also have a good understanding of theory, practice and the assessment of competence using the PCEPS. Supervision of PCE-CfD practice requires a highly specialist appreciation of the approach and so a dedicated PCE-CfD supervision training is available and recommended.

As with PCE-CfD counsellor training, PCE-CfD supervisor training builds on core supervisory skills and knowledge. Knowledge of the PCE approach is essential and therefore it is important for PCE-CfD supervisors to have undergone initial training in this modality. Likewise, familiarity with the PCE-CfD competence model is important and so it is desirable for supervisors themselves to have trained as PCE-CfD counsellors. Considerable experience of working as a therapist is preferable, particularly within healthcare settings. It is also helpful for PCE-CfD supervisors to have an understanding of multidisciplinary working and the stepped care model used in IAPT services. This type of knowledge can support counsellors in assessing clients and making appropriate referrals. Supervisors' understanding of depression and the elevated risk of suicide among this population of clients can be essential in helping counsellors identify and manage risk of suicide and self-harm among their clients. In their competence framework for supervisors, Roth and Pilling (2009) describe a wide range of core skills and knowledge, too exhaustive to set out here. Some examples, however, include the ability to: enable ethical practice; foster competence in working with difference; form and maintain a supervisory alliance; structure supervision sessions; help the supervisee present information about clinical work; help the supervisee to reflect on his or her work and on the usefulness of supervision; use a range of methods to give accurate and constructive feedback; manage serious concerns about practice.

In addition to these areas of core knowledge and skill there are a number of supervision competences which have been adapted from Roth and Pilling's (2009) supervision framework that are of specific relevance to the supervision of PCE-CfD counsellors. They fall into three areas, outlined below.

Understanding and application of PCE-CfD

Supervisors need to draw upon a sound knowledge of the principles underpinning the PCE approach and the PCE-CfD model. In the PCE-CfD competence framework the overarching competence that attempts to summarise the whole approach is the ability to offer a therapeutic relationship which facilitates experiential exploration within a relational context. This descriptor emphasises two key elements. The first is that 'experiencing' is at the centre of human psychological functioning. Experiencing is defined as thinking, perceiving, sensing, remembering and feeling, along with the inherent meanings and actions associated with these. It follows, therefore, that effective therapy should track and facilitate exploration of the client's experiencing.

The second element is that people are essentially relational beings and are best helped through authentic, person-to-person relationships. The implication of this is that the therapeutic relationship is the major vehicle for change. Additional, but no less important principles are that human beings are free to act in relation to their worlds, and consequently therapeutic change will be largely founded on self-direction.

Also, people tend to be motivated towards self-maintenance, psychological growth and development, and hence the realisation of their potential, a process which operates throughout the life span. Knowledge of depression and the ability to conceptualise this condition from the PCE perspective are also important. Supervisors need to be able to draw upon these principles to help supervisees review and apply their own knowledge of PCE-CfD, and link concepts and principles to therapeutic strategies and methods.

The PCE-CfD supervisory stance

The relational stance adopted by the supervisor needs to place the primary focus on the exploration of client issues and the therapist's experience of the client, rather than on developing immediate solutions to problems. Therefore the ability to empathically understand the supervisee's perceptions, experience and responses to their work, including those which may be on the edge of awareness, is of paramount importance. Allied to this is the ability to be reflective and to self-monitor the emotional and interpersonal processes associated with supervisor–supervisee interactions.

In IAPT settings where the focus is on PCE-CfD specifically, the supervisor stance must also be very clearly distinguished from the role of case manager. In case management of PCE-CfD, if it is mixed with clinical supervision, the agenda can shift away from the client–therapist relationship and the adherence to the approach to one of performativity. Here the therapist is placed under scrutiny regarding the rate of change according to the measures and calculations on expected change and the numbers of sessions, together with pressures for meeting service level targets; these will inevitably become the focus of the discussion. This was highlighted in the study by Drewitt et al. (2017) that presented the experiences of qualified PCE-CfD practitioners following their training having returned to the IAPT setting. It should be stated that PCE-CfD supervision is not to be confused with case management.

Maintaining the PCE-CfD therapeutic focus

Part of the role played by supervision is also to help the supervisee maintain a primary focus on clients' affective experience and for the supervisee to reflect on their own experience of the therapeutic relationship (including their affective, cognitive and somatic reactions to the client). This is central to an experiential approach to therapy and is mirrored in the experiential approach to supervision. In maintaining an empathic and congruent supervisory relationship that supports supervisees' capacity to be honest and open about their experience of offering therapy, supervision can help supervisees become more flexible and spontaneous in their therapeutic role. The modelling of the relationship conditions (empathy, non-possessive warmth, genuineness) in the supervisory relationship is also an important aspect of maintaining an experiential focus.

Throughout this book, it has been emphasised how the use of measures can support effective and reflective practice. This principle applies equally to

PCE-CfD supervision. For example, not only is the PCEPS a valuable tool for research and training but it can also be useful in the supervisory context. This is particularly central to the role of the supervisor supporting candidates through the PCE-CfD training programme. Significant learning can emerge from reviewing recordings of therapy sessions in supervision, and applying the PCEPS in a collaborative and reflective manner. This can help to identify areas of strength and weakness and provide a basis for further training and skills development (Slovák, Thieme, Murphy, Tennent, Olivier & Fitzpatrick, 2015; Murphy, Slovák, Thieme, Jackson, Olivier & Fitzpatrick, 2017). The shared use of a standardised tool also ensures that practice remains 'on model' and doesn't become randomly eclectic.

Additionally, in IAPT and other psychological therapy services, it has become the norm to use sessional measures to track and monitor the client's progress (see Chapter 7). This provides important data on how services are being used, who the clients are that are using the service and how effective the service is in reducing clients' levels of distress. While accepting the general benefits of this process, individual therapists have at times expressed concern that the collection of this data may disrupt the client–counsellor relationship. Asking clients to complete questionnaires when they are distressed or have urgent concerns to discuss can take valuable time away from the session. However, used judiciously, measures can provide an additional support to the therapeutic process. Brief sessional measures, such as those discussed in the previous chapter, can be completed by clients in just a few minutes. They can then serve as a basis for reviewing with the client how they have been feeling since the last session. Problem areas can be identified and focused on, if the client wishes this, and more nuanced and subjective discussions of the problem areas entered into. Repeating this process on a sessional basis encourages clients to review their progress and reflect on their levels of wellbeing over time. This tends to foster self-reflection and self-care, helping clients self-manage their problems with a greater degree of autonomy. Bringing data from these measures into supervision can similarly produce benefits, where the discussion can focus on key areas of difficulty for the client and creative ways of working with such difficulties.

The outcome data can also provide an indication of which clients seem to be doing well and which are either not improving or deteriorating. Studies have found (Harmon et al., 2007) that around 8 per cent of clients in psychological services deteriorate and that routine outcome data is more reliable in identifying clients who deteriorate than counsellors' own professional judgement alone. As such these data represent a valuable additional source of information that can be used in supervision to benefit clients. Accurately identifying clients who are not doing well can prompt supervisors to focus on providing support to supervisees, helping them to adapt the way they are working with a deteriorating client or make an appropriate referral. The active use of this data in supervision can help to reverse the process of deterioration and lead to improvements in the overall effectiveness of services. Given the elevated risk of suicide among clients who deteriorate and the high costs of hospitalisation where a client can no longer be treated as an outpatient, this is an important role supervision can play. This element of the supervisory role is not to be confused with case management. Case management is where the processing of clients 'through and not in therapy' is the purpose of the meeting. Data collected from measures can be used in supervision to support the client 'in therapy'.

It should be noted that the use of such quantitative measures in the supervision should always be secondary to the focus on the therapist's development of congruence in the therapy relationship. If there is not sufficient time for focusing on the development of the relationship in supervision due to the focus on outcomes, then it is advised that additional supervision be arranged or the focus on outcomes is ring fenced for case management meetings. Supervision in PCE-CfD has to be about more than simply efficiency.

Two experiences of CfD training, supervision, assessment and practice

In the following section two case vignettes are provided which illustrate the experiences of PCE-CfD training and its implementation in the workplace. The first of these is provided by Bill Miller and offers a longitudinal view covering a period of several years from training as a PCE-CfD therapist and then supervisor and offers an update since the last edition of this book. The second is a new illustration from Laura Arnold and explores the issues faced when working in a modality that is shared by only a few colleagues in her service.

Case vignette 1: Bill Miller

First impressions

Arriving on day one I felt pleased to step off the treadmill of full-time counselling work to spend time engaging with some core therapeutic values in a supportive learning environment. The course structure allowed time and space for reflection on theory and practice. During the week I began walking each day after lunch reflecting on each morning's work – a challenging and refreshing process.

The training week

The training involved taught sessions that explained the origins of IAPT, EBP and counselling's position within this new context. This set the scene for referring to the recently developed PCE-CfD competence framework which articulates the features of counselling that are evidently effective in 'treating' depression. This framework has been designed to describe the skills that are brought into use by effective counsellors working with depression. These competences are explained in clear and accessible terms and are linked to evidence of effective practice.

(Continued)

(Continued)

Many course participants expressed a sense of being marginalised by the recent and growing dominance of the CBT approach. Even though counsellors are valued within many NHS services, without NICE recognition and ongoing approval as an evidence-based therapy, counselling will not continue to be commissioned. CBT's success is based on the findings of many RCTs and it has developed its own competence framework – a manual laying out the skills involved in that approach.

The competence framework for CfD, based on a person-centred/experiential model, is the result of painstaking efforts to capture the essential attitudes and skills of this approach. This work, I would argue, has significantly improved the prospects for counsellors working within the NHS.

This framework was explored during the training week, through many experiential exercises and discussions. As a fundamentally person-centred practitioner, I felt at ease in this process. However, for others whose approach was more integrative, there seemed to be more anxiety about practising within the framework. The subtlety of the person-centred approach was similarly illustrated, discussed and practised in various exercises related to the competence framework.

The course provided ample time for discussion and practice and at the end of the week we worked in pairs as counsellors and clients, video recording sessions that were assessed for adherence to the competence framework.

Reflecting on my practice

On returning to my counselling work, I began audio recording counselling sessions with those of my NHS clients who gave consent. With up to 20 clients a week I felt relaxed about producing four recordings that evidenced my adherence to the PCE-CfD competence framework to pass the course. I was able to review many of these recordings, becoming newly aware of how I actually work. I learned, for example, that my genuineness was consistently evident, along with warmth and acceptance. I also realised that when feeling pressured to get results I can, without sufficient self-awareness, be prone to losing touch with my client's perspectives in favour of my own. I found this to be a very helpful learning process.

Supervision and post-qualification experience

Trainees proceed to a period of supervised practice following assessment of their video recordings on the taught course. Feedback from tutors on audio-recorded sessions was usefully discussed in supervision. From initial supervision sessions, recordings were eligible for assessment, and feedback received and acted on. I found feedback from tutors, my use of supervision and my ability to self-assess supported my use of the competence framework, which boosted my confidence. In fact, my PCE-CfD adherence scores were mostly well above the pass mark so I could trust in my ability to practise, reducing my anxiety about having to fit in with an external framework. This eventually led to my being awarded the certificate of competence later in the year.

Since being awarded the certificate of competence I have attended PCE-CfD supervision training and taken a PCE-CfD training course, passing on some practical tips and encouragement to new PCE-CfD trainees. My sense is that PCE-CfD is at the forefront of developing counselling in terms that are consistent with NICE clinical guidelines.

2018 update

Since qualifying as PCE-CfD supervisor in 2013 I have met with counsellors face to face in my home town and across the country by Skype or telephone. This has been hugely enriching and at times very challenging.

Counsellors working in IAPT, particularly those on substantive contracts, are increasingly expected to complete PCE-CfD training in order to be NICE and IAPT compliant. For those whose core training is person-centred, feedback suggests that there is a sense of 'coming home' in fulfilling the course through practice, recording sessions and supervision. For those whose practice integrates other approaches including, for example, psychodynamic or CBT there is often, in my experience, a stronger sense reported by practitioners of being deskilled in order to pass the course.

For those who persist in the face of such hurdles there is a sense of discovering or rediscovering a way of being that is focussed on client experience; a simple but disciplined approach that keeps close empathic watch on client perspectives, feelings and associated meanings. The PCE-CfD approach seems to facilitate deeper reflection in the moment within clients and therapists alike, enabling growth of insight and resourcefulness.

NICE have promised to take into account stakeholder feedback, current research and evidence before republishing its guidance for treating depression in adults. Current evidence shows that counselling is as effective as CBT for depression, which bodes well for the standing of PCE-CfD for the future.

Of course, the next challenge will be in proving suitable evidence of efficacy of counselling with other presentations, such as anxiety, which is a major theme in referrals to primary care talking therapy services.

Next is an account from Laura Arnold who has described the process of going from initial practitioner training through to being a PCE-CfD supervisor providing supervision to both trainees and experienced PCE-CfD practitioners in their IAPT setting.

Case vignette 2: Laura Arnold

My initial experience of working as a counsellor for IAPT could be likened to that of salmon swimming upstream: energetic and willing to face a challenge, whilst meeting a constant flow of CBT practitioners moving swiftly in the opposite direction.

(Continued)

(Continued)

PCE-CfD therefore came along at a perfect time for me. Having spent four years as the only counsellor within a Healthcare Foundation Trust, I felt I was beginning to sink. There seemed to be a surge of evidence surrounding CBT, a language of cognitive restructuring, core beliefs and RCTs but little potential for change on the horizon, regarding the development of other modalities.

Therefore, I embraced the prospect of an IAPT-endorsed humanistic modality when offered a training place at the University of Nottingham. The simple act of entering a room full of counsellors was a novelty in itself. To hear the terminology of my own training, to immerse myself again in the language of the person-centred approach, was a breath of fresh air.

The five-day training course itself was split into various topics. These included an introduction to IAPT and how it had evolved. This also incorporated a lively discussion about counselling and, chiefly its place in IAPT. This was an affirming experience, outlining for me that many counsellors felt the same sense of difference as me. There seemed to be an implicit sense of doubt regarding counselling. A subtle atmosphere of 'Where's your evidence base and core profession?' However, here finally was an IAPT-endorsed, NICE-approved, evidence-based therapy for depression, with a framework designed to promote unity of approach, and therefore make outcome measures easier to achieve. We spent time looking at the PCEPS, which was helpful. This is a criteria-based framework, which outlines the specific person-centred and emotion-focused qualities required in order to meet adherence to the model. Beginning this training felt like a long-awaited answering call to those who saw counselling as 'just counselling' or necessary but by no means sufficient.

On the final day, having had time to work in pairs and reflect on the competences required, we each completed a video recording. These recordings formed part of our overall assessment. As with all the recordings, thorough, timely and thoughtful feedback was offered.

Development of practice

We were encouraged to record as many of our PCE-CfD sessions as possible. Whilst this felt daunting initially, I found that people were happy to complete the required consent forms and partake in audio-recorded sessions. Recording with up to 20 clients a week gave me numerous opportunities to consider audio recordings for submission. However, through the use of supervision, I learnt to submit sparingly, and develop my practice from the feedback of previous recordings. I found the feedback detailed and accepting, enabling me to build on my competences and overall approach.

Supervision of training practice

We were provided with six supervision sessions as part of our initial training. This was primarily to listen to audio recordings, and to reflect on whether or not to submit a recording for marking and feedback. We were required to pass four session recordings, meeting adherence to the PCEPS. Although supervision is offered on an individual basis, we opted to share our supervision time, learning together as a group. This was beneficial as it gave us the opportunity to listen to other counsellors, and their application of CfD. It also gave us an increased understanding of meeting adherence to the PCEPS, and increased confidence in rating ourselves and others. It also gave us the opportunity to reflect on feedback offered on audio recordings. When I qualified as a PCE-CfD practitioner, I felt my person-centred counselling training had been further embedded and validated by the CfD training.

PCE-CfD supervision training

Following two years of employing PCE-CfD within an IAPT service, with approximately 20 clients per week, I felt that I was strengthening my CfD practice. I felt confident in my ability to offer the competences, and the emotion-focused elements of the approach became an integral part of my work. Our local IAPT service had a consultation and a key request from staff was that we have more PCE-CfD available to the service. With this in mind, I was asked to return to Nottingham and complete the PCE-CfD Supervisor training, in anticipation of recruiting more counsellors.

A prerequisite for the PCE-CfD supervision training was our completion of the practitioner training. Therefore all participants already had a solid grounding in the PCEPS, and the practicalities and challenges of meeting adherence. During the two-day course, we looked at our own experiences of training and PCE-CfD supervision. We also spent time looking at the PCEPS and considering some challenges for course participants trying to meet adherence for their practitioner qualification.

Initially the PCE-CfD supervisor role was focused more on supporting trainee therapists to meet adherence. Therefore our own understanding of the PCEPS and our ability to model the process within supervision were key areas. We were introduced to the supervision adherence scale. As part of the trainee PCE-CfD supervision requirements, we once again audio-recorded sessions to demonstrate our adherence to the supervisory stance, receive feedback and continuing development. As with all the PCE-CfD training, I found the course helpful, detailed and appropriate. The feedback given was supportive and timely for developing my supervision practice. The supervision of audio-recorded sessions was supportive and modelled the PCE-CfD supervisory stance well.

I am happy to report that PCE-CfD supervision has developed further now, as PCE-CfD becomes an integral part of IAPT. Whilst we still support trainee practitioners, we now increasingly work with trained PCE-CfD practitioners within IAPT. This goes beyond the initial training, focused on adherence, giving the opportunity to develop practitioners, and embed the approach. In doing so I feel I am further contributing to the long-term development of a robust, effective and evidence-based counselling approach.

(Continued)

Research evidence for the effectiveness of PCE therapy with depression

To conclude this chapter the question 'Does it work?' will be considered. This section briefly reviews three sets of research on the effectiveness of PCE therapy with depression: first, a brief review of the most recent evidence used in a meta-analysis that is currently being conducted on PCE therapy and depression (Sharbanee, Elliott & Bergman, 2015); second, a section that considers the evidence that was used when constructing the original PCE-CfD evidence base; and third, Elliott, Watson, Greenberg, Timulak and Freire's (2013) meta-analysis of 27 studies of humanistic psychotherapy and counselling, the latter having a much broader focus than the former.

PCE therapy and depression – a brief update

A meta-analysis is an analysis of analyses, carried out over several stages. Initially, several studies examining the same research question are collected and their relevant characteristics coded (e.g. number of participants, measures used, whether participants were randomly assigned to treatments). The next step involves putting the measures in all the individual studies onto the same metric, so that they can be combined and compared. This common metric is called an effect size (ES). The most frequently used ES measure is called the 'standardised mean difference', which is, in the case of this meta-analysis, the difference between the average pre-therapy score and the average post-therapy score divided by the pooled standard deviation. Standard deviation is a measure of the variability associated with an average.[2] The last step in a meta-analysis is analysing all the analyses (i.e. the 'meta' part of the process), running various corrections, coming up with summary values, and looking for variables that might explain differences in ESs (e.g. randomisation or level of therapists' experience).

A recent report of an ongoing meta-analytic research study looked at seven studies of humanistic therapies on pre–post scores for depression (Sharbanee et al., 2015). Therapies were considered suitable for inclusion if they were person-centred, emotion-focused, supportive counselling (so long as the focus was on empathy or experiencing), Gestalt, psychodrama and focusing therapy. The dataset was generated by way of updating that of Elliott et al. (2013) so only studies published from 2008 onwards were included. Two databases were searched (Medline and PsychINFO) and in the final analysis 20 studies were identified as suitable from a total of 200 full texts reviewed. First, an overall pre–post ES was calculated to compare scores on depression indicators before and after therapy. Only seven studies reported pre–post data representing

---

[2] For more information on the calculation of standard deviation and effect size, see Sanders and Wilkins (2010).

findings for N = 631 participants; an ES was calculated g = 0.89 (95% CI: 0.5 to 1.22), which suggested a pretty large effect. However, a test for heterogeneity showed that there was significant variability in the findings and that 'researcher allegiance' statistically significantly moderated the findings. That means, much of the variance in ESs could be accounted for by the allegiance of the research teams.

Using the same data set, a comparison of ESs between humanistic therapies and other interventions was made. This was comparing effects for humanistic therapy with a control group, another active therapy such as CBT or with treatment as usual. Based on a total of 12 comparisons representing N = 1,696 participants, there was virtually no difference in effects g = 0.08 (95% CI -0.13 to 0.30). Once again there was significant moderation. This time researcher allegiance and comparison type were both moderating variables. Finally, there were five studies with N = 855 participants that made comparisons between either person-centred or EFT and CBT. Overall these approaches were no different from CBT g = -0.07 (95% CI -0.21 to 0.08) and there was no heterogeneity for these comparisons.

In concluding this review, Sharbanee et al. (2015) stated that there are very few new research studies that have been conducted which include humanistic therapies as anything other than an 'intent to fail' condition. This is perhaps reflective of a paucity of research being conducted by those interested in the field of humanistic therapy. Also, whilst finding a large pre–post effect, and a significant difference in favour of humanistic therapy to treatment as usual, the comparisons to CBT were confounded by researcher allegiance. Overall, what this tells us is that the approach continues to be able to demonstrate good effects and that it is possible the reasons why the approaches are not recommended in guidelines is rather more likely to be political than empirical.

Previous studies used as the PCE-CfD evidence base

Five studies reviewed below formed the basis of the evidence for the effectiveness of PCE-CfD as it was included in the NICE (2009) guideline. Bedi et al. (2000) compared the effectiveness of counselling vs. antidepressants. No significant differences between the two types of treatment were found and at 12-month follow-up clinician-reported depression scores were significantly lower in the antidepressant group when compared with counselling. The finding from this suggests the study outcome is inconclusive and not supporting a conclusion that counselling and antidepressants were equivalent. The NICE 2009 Guidance Development Group (GDG) stated that this study should be treated with some caution as the introduction of a patient preference element to the trial led to considerable differences in baseline severity measures between the two arms.

Two studies (Goldman, Greenberg & Angus, 2006; Greenberg & Watson, 1998) compared two distinct types of PCE therapy (client-centred and emotion-focused). In Goldman et al. (2006) the comparison of client-centred counselling and EFT favoured EFT. In Greenberg and Watson (1998) the comparison of client-centred counselling and EFT (referred to as process-experiential coun-selling)[3] findings indicated that there was no significant difference between treatments in the reduction of self-reported depression scores. The GDG urged caution in the interpretation of these results because of what it considered to be small sample sizes.

Simpson, Corney, Fitzgerald and Beecham (2003) compared the combina-tion of psychodynamic counselling plus GP care with usual GP care alone and found no important clinical benefit of therapy plus GP care. Watson, Gordon, Stermac, Kalogerakos and Steckley (2003) compared EFT with CBT. The GDG criticised this study based on its sample size, judging it to be small and con-cluding that the study produced insufficient evidence to reach any definite conclusion about the relative effectiveness of the two treatments.

Despite several studies having major depression as a criterion for the recruitment of participants, the GDG concluded that participants in the reviewed studies were predominantly drawn from groups in the mild-to-moderate range of depression (mean baseline BDI scores between 18 and 26) and two trials included people with minor depression (BDI scores starting from 14) (Bedi et al., 2000 and Ward et al., 2000). Because of this the GDG concluded that evidence supported the effectiveness of counselling for mild-to-moderate depression but not for severe depression. The evidence was also seen to be limited by the small size of the samples of participants recruited into the studies, resulting in studies with low *power* to reliably detect differ-ences between groups within trials. The concept of *power* refers to whether the sample size of a trial is large enough to detect differences that might exist between groups at a better than chance level. A relatively small sample size can be used where the differences between groups are expected to be large, such as where a therapy is compared with no-treatment. Where two active treatments are compared such as EFT and CBT (Watson et al., 2003) and dif-ferences would be expected to be small, a much larger sample size would have been needed to detect differences. The evidence reviewed was therefore judged to be limited partly because of small sample sizes. Another issue, relat-ing to sample selection, is whether or not participants meet the criteria for depression. NICE guidelines are disorder specific and so it follows that the guidelines for depression should be based on studies of participants who were clearly depressed. Therefore studies of participants who did not meet the full diagnostic criteria for depression or who had other prominent psychological problems besides depression were excluded from the evidence review.

The fact that some clients may have strong preferences for treatments pre-sents a further problem for the randomisation process in RCTs. If allocated to a treatment they do not want, these participants may become demoralised, hence affecting the outcomes of the treatment they receive. Random allocation to groups is therefore predicated on the notion that clients have no strong prefer-ence for treatment. Where strong preferences exist, *patient preference* trials have

---

[3]Note that 'process-experiential' and 'emotion-focused' are two names for the same therapy.

been designed to enable those without strong preferences to be randomly allocated and those with strong preferences to be given the intervention they wish to receive. Whereas this is more ethical and helps with recruitment, it can have the effect of setting up the differences between groups that random allocation intends to prevent. This is a criticism levelled at the Bedi et al. (2000) study.

The GDG considered studies that compared two different forms of PCE therapy (client-centred and EFT) (Goldman et al., 2006; Greenberg & Watson, 1998) as problematic because they only evaluated the effects of two quite similar interventions. Had these therapies been compared with a no-treatment control group or comparison with a recommended treatment such as CBT, then the effectiveness of these therapies would have been more clearly established.

Elliott et al. (2013) meta-analysis

In their meta-analysis of outcome studies of humanistic-experiential therapies, Elliott et al. (2013) took a much more inclusive approach to the evidence review process than is commonly used by NICE. There were several reasons for this. First, when Elliott and colleagues began meta-analysing person-centred-experiential outcome research (Greenberg, Elliott & Lietaer, 1994), there was little research available and so they wanted to use all the available data, including evidence for emerging versions of PCE therapy and applications to new client populations. Second, they were concerned that selecting studies based on judgements of quality would introduce bias: if you don't like the results of a study, it is extremely easy to find faults with the statistics and design. Third, following the original philosophy behind meta-analysis (Glass, McGaw & Smith, 1981), a wide range of studies using different methods was included and methodological features of studies were coded to make it possible to see what difference these made for the results. For example, there is an assumption that non-randomised studies are biased and so produce different results from randomised studies.

In any event, Elliott et al. (2013) looked at approximately 200 studies of the outcome of PCE therapies (which they referred to as 'humanistic-experiential psychotherapies' or HEPs). Within this data set were five types of client presenting problem: depression, relationship problems, coping with chronic medical problems (e.g. HIV), habitual self-damaging behaviours (substance misuse, eating disorders) and psychosis. Of these, there were more studies of depression than any other client presenting problem. Twenty-seven studies of depression were included in the meta-analysis and form the basis of the discussion here. There were 34 samples of clients within the 27 studies, comprising a total of 1,287 clients. The types of therapy tested were most commonly PCT (10 samples), supportive therapy (often used as a control condition) (nine samples), or EFT (eight samples). Other types of experiential therapy, such as gestalt or psychodrama, were also included.

The 27 studies fell into two broad categories: those which measured levels of distress pre- and post-therapy without the use of a control or comparison group (n = 19), and similar studies which made use of comparison/control groups (n = 8). Analyses were based on the calculation of ES, where 0.2 is viewed as small, 0.5 as medium and 0.8 as large (Cooper, 2008). The weighted mean pre–post ES across all 34 samples was large. On the other hand, the ES across just the eight comparison/control studies was somewhat weaker, but still a statistically significant weighted effect in the small to medium range. Within this latter group of studies were two outliers (Maynard, 1993; Tyson & Range, 1987), where negative outcomes were found for the interventions compared with no-treatment groups. Both of these studies had small samples and used group interventions which were not bona fide PCE therapies.

Where PCE is compared with other types of therapy (23 studies), most commonly CBT, the outcomes are broadly equivalent: positive and negative comparative results are evenly balanced across the studies. Within the range of PCE therapies there is some preliminary support that process-guiding approaches may have some superiority over approaches that do not use these methods with depressed clients. Four studies made comparisons between more and less process-guiding therapies involving depressed clients (Beutler et al., 1991; Goldman et al., 2006; Greenberg and Watson, 1998; Tyson & Range, 1987). A significant small to medium mean ES was found across these studies. However, there was a degree of heterogeneity in the interventions tested: Greenberg and Watson (1998) and Goldman et al. (2006) compared EFT with CCT; Beutler et al. (1991) compared focused-expressive group therapy with a supportive group involving bibliotherapy; and Tyson and Range (1987) compared group gestalt therapy with an active expression group.

Two clusters of evidence on depression are worth noting. First, there are the three well-designed comparative treatment RCTs testing EFT for depression (Goldman et al., 2006; Greenberg & Watson, 1998; Watson et al., 2003), comparing EFT with other therapies in the treatment of MDD, using medium-sized samples and conducted by two different research teams.[4] Goldman et al. (2006) found that EFT had significantly better outcomes (including very low relapse rates) when compared with PCT. Watson et al. (2003) found generally equivalent (and on some measures better) results compared with CBT. Second, there were four well-designed RCTs of PCT for perinatal depression with medium to large sample sizes that either showed superiority to treatment as usual (Holden, Sagovsky, & Cox, 1989; Morrell et al., 2009; Wickberg & Hwang, 1996), or no difference in comparison with CBT (Cooper, Murray, Wilson & Romaniuk, 2003) or short-term psychodynamic therapy (Cooper et al., 2003; Morrell et al., 2009). Both clusters of well-controlled studies met Chambless and Hollon's (1998) criteria for *efficacious and specific* treatments: that is, they were well-designed, conducted by at least two different research teams, and were either superior to some other treatment or superior to a recognised efficacious treatment.

---

[4]These studies, also discussed earlier in this chapter, were brought to the attention of the 2009 NICE GDG in the review process but were generally dismissed for being relatively small and for comparing related treatments.

Key recent studies include Cooper et al. (2003) and Morrell et al. (2009), both with perinatal depression as mentioned above, and two studies by Mohr on depression in a medical population (Mohr, Boudewyn, Goodkin, Bostrom & Epstein, 2001; Mohr et al., 2005). The other recent substantial study is Stice, Rohde, Gau and Wade (2010), in which adolescents with mild to moderate depression were randomised to one of four conditions: supportive group therapy vs. CBT group therapy vs. CBT bibliotherapy vs. controls. Participants seen in supportive therapy showed benefits comparable with those in CBT which were sustained to two-year follow-ups and did much better than control group clients.

In addition to these studies listed above there will soon be the results of the PRaCTICED trial to be added. Barkham and colleagues at the University of Sheffield will be concluding their findings very shortly and the results of this trial will be the first to test the PCE-CfD approach as it is defined and set out in this text. The results of the trial could have significant impact on the availability of the approach in statutory settings both in the UK or in managed care settings in the US.

In this chapter the topics of training and supervision and research have been covered. Training in PCE-CfD is a great opportunity for experienced practitioners to help reorient themselves to an approach to practice that has often been lost or even forgotten under the strain of the IAPT work context. The pressure of working in IAPT is significant (Marzouk, 2019) and this makes the role of supervision all the more important. Investment in well-trained and experienced supervisors for supporting the PCE-CfD therapists is essential for the maintenance of wellness at work.

9

Future Orientations and Conclusions

Chapter overview

- To the future
- Personal reflection

This short, final, chapter will consider some of the potential future orientations for PCE-CfD and provide some conclusions that have been arrived at through the process of writing this second edition. The aim is to be both reflective and discursive and to write something more personal than perhaps has so far been put forward in the previous chapters. I will present some of my thoughts about how PCE-CfD might proceed in the years ahead and consider some of the issues that might impact on its development, especially within the field of statutory health care provision. I will also explore some of the personal difficulties and challenges that I have faced in bringing this project to completion and examine these with the view to seeing how they might resonate with readers' feelings and thoughts about the PCE-CfD project.

To the future

First, in order to look forward, let's just briefly take stock of where we have come to in the development of PCE-CfD. Several years ago, person-centred counselling was on the verge of being discontinued in the NHS. That's proba-bly not overstating the case. There has been an ideological shift in psycholog-ical therapies over the last few decades where a number of factors are influencing the way that therapy is being provided, the purpose it is seen to fulfil within society and therefore the means by which it can be funded. When the previous NICE (2009) guidelines for depression in adults were presented, PCE counselling was nowhere to be seen, the future looked bleak. However, the development of the competences through the accumulation of research evidence was just about enough to see the continuation of the approach within the statutory health sector. Since then, hundreds of therapists working in IAPT settings have been trained, supervisors are now embedded in IAPT services, and in some locations PCE-CfD teams have been formed and considered to be on a level pegging with their CBT colleagues when considering clients seeking therapy for depression. Or at least that's the rhetoric. As we shall see below the reality is probably somewhat different. On top of this, the BACP Research Foundation have commissioned the PRaCTICED trial to test for the non-inferiority of PCE-CfD to CBT. The findings of this trial, which are not availa-ble at the time of writing, are going to be pivotal for the future of PCE-CfD in IAPT settings. I should stress that what is at risk is PCE-CfD and not PCE therapy per se. The PCE approach is thriving in many areas of social and cul-tural life, and what happens within the NHS is only one element of this evolv-ing paradigm. Some (me included) even question whether even having PCE therapy in the health service is beneficial to the development of society and whether its place in the health sector potentially limits the development of the PCE approach more broadly. More on this later.

The relation between IAPT and NICE will continue to play a significant role in the longevity and availability of PCE-CfD in the NHS. IAPT services are required to provide evidenced-based therapies that are recommended by NICE. This means that if the PCE-CfD approach is to continue to be available in NHS settings, it will need to generate the evidence required. As we have seen above there is still a significant gap in the literature and few studies are conducted that specifically aim to test the effectiveness of PCE therapy under trial conditions. If PCE-CfD does not feature as a therapy recommended by NICE, then it will be vulnerable to once again being marginalised when new services are being commissioned.

On the positive side, the updated IAPT manual (NCCMH, 2018) has posi-tioned PCE-CfD as a high-intensity therapy that should be available through all commissioned IAPT services. At present this is done despite there being very little evidence available and one might question both the rationale for this and how long this could continue in the absence of such little support from NICE. Another problem with this is that within the IAPT manual, only the term 'CfD' is used and it is referred to as a 'particular type of counselling developed for people with depression' (p. 16). Whilst this sounds positive, the difficulty is that as the manual is the main document used by commissioners, it does not refer to 'PCE-CfD' and instead reverts to the use of generic termi-nology and 'CfD'. This is not unintentional and could have been amended as per the requests made by the PCE-CfD trainers group to IAPT. One crucial step for the future of PCE-CfD is to ensure that those running the IAPT initiative, the professional associations such as BACP, and all those associated with PCE-CfD, use the correct acronym. One reason that this is so important is that the emerging research evidence from the PRaCTICED trial will be squarely situated within the PCE theoretical paradigm. As the evidence begins to emerge in support of PCE-CfD, consistent reference to the approach through the correct acronym will be crucial to separate PCE-CfD from the use of the generic term 'counselling'.

In this book, PCE therapy, and its conceptualisation of depression, have been positioned to be at odds with the medical model of psychological distress. This inevitably positions the approach as an awkward partner in the context of IAPT. After all, IAPT is inherently geared up to deliver talking therapy in a way that advances a medical model of distress. A major issue for PCE-CfD in the future is the extent to which this position can be sustained without compromising the central message of the PCE paradigm. Going forward, PCE-CfD practitioners must equip themselves with the skills and knowledge required to engage critically with the field in which it is situated. The future doesn't have to be the same as things are now. The status quo does not have to be maintained. There is the chance that the basis upon which the provision of talking therapies are currently made available in the NHS can change.

It was stated previously, in this book, that some people have been working away at bringing about change from within the system. This must be continued by those practising this approach. Change is possible. For example, fundamental questions continue to be asked about the benefits of manualisation of therapy. A recent meta-analysis that compared the effects of manualised and non-manualised therapies has placed further doubts surrounding the principle of manualisation. Truijens, Zülke-van-Hulzen and Vanheule (2018) tested three hypotheses. First, they wanted to know whether manualised and non-manualised therapies are as effective as each other; second, whether manualised therapies are more effective than control groups; third, whether manual adherence is indicative of manual efficacy. They found that none of the studies supported the view that manualised therapies are more effective than non-manualised. Of eight studies comparing manualised therapies with controls, only three showed better effects for manualised therapy whilst five did not. Fourth, in looking at one meta-analysis and 15 additional studies, they found that there is at best inconclusive evidence as to whether adherence affects outcome. These findings cast doubt over the very premise upon which so much in NICE, IAPT and the field of psychological therapies is founded. PCE-CfD therapists need to be knowledgeable about and be able to engage in meaningful debate with funders and policy makers at all levels of the system in order to have an influence. Understanding these issues and many others is crucial. Practitioners and researchers in the field of PCE therapy cannot afford to have their heads in the sand.

Influencing the system from inside, however, is going to be difficult. Engaging in research when the opportunity arises is one way that PCE-CfD therapists in IAPT can contribute. It is also possible for IAPT therapists, including PCE-CfD therapists, to influence their Trusts or other providers/employers and request they adopt any of the range of measures suggested in this book. These measures can be proposed as either to replace, or more likely be used in addition to, those currently included in the National Minimum Data Set (NMDS). PCE-CfD therapists can contribute to this by asking their clinical leads, their service managers or directly to the local commissioners, if they can add to the measures something that can show how change happens in diverse ways within different therapies. When doing so, it will be useful to explain why these measures might be worth adopting. They can tell their managers and commissioners that what PCE-CfD can offer that other IAPT modalities cannot is the theoretical underpinning to therapy, reflected in the measures, that rests on the growth paradigm. By presenting the PCE-CfD model as a positive psychology of mental health, explaining how mental wellbeing in this theory is not merely about an absence of symptoms, will be a convincing and potentially attractive idea for commissioners.

Whether PCE therapists will engage with the system in this way is obviously an entirely individual decision. However, every PCE therapist working in IAPT must know the impact of their decision to act or not, in whatever way they choose, is to influence the medical model system. It must be acknowledged that engaging in any kind of 'guerrilla' tactic is not risk free and might even come at a cost. For example, some might think the next logical step in changing the system from the inside would be to develop evidence and competences for PCE therapy for working with other prevalent client presentations (e.g. clients who are traumatised or clients who present with anxiety). The benefits of this are easy to see and would certainly offer the opportunity to gain a further foothold within the IAPT context. It could be argued that this will be a necessity if the practitioners of the approach want to be included in additional NICE guidelines; however, generating the evidence will be an essential first step. But what might it cost the PCE approach if it were to continue down this road? One potential cost is that the approach risks becoming just another therapy that is 'treating' individualised presentations of distress as if they were medical conditions. All PCE therapists must be aware that they can never be both a part of the medical model and remain true to the PCE approach. There must be a compromise. This is an issue that each PCE therapist must critically examine and decide for themselves, and determine where they are prepared to venture and where their personal limits might be reached.

The future of PCE-CfD is also contingent on the continued funding for training places. At present, places are funded across the country by the NHS. All IAPT services are required to offer a range of therapies for a given client presentation where there are alternative therapies available that are recognised as evidence based. This should mean that PCE-CfD training continues to be invested in at the national level as all IAPT funded providers are required to include the approach as one of the choices available to clients. However, if PCE-CfD does not get included in the forthcoming NICE guidelines for depression in adults (due out in 2019), this might present a difficulty for education/training commissioners' funding of places. That is not to say that commissioners do not look at other sources of evidence, and they should be encouraged by PCE-CfD practitioners in their local areas and take note of the evidence drawn from practice-based studies. This is very favourable to PCE-CfD and shows that when implemented on the ground, counselling is effective. PCE-CfD therapists should ensure that they present the findings of such studies (Pybis et al., 2017) to their commissioners in a bid to address any moves to dismantle the current level of provision of PCE-CfD within IAPT.

As is apparent in the paragraphs above, the position of PCE-CfD in the IAPT context remains precarious. This is likely to continue for some time.

Some personal reflections

In these closing few paragraphs of this book, I would like to share a few personal reflections. Writing this book has presented me with one of the deepest personal and ethical conflicts that I have faced in almost two decades as a PCE therapist. Agreeing to write the second edition of this book has certainly felt like 'doing my bit' for the cause. The cause being to ensure that the PCE approach does not disappear entirely from the NHS. And whilst I am in a position where I can have some influence, it would be remiss of me to not accept that responsibility fully. However, that is not the same as saying that I took this project on lightly, and without significant soul searching and a fair degree of reserve. For many years, NHS psychotherapy services were dominated first by the psychoanalytic psychotherapists and then cognitive-behavioural therapists. Psychotherapy services and secondary mental care has never been the place where person-centred practitioners have been able to work with clients. However, primary care was once the place where PCT could be practised, and was, almost ubiquitously provided by counsellors in GP surgeries up and down the country. The assault on these counsellors (of whom I was one) came through the advancement of NICE guidelines and the IAPT roll out. Psychological distress within primary care was medicalised through these two sets of apparatus. Whilst the rhetoric at the time was that IAPT and CBT would be in addition to existing services and that counselling services should not be decommissioned, that is exactly what did happen. PCE-CfD is a reaction of the medicalisation of distress, and none of us should be under any illusion of that fact. If distress at the primary care level was not medicalised to the point that it has been today, there would have been no need to develop the competences. The competency and manual makers will defend their logic and so they should. But there is no evidence that counselling services in primary care have become any more effective as a result of IAPT and the large-scale roll out of CBT. In fact, there is probably sufficient data out there to suggest that the results will be marginally worse than pre-IAPT. Writing this book, I have never felt more incongruent with my values and my understanding of the nature of human suffering, psychological distress, and how best to respond to it. I cannot cosy up to the idea of the medical model so that the person-centred approach finds a place inside the system. Not when that system is designed in order to maintain the medical model. I do, however, feel that people can benefit from PCE-CfD, and that it is a humane and ethical form of therapy that needs to be available to as many people that might benefit from it, especially people who cannot otherwise afford to pay for it. This has been my dilemma in writing this book, and it is important to me to be open about it. This has meant that some of the language used in the book is not wholly reflective of exactly how I would like to have said things. I have been mindful of how the words might be received in some places. The tone in the book is certainly more conciliatory towards IAPT and NICE than how I feel personally. I feel angry that those people with significant power and influence over IAPT, NICE, and how the system could be organised, do not do what is 'right' rather than what serves ideological interests that they might even be barely aware of.

How have I managed to reconcile myself with this incongruence? How have I managed to balance the tension between writing to support a mode of practice that will be inside the medical model settings in IAPT, whilst being fundamentally opposed to the medical model of psychological distress and all of its 'apparatus' (to use Sanders', 2006 term)? One way has been to see the entire PCE-CfD project as a kind of Trojan horse metaphor; using the 'idea' of competences and manualised forms of therapy to get inside the system, only for the doors to be opened and the true nature of the PCE approach to be released once on the inside. This has been something of a saving grace. It was certainly the case that, when I was working as a PCE-CfD trainer, people attending the course reported how much they valued being able to attend and train in the approach. They enjoyed the chance to once again feel connected to something that they felt passionate about. When they had lost their connections to the PCE approach after years of working in IAPT, and sometimes even having been forced to retrain and practise CBT or else lose their jobs, attending PCE-CfD training was a significant event. For those therapists, the agony was visible. They felt, and I could sense the pain, that having to practise CBT was an approach that they simply considered to be unethical in the face of human distress. Of course, using CBT manuals isn't unethical from the medical model point of view. Once outside the medical model of distress, it can't be considered anything else. Being part of the PCE-CfD project has been meaningful for those reasons mentioned above. This book will hopefully contribute to enabling more people to attend the courses, return to their IAPT fortresses, now with their own Trojan horse. This book is for the PCE therapists working in settings where they can establish therapeutic relationships in which clients can grow. The extent that IAPT allows this to happen is another matter altogether.

Appendix 1

Lists of Competences

Generic

G1-Knowledge and understanding of mental health problems

G2-Knowledge of depression

G3-Knowledge of, and ability to operate within, professional and ethical guidelines

G4-Knowledge of a model of therapy, and the ability to understand and employ the model in practice

G5-Ability to work with difference (cultural competence)

G6-Ability to engage client

G7-Ability to foster and maintain a good therapeutic alliance, and to grasp the client's perspective and 'world view'

G8-Ability to work with the emotional content of sessions

G9-Ability to manage endings

G10-Ability to undertake a generic assessment

G11-Ability to assess and manage risk of self-harm

G12-Ability to use measures to guide therapy and to monitor outcomes

G13-Ability to make use of supervision

Basic

B1-Knowledge of the philosophy and principles that inform the therapeutic approach

B2-Knowledge of person-centred theories of human growth and development and the origins of psychological distress

B3-Knowledge of the person-centred conditions for, and goals of, therapeutic change

B4-Knowledge of the PCE conceptualisation of depression

B5-Ability to explain and demonstrate the rationale for counselling

B6-Ability to work with the client to establish a therapeutic aim

B7-Ability to experience and communicate empathy

B8-Ability to experience and to communicate a fundamentally accepting attitude to clients

B9-Ability to maintain authenticity in the therapeutic relationship

B10-Ability to conclude the therapeutic relationship

Specific

S1-Ability to help clients to access and express emotions

S1.1-An ability to identify the ways in which clients manage and process their emotions, including the ability to recognise when clients are finding it difficult to access these

S1.2-An ability to help clients experience feelings which may be out of current awareness, e.g.:

- by helping clients focus their attention inwards in order to become more aware of their feelings
- by helping clients find ways of describing emotions which seem difficult to access
- by listening empathically for feelings that are implicit and not yet fully in awareness
- by focusing the client's attention on bodily sensations
- by making empathic conjectures about feelings that have not yet been expressed

S1.3-An ability to judge when it is appropriate to help clients reduce the extent to which they avoid experiencing underlying feelings

S1.4-An ability to use methods that help clients increase contact with avoided emotion e.g.:

- by helping clients explore what might be making it difficult for them to acknowledge and/or experience feelings
- by identifying moments when clients seem to be having difficulty acknowledging and/or experiencing underlying feelings and drawing their attention to this
- by helping clients explore the ways in which they avoid acknowledging and/or experiencing underlying feelings, and possible factors that may influence this e.g.:

> ○ previous negative experiences of expressing emotions to others
> ○ cultural and family attitudes to the expression of emotion

S1.5-An ability to help clients achieve a level of emotional arousal that is optimal for exploring their feelings, e.g.:

- helping clients who are overwhelmed by feelings e.g. by offering a calming and containing presence, containing imagery, or help to self-soothe
- enabling clients who are out of touch with their feelings to increase emotional contact, for example by:
  - ○ helping them review current concerns and focus on the most significant
  - ○ helping them bring to mind and discuss previous episodes when they experienced heightened emotion
  - ○ the counsellor using vivid imagery or language aimed at promoting feelings in the client
  - ○ suggesting active methods that promote emotional expression (e.g. encouraging clients to repeat a phrase more forcefully)

S1.6-An ability to help the client differentiate between feelings that are appropriate to (and hence useful for) dealing with a current situation and those that are less helpful to them, for example:

- because they are emotional responses relating to previous experiences rather than the present context
- because they are reactions to other, more fundamental, emotions

S2-Ability to help clients articulate emotions

S2.1-An ability to help the client clarify and find appropriate words to describe their emotions

S2.2-An ability to help the client verbalise the key concerns, meanings and memories which emerge out of emotional arousal

S2.3-An ability to help the client identify and verbalise the wishes, needs, behaviours and goals associated with feelings and emotions (i.e. the 'action tendency' inherent in emotions)

S2.4-An ability to suggest imagery and metaphor to help the client become more aware of and to articulate the meaning of their experiences

S2.5-An ability to work with images or metaphors in a way that is helpful to clients: by communicating in a manner that helps clients focus on their experiencing:

- by checking the 'fit' of images or metaphors with the client's experience
- by working with the client to elaborate the image or metaphor

S3-Ability to help clients reflect on and develop emotional meanings

S3.1-An ability to help clients explore their implicit central assumptions about self, others and the world

S3.2-An ability to help clients adapt central assumptions in the light of experience

S3.3-An ability to help the client explore alternative ways of understanding their emotional difficulties and the ways in which they experience themselves and others

S3.4-An ability to help clients explore and evaluate new perspectives on their experiences in order for them to:

- develop alternative ways of understanding their experiences
- revise their views of themselves
- develop new narratives relating to themselves and their world

S3.5-An ability to help the client develop metaphors for themselves that fit with their newly-emerging experience

S3.6-An ability to help the client reflect on any new meanings that emerge:

- to check the accuracy of meanings against experience
- to assess the implications of the new meanings
- to re-examine behaviour and where appropriate consider alternative forms of action

S3.7-An ability to help clients evaluate new perspectives in terms of their social context, personal values and goals in life

S4-Ability to help clients make sense of experiences that are confusing and distressing

S4.1-An ability to recognise and to help clients reflect on reactions that they experience as problematic and/or incongruent (e.g. when they over- or under-react to a situation, or react in ways which they describe as being out of character)

S4.2-An ability to help the client describe both their emotional reactions and the external situation, in ways that encourage the client:

- to identify how they were feeling before they encountered the situation
- to re-imagine the situation
- to identify the moment when the reaction was triggered
- to explore their reaction to the situation

- to make links between their reactions and the way they construed the situation
- to develop new ways of understanding the situation and their responses to it

Metacompetences

M1-Capacity to implement CfD in a flexible but coherent manner

M2-Capacity to adapt interventions in response to client feedback

M3-Working with the whole person

- M3.1-An ability, when working with clients, to maintain a holistic perspective (recognising the integral nature of intrapersonal, interpersonal, contextual, and spiritual aspects of the person)
- M3.2-An ability to take fully into account the clients' cultural and social context in order to empathise with their frame of reference

M4-Maintaining a person-centred stance

- M4.1-An ability to balance any tensions between the maintenance of the therapeutic relationship and the achievement of therapeutic tasks
- M4.2-An ability to maintain a balance between directive and non-directive dimensions of the therapeutic process
- M4.3-An ability for the counsellor to adopt an accepting and non-judgemental attitude towards the client while acknowledging their feelings for, and reactions to, the client.

M5-Maintaining safety in the therapeutic relationship

- M5.1-An ability to balance the maintenance of a person-centred stance with the need to attend to issues of client safety and risk
- M5.2-An ability to hold authority and contain the therapeutic process while sharing power appropriately with the client

M6-Maintaining psychological contact

- M6.1-An ability to establish and maintain psychological contact with the client at both explicit and implicit levels

M7-Capacity to balance therapeutic tasks

- M7.1-An ability to balance the need for warmth and acceptance with the need to be congruent and transparent with clients
- M7.2-An ability to attend to both process and content in the therapeutic relationship

- M7.3-An ability to balance emotional arousal with the need for understanding and meaning making in the therapeutic relationship
- M7.4-An ability to balance levels of support and challenge in the therapeutic relationship
- M7.5-An ability to hold in mind and to monitor the client's emotional needs and capacities when devising and undertaking therapeutic tasks

M8-Integrating the therapist's experience into the therapeutic relationship

- M8.1-An ability for the counsellor to make use of 'metacommunication' (describing the impact of the client's behaviour and communications on them), and a capacity to:
  - judge when metacommunication might be helpful to the client
  - convey the intention behind the counsellor's communication
  - explore the impact of the counsellor's communication on the client
- M8.2-An ability for the counsellor to recognise their own contribution to the construction of meaning in the therapeutic relationship

Ability to offer a therapeutic relationship that facilitates experiential exploration within a relational context

Generic therapeutic competences

- Knowledge and understanding of mental health problems
- Knowledge of, and ability to operate within, professional and ethical guidelines
- Knowledge of a model of therapy, and the ability to understand and employ the model in practice
- Ability to engage client
- Ability to foster and maintain a good therapeutic alliance, and to grasp the client's perspective and 'world view'
- Ability to work the emotional content of sessions
- Ability to manage endings
- Ability to undertake generic assessment (relevant history and identifying suitability for intervention)
- Ability to make use of supervision

Basic humanistic psychological therapy competences

- Knowledge of the basic assumptions and principles of humanistic psychological therapies
- Ability to initiate therapeutic relationships
- Ability to explain and demonstrate the rationale for humanistic approaches to therapy
- Ability to work with the client to establish a therapeutic aim
- Ability to maintain and develop therapeutic relationships
- Ability to experience and communicate empathy
- Ability to experience and to communicate a fundamentally accepting attitude to clients
- Ability to maintain authenticity in the therapeutic relationship
- Ability to conclude the therapeutic relationship

Specific humanistic psychological therapy competences

- Approaches to work with emotions and emotional meaning
- Ability to help clients access and express emotions
- Ability to help clients articulate emotions
- Ability to help clients reflect on and develop emotional meanings
- Ability to help clients make sense of experiences that are confusing and distressing
- Ability to make use of methods that encourage active expression
- Approaches to working relationally
- Ability to maintain a client-centered stance
- Ability to work with the immediate therapeutic relationship

Specific humanistic adaptations

- Process Experimental/ Emotional Focused Therapy

Metacompetences

- Generic metacompetences
- Capacity to use clinical judgement when implementing treatment models
- Capacity to adapt interventions in response to client feedback
- Humanistic metacompetences
- Metacompetences specific to humanistic psychological therapies competences

Figure A1.1 The competency map

Appendix 2

Person-Centred & Experiential Psychotherapy Scale (PCEP)

Therapist rating scale

PERSON–CENTRED & EXPERIENTIAL PSYCHOTHERAPY SCALE-10-T

(THERAPIST VERSION, v. 1.1, 16/09/2016)

© 2016 Robert Elliott & Graham Westwell. (Permission is granted to reproduce this form for educational, training, or supervision purposes, on the condition that it is not changed or sold).

Rate the items according to how well you think you did on each during this therapy session.

---

1. CLIENT FRAME OF REFERENCE/TRACK:

How much did my responses convey an understanding of my client's experiences as they themselves understood or perceived these? To what extent was I following my client's track?

Rating Notes: Did my responses convey an understanding of my client's immediately expressed inner experience or point of view? Or conversely, how did my responses impose meaning based on my own frame of reference?

Were my responses right on client's track? Conversely, were my responses a diversion from my client's own train of thoughts/feelings?

1	**No tracking**: My responses conveyed no understanding of my client's frame of reference or added meaning based completely on my own frame of reference.
2	**Minimal tracking**: My responses conveyed a poor understanding of my client's frame of reference or added meaning partially based on my own frame of reference rather than my client's.

3	**Slight tracking**: My responses came close but don't quite reach an adequate understanding of my client's frame of reference; my responses were slight "off" of my client's frame or reference.
4	**Adequate tracking**: My responses conveyed an adequate understanding of my client's frame of reference.
5	**Good tracking**: My responses conveyed a good understanding of my client's frame of reference.
6	**Excellent tracking**: My responses conveyed a highly accurate understanding of my client's frame of reference in which I added no meaning from my own frame of reference.

2. PSYCHOLOGICAL HOLDING:

How well did I metaphorically hold my client when they were experiencing painful, scary, or overwhelming experiences, or when they were connecting with their vulnerabilities?

> *Rating Notes: High scores refer to me maintaining a solid, emotional and empathic connection even when my client was in pain or overwhelmed.*

> *Low scores refer to situations in which I avoided responding or acknowledging painful, frightening or overwhelming experiences of my client.*

1	**No holding**: I was oblivious to my client's need to be psychologically held; I avoided responding, acknowledging or addressing their experience/feelings.
2	**Minimal holding**: I was aware of my client's need to be psychologically held but was anxious or insecure when responding to client and diverted or distracted them from their vulnerability.
3	**Slight holding**: I conveyed a bit of psychological holding, but not enough and with some insecurity.
4	**Adequate holding**: I managed to hold my client's experience sufficiently.
5	**Good holding**: I calmly and solidly held my client's experience.
6	**Excellent holding**: I securely held my client's experience with trust, groundedness and acceptance, even when they were experiencing, for example, pain, fear or being overwhelmed.

3. EXPERIENTIAL SPECIFICITY:

How much did I appropriately and skilfully work to help my client focus on, elaborate or differentiate specific, idiosyncratic or personal experiences or memories, as opposed to abstractions or generalities?

> *Rating Notes: E.g., By my reflecting specific client experiences using crisp, precise, differentiated and appropriately empathic reflections; by asking for examples or for my client to specify feelings, meanings, memories or other personal experiences.*

1	**No specificity**: I consistently responded in a highly abstract, vague or intellectual manner.
2	**Minimal specificity**: I had the concept of specificity but didn't implement it adequately, consistently or well; I was either somewhat vague or abstract or generally failed to encourage experiential specificity where appropriate.
3	**Slight specificity**: I was often or repeatedly vague or abstract; I only slightly or occasionally encouraged experiential specificity; sometimes I responded in a way that pointed to experiential specificity, but often I failed to do so, or did so in an awkward manner.
4	**Adequate specificity**: Where appropriate, I generally encouraged client experiential specificity, with only minor, temporary lapses or slight awkwardness.
5	**Good specificity**: I did enough of this and did it skilfully, where appropriate trying to help my client to elaborate and specify particular experiences.
6	**Excellent specificity**: I did this consistently, skilfully, and even creatively, where appropriate, offering the client crisp, precise reflections or questions.

4. ACCEPTING PRESENCE:

How well did I convey unconditional acceptance of whatever my client brought?

Rating Notes: Did my responses convey a grounded, centred, and acceptant presence?

1	**Explicit nonacceptance**: I explicitly communicated disapproval or criticism of my client's experience/meaning/feelings.
2	**Implicit nonacceptance**: I implicitly or indirectly communicated disapproval or criticism of my client's experience/meaning/feelings.
3	**Incongruent/inconsistent nonacceptance**: I conveyed anxiety, worry or defensiveness instead of acceptance; or I was not consistent in communicating acceptance to my client.
4	**Adequate acceptance**: I demonstrated calm and groundedness, with at least some degree of acceptance of my client's experience.
5	**Good acceptance**: I conveyed clear, grounded acceptance of my client's experience; I did not demonstrate any kind of judgment towards my client's experience/behaviour
6	**Excellent acceptance**: I skilfully conveyed unconditional acceptance while being clearly grounded and centred in myself, even in the face of intense client vulnerability.

5. CONTENT DIRECTIVENESS:

How much did my responses intend to direct my client's content?

Rating Notes: Did my responses introduce explicit new content? e.g., Did my responses convey explanation, interpretation, guidance, teaching, advice, reassurance or confrontation?

1   **"Expert" directiveness**: I overtly and consistently assumed the role of expert in directing the content of the session

2   **Overt directiveness**: My responses directed my client overtly towards new content.

3   **Slight directiveness**: My responses directed my client clearly but tentatively towards a new content.

4   **Adequate nondirectiveness**: I was generally nondirective of content, with only minor, temporary lapses or slight content direction.

5   **Good nondirectiveness**: I consistently followed my client's lead when responding to content.

6   **Excellent nondirectiveness**: I clearly and consistently followed my client's lead when responding to content in a natural, inviting and unforced manner, with a high level of skill.

6. EMOTION FOCUS:

How much did I actively work to help my client focus on and actively articulate their emotional experiences and meanings, both explicit and implicit?

Rating Notes: E.g., By helping my client focus their attention inwards; by focusing my client's attention on bodily sensations; by reflecting toward emotionally poignant content, by inquiring about client feelings, helping my client intensify, heighten or deepen their emotions, by helping my client find ways of describing emotions; or by making empathic conjectures about feelings that have not yet been expressed. Lower scores reflect ignoring implicit or explicit emotions; staying with non-emotional content; focusing on or reflecting generalized emotional states ("feeling bad") or minimizing emotional states (e.g., reflecting "angry" as "annoyed").

1   **No emotion focus**: I consistently ignored emotions or responded instead in a highly intellectual manner while focusing entirely on non-emotional content. When my client expressed emotions, I consistently deflected my client away from them.

2   **Minimal emotion focus**: I understood [what] emotion focus is but didn't implement it adequately, consistently or well. For example, I generally stayed with non-emotional content; I generally but not always deflected my client way from their emotion; I reflected only general emotional states (e.g., "bad"); or I minimized my client's emotions.

3   **Slight emotion focus**: I often or repeatedly ignored or deflected my client away from emotion; I only slightly or occasionally helped my client to focus on emotion; while I sometimes responded in a way that pointed to client emotions, at times I failed to do so, or did so in an awkward manner.

4   **Adequate emotion focus**: Where appropriate, I generally encouraged my client to focus on emotions (by reflections or other responses), with only minor, temporary lapses or slight awkwardness.

5   **Good emotion focus**: I did enough of this and did it skilfully, where appropriate trying to help my client to evoke, deepen and express particular emotions.

6   **Excellent emotion focus**: I did this consistently, skilfully, and even creatively, where appropriate offering the client powerful, evocative reflections or questions, while at the same time enabling the client to feel safe while doing so.

7. DOMINANT OR OVERPOWERING PRESENCE:

To what extent did I project a sense of dominance or authority in the session with my client?

Rating Notes: Low scores refer to situations in which I was taking charge of the process of the session; acting in a self-indulgent manner or taking over attention or focus for myself; interrupting, talking over my client, being silent or controlling the process; or acting in a definitive, lecturing, or expert manner.

High scores refer to situations in which I offered my client choice or autonomy in the session, allowing my client space to develop their own experience, waiting for them to finish their thoughts, being patient with them, or encouraging them to feel empowered in the session.

1	**Overpowering presence**: I overpowered my client by strongly dominating the interaction, controlling what they talked about or did in the session; clearly made myself the centre of attention; or was patronizing toward my client.
2	**Controlling presence**: I clearly controlled my client's process in the session, acting in an expert, or dominant manner.
3	**Subtle control**: I subtly, implicitly or indirectly controlled what and how my client was in the session.
4	**Noncontrolling presence**: I generally respected my client's autonomy in the session; I did not try to control my client's process.
5	**Respectful presence**: I consistently respected my client's autonomy in the session.
6	**Empowering presence**: I clearly and consistently promoted or validated my client's freedom or choice, allowing them space as they desired.

8. CLARITY OF LANGUAGE:

How well did I use language that communicated simply and clearly to my client?

Rating Notes: E.g., my responses were not too wordy, rambling, or unnecessarily long; I did not use language that was too academic or too abstract; my responses did not get in my client's way.

1	**No clarity**: My responses were long-winded, tangled, and *confusing*.
2	**Minimal clarity**: My responses were wordy, rambling or *unfocused*.
3	**Slight clarity**: My responses were *somewhat clear*, but a bit too abstract or long.
4	**Adequate clarity**: My responses were *clear but a bit too long*.
5	**Good clarity**: My responses were *clear and concise*.
6	**Excellent clarity**: My responses were very clear and concise, even *elegantly* capturing *subtle* client experiences in a few choice words.

9. CORE MEANING:

How well did my responses reflect the core, or essence, of what my client was communicating or experiencing in the moment?

Rating Notes: My responses were not just a reflection of surface content but showed an understanding of my client's central/core experience or meaning that was being communicated either implicitly or explicitly in the moment; my responses did not take away from the core meaning of my client's communication.

1	**No core meaning**: My responses addressed *only* the cognitive content or stayed **exclusively** in the superficial narrative.
2	**Minimal core meaning**: My responses addressed *mainly* the cognitive content or the superficial narrative but brought occasional *glimpses* into the underlying core feeling/experience/meaning.
3	**Slight core meaning**: My responses *partially but incompletely* addressed the core meaning/feeling/experience underneath my client's expressed content.
4	**Adequate core meaning**: My responses were *close* to the *core* meaning/feeling/experience that was underneath my client's expressed content but did not quite reach it.
5	**Good core meaning**: My responses accurately addressed the *core* meaning/feeling/experience that was underneath my client's expressed content.
6	**Excellent core meaning**: My responses addressed with a high degree of accuracy the **core** meaning/feeling/experience that was underneath my client's expressed content.

10. EMOTION REGULATION SENSITIVITY:

How much did I actively work to help my client adjust and maintain the level of emotional arousal they needed for productive self-exploration?

Rating Notes: Client agency is central here; this is not to be imposed by me. There are three possible situations:

(a) If my client was overwhelmed by feelings and wanted help in moderating them, did I try to help my client to manage these emotions? E.g., By offering a calming and holding presence; by using containing imagery; or by helping my client self-soothe vs. allowing them to continue to panic or feel overwhelmed or unsafe.

(b) If my client was out of touch with their feelings and wanted help in accessing them, did I try to help them appropriately increase emotional contact? E.g., by helping them review current concerns and focus on the most important or poignant; by helping them remember and explore memories of emotional experiences; by using vivid imagery or language to promote feelings vs. increasing distance from emotions.

(c) *If my client was at an optimal level of emotional arousal for exploration, did I try to help them continue working at this level, rather than either heightening or flattening their emotions?*

1	**No facilitation**: I consistently ignored possible concerns about emotional regulation on the part of my client, or generally worked against the client regulating their emotions, that is by allowing them to continue feel overwhelmed or distanced.
2	**Minimal facilitation**: I understood the principle of facilitating client emotional regulation but didn't implement it adequately, consistently or well; I generally ignored my client's desire to contain overwhelmed emotion or to approach distanced emotion; or I sometimes misdirected my client out of a productive, optimal level of emotional arousal, into either stuck or overwhelmed emotion or emotional distance/avoidance.
3	**Slight facilitation**: I often ignored or deflected my client away from the level of emotional regulation they experienced as productive for self-exploration; or I only slightly facilitated productive self-exploration. While I sometimes responded in a way that facilitated client productive emotional regulation, at times I failed to do so, or did so in an awkward manner.
4	**Adequate facilitation**: Where appropriate, I generally encouraged client emotional regulation (e.g., by helping them approach difficult emotions or contain excessive emotional distress as they desired), with only minor, temporary lapses or slight awkwardness.
5	**Good facilitation**: I did enough emotional regulation facilitation and did it skilfully and in accordance with my client's desires, where appropriate trying to help them to maintain a productive level of emotional arousal.
6	**Excellent facilitation**: I did this consistently, skilfully, and even creatively, where desired by my client, offering them evocative or focusing responses to help them to approach difficult emotions when they were too distant or to contain overwhelming emotions when these were too much, all within a safe, holding environment.

Rater emotional reaction to therapist form

RATER EMOTIONAL REACTION TO THERAPIST FORM (v1.0; 20.07.17).

©2017, Graham Westwell & Robert Elliott. (Permission is granted to reproduce this form for educational, training, or supervision purposes, on the condition that it is not changed or sold).

Please rate your emotional reaction to the therapist for each segment. Use the item descriptors below to pick the item that *fits best* with your experience. You do not have to agree with *all* of the descriptions – choose the one that *most* accurately matches your emotional reaction to the therapist.

1. **Strongly dislike therapist:** I found it really hard to listen to this therapist; this really didn't sound like good therapy; I found it really hard to listen all the way through; I felt upset, angry or distressed when listening to this; I felt concerned for the client.
2. **Quite dislike therapist**: I found it hard to listen to the segment in places; I wanted to help out the client in places; I was bothered to some degree by listening to this; I wanted to stop the therapist in places.
3. **No significant reaction**: I found this therapist OK to listen to; I didn't feel strongly bothered by the therapist, one way or another.
4. **Quite like therapist**: I enjoyed listening to most of the therapist responses; I thought that the client was getting something out of the session; I felt like the therapist was trying their best; I felt mostly comfortable listening to this therapist.
5. **Strongly like therapist**: I was really impressed with this therapist; I felt like I had learned something from their practice; I felt like the client had had a good experience; I found this therapist really easy to listen to; I felt warm and positive towards the therapist.

Notation system for PCEPS-10 raters

NOTATION SYSTEM FOR PCEPS-10 RATERS (v1.0, 17.08.17)

©2017, Graham Westwell & Robert Elliott. (Permission is granted to reproduce this form for educational, training, or supervision purposes, on the condition that it is not changed or sold).

Notation system for PCEPS-10 raters

Notation	Meaning of notation.
*	Therapist response seems to be helpful for the client (e.g. response addresses core meaning; response names accurate emotion; psychologically holds the client).
**	Therapist response seems to be *very* helpful for the client (as above but with greater mastery).
M/E	Therapist response is a minimal encourager.
E/R	Therapist response is an empathic reflection.
Tr	Therapist response is an empathic tracking response.
EFR	Therapist response is an empathic following response (e.g. word-for-word reflection).
EXP	Therapist response is focused towards greater client experiential specificity.
Q	Therapist has asked a question.
(?)	Rater is not sure why therapist has offered this response.
FOR?	Rater wonders if this response is from the therapist's frame of reference.

Notation	Meaning of notation.
Cont?	Rater wonders if therapist is making a content directive response.
Missed?	Rater thinks that something important (e.g. core meaning) has been missed by the therapist; or therapist is simply not responding to the client for a significant period.
Emotion?	Rater thinks that therapist is missing responding to the client's emotions.
\	Therapist is talking over the client (*notation are lines made across the central divide, between therapist column and client column, to indicate cross-talk).
/	
\	
/ *	

Appendix 3

PCE-CfD Supervision Adherence Scale

Person-Centred Experiential Counselling for Depression

Supervision Adherence Scale

Use the scale below to rate the items according to the quality and frequency of each activity during the supervision segment to which you've just listened.

SA 1. Understanding and application of PCE- CfD (0–4 marks)

- An ability for the supervisor to draw on knowledge of the principles underpinning PCE – Counselling for Depression
- An ability to link PCE-CfD concepts and principles to the therapist's way of being with the client.
- An ability to help supervisees review and apply their knowledge of PCE Counselling for Depression.
- An ability to help supervisees think about their values and intentions with their interventions and to explore the consistency or inconsistency of these with the values and attitudes of CfD.

Shows no evidence of	Shows some evidence of	Shows moderate evidence of	Shows good evidence of	Shows very good evidence of
0	1	2	3	4

SA 2 Understanding and application of marking using PCEPS

- Ability for the supervisor to draw on their knowledge of the subscales of the PCEPS

- Ability to link the subscales of the PCEPS with what they hear of the supervisee's work.
- An ability to help the supervisee think about how their recordings will be marked using the PCEPS.

Shows no evidence of	Shows some evidence of	Shows moderate evidence of	Shows good evidence of	Shows very good evidence of
0	1	2	3	4

SA 3. The PCE supervisory stance (0–4 marks)

- An ability to adopt an approach to supervision which places the primary focus on the exploration of the therapist's experience of the client, rather than on the client issues or developing immediate solutions to problems
- An ability to be reflective and to self-monitor the emotional and interpersonal processes associated with supervisor-supervisee interactions
- An ability to employ empathic understanding to sense the supervisee's perceptions, experience and responses to their work

Shows no evidence of	Shows some evidence of	Shows moderate evidence of	Shows good evidence of	Shows very good evidence of
0	1	2	3	4

SA 4. Maintaining the PCE therapeutic focus (0–4 marks)

An ability to help the supervisee:

- to maintain a primary focus on clients' affective experience
- to reflect on their experience of the therapeutic relationship (including their affective, cognitive and somatic reactions to the client)

Shows no evidence of	Shows some evidence of	Shows moderate evidence of	Shows good evidence of	Shows very good evidence of
0	1	2	3	4

Maximum score 16
Adherence is from a score of 8 or above.

Appendix 4

Measurement Scales

Patient Health Questionnaire – 9: PHQ-9

Table A4.1 Patient Health Questionnaire – 9: PHQ-9

Over the last 2 weeks, how often have you been bothered by any of the following problems? (Use "☐" to indicate your answer)	Not at all	Several days	More than half the days	Nearly every day
1. Little interest or pleasure in doing things	0	1	2	3
2. Feeling down, depressed or hopeless	0	1	2	3
3. Trouble falling or staying asleep, or sleeping too much	0	1	2	3
4. Feeling tired or having little energy	0	1	2	3
5. Poor appetite or overeating	0	1	2	3
6. Feeling bad about yourself – or that you are a failure or have let yourself or your family down	0	1	2	3
7. Trouble concentrating on things, such as reading the newspaper or watching television	0	1	2	3
8. Moving or speaking slowly that other people could have noticed? Or the opposite – being so fidgety or restless that you have been moving around a lot more than usual	0	1	2	3
9. Thoughts that you would be better off dead or of hurting yourself in some way	0	1	2	3
For office coding	+	+	+	
		=Total Score:		
If you have checked off any problems, how difficult have these problems made it for you to do your work, take care of things at home, or get along with other people?				
Not difficult at all ☐	Somewhat difficult ☐	Very difficult ☐	Extremely difficult ☐	

Source: Developed by Drs Robert L. Spitzer, Janet B.W. Williams, Kurt Kroenke and colleagues, with an educational grant from Pfizer Inc. No permission required to reproduce, translate, display or distribute.

Unconditional Positive Self-Regard Scale (UPSR Scale)

Below is a list of statements dealing with your general feelings about yourself. Please respond to each statement by circling your answer using the scale '1 = Strongly Disagree' to '5 = Strongly Agree'.

Table A4.2   Unconditional Positive Self-Regard Scale (UPSR Scale)

		Strongly Disagree	Disagree	Unsure	Agree	Strongly Agree
1	I truly like myself.	1	2	3	4	5
2	Whether other people criticise me or praise me makes no real difference to the way I feel about myself.	1	2	3	4	5
3	There are certain things I like about myself and there are other things I don't like.	1	2	3	4	5
4	I feel that I appreciate myself as a person.	1	2	3	4	5
5	Some things I do make me feel good about myself whereas other things I do cause me to be critical of myself.	1	2	3	4	5
6	How I feel towards myself is not dependent on how others feel towards me.	1	2	3	4	5
7	I have a lot of respect for myself.	1	2	3	4	5
8	I feel deep affection for myself.	1	2	3	4	5
9	I treat myself in a warm and friendly way.	1	2	3	4	5
10	I don't think that anything I say or do really changes the way I feel about myself.	1	2	3	4	5
11	I really value myself.	1	2	3	4	5
12	Whether other people are openly appreciative of me or openly critical of me, it does not really change how I feel about myself.	1	2	3	4	5

Scoring Key for the UPSR Scale*: Strongly Disagree = 1; Disagree = 2; Unsure = 3; Agree = 4; Strongly Agree = 5

*Items 3 & 5 are reverse scored.

Scores on the total scale have a possible range of 12 to 60, and a possible range of 6 to 30 on each of the two subscales. On the 'Self-Regard' subscale, high scores indicate presence of positive self-regard while low scores indicate absence of positive self-regard. On the 'Conditionality' sub-scale, high scores indicate *unconditionality* of self-regard, while low scores indicate *conditionality* of self-regard.

Subscales: Items 1 + 4 + 7 + 8 + 9 + 11 = Self-Regard Subscale;

Items 2 + 3 + 5 + 6 + 10 + 12 = Conditionality Subscale

Source: Patterson, T. G., & Joseph, S. (2006). Development of a measure of unconditional positive self-regard. *Psychology and Psychotherapy: Theory, Research, and Practice, 79*, 557–570.

Authenticity Scale

Table A4.3 Authenticity Scale

Authenticity Scale	
Scoring Instructions	
All items are presented on a 1 (*does not describe me at all*) to 7 (*describes me very well*) scale.	
1. 'I think it is better to be yourself, than to be popular.'	
2. 'I don't know how I really feel inside.'	
3. 'I am strongly influenced by the opinions of others.'	
4. 'I usually do what other people tell me to do.'	
5. 'I always feel I need to do what others expect me to do.'	
6. 'Other people influence me greatly.'	
7. 'I feel as if I don't know myself very well.'	
8. 'I always stand by what I believe in.'	
9. 'I am true to myself in most situations.'	
10. 'I feel out of touch with the "real me."'	
11. 'I live in accordance with my values and beliefs.'	
12. 'I feel alienated from myself.'	

To score the scale, total:

Items: 1, 8, 9, and 11 for Authentic Living;
Items: 3, 4, 5, and 6 for Accepting External Influence; and
Items: 2, 7, 10, and 12 for Self-Alienation.

To obtain a score where high authenticity is represented by a high score, the following items need to be reverse scored: 2, 3, 4, 5, 6, 7, 10, 12.

Source: Wood, A. M., Linley, P. A., Maltby, J., Baliousis, M., & Joseph, S. (2008). The authentic personality: A theoretical and empirical conceptualization and the development of the Authenticity Scale. *Journal of Counseling Psychology*, 55(3), 385–399.

Short Depression-Happiness Scale (SDHS)

Table A4.4   Short Depression-Happiness Scale (SDHS)

	Never	Rarely	Sometimes	Often
1. I felt dissatisfied with my life				
2. I felt happy				
3. I felt cheerless				
4. I felt pleased with the way I am				
5. I felt that life was enjoyable				
6. I felt that life was meaningless				

Strathclyde Inventory

Client ID _____ Male □ Female □ Age _____ Date ___/___/___ Session_____

Please read each statement below and think how often you sense it has been true for you DURING THE **LAST MONTH**. Then mark the box that is closest to this. There are no right or wrong answers – it is only important what is true for you individually.

Table A4.5   Strathclyde Inventory

OVER THE LAST MONTH	Never	Only occasio-nally	Some-times	Often	All or most of the time
1. I have been able to be spontaneous	$\square_0$	$\square_1$	$\square_2$	$\square_3$	$\square_4$
2. I have condemned myself for my attitudes or behaviour	$\square_4$	$\square_3$	$\square_2$	$\square_1$	$\square_0$
3. I have tried to be what others think I should be	$\square_4$	$\square_3$	$\square_2$	$\square_1$	$\square_0$
4. I have trusted my own reactions to situations	$\square_0$	$\square_1$	$\square_2$	$\square_3$	$\square_4$
5. I have experienced very satisfying personal relationships	$\square_0$	$\square_1$	$\square_2$	$\square_3$	$\square_4$
6. I have felt afraid of my emotional reactions	$\square_4$	$\square_3$	$\square_2$	$\square_1$	$\square_0$
7. I have looked to others for approval or disapproval	$\square_4$	$\square_3$	$\square_2$	$\square_1$	$\square_0$

(Continued)

Table A4.5   (Continued)

OVER THE LAST MONTH	Never	Only occasio- nally	Some- times	Often	All or most of the time
8. I have expressed myself in my own unique way	$\square_0$	$\square_1$	$\square_2$	$\square_3$	$\square_4$
9. I have found myself 'on guard' when relating with others	$\square_4$	$\square_3$	$\square_2$	$\square_1$	$\square_0$
10. I have made choices based on my own internal sense of what is right	$\square_0$	$\square_1$	$\square_2$	$\square_3$	$\square_4$
11. I have listened sensitively to myself	$\square_0$	$\square_1$	$\square_2$	$\square_3$	$\square_4$
12. I have felt myself doing things that were out of my control	$\square_4$	$\square_3$	$\square_2$	$\square_1$	$\square_0$
13. I have lived fully in each new moment	$\square_0$	$\square_1$	$\square_2$	$\square_3$	$\square_4$
14. I have been aware of my feelings	$\square_0$	$\square_1$	$\square_2$	$\square_3$	$\square_4$
15. I have hidden some elements of myself behind a 'mask'	$\square_4$	$\square_3$	$\square_2$	$\square_1$	$\square_0$
16. I have felt true to myself	$\square_0$	$\square_1$	$\square_2$	$\square_3$	$\square_4$
17. I have felt myself doing things that are out of character for me	$\square_4$	$\square_3$	$\square_2$	$\square_1$	$\square_0$
18. I have accepted my feelings	$\square_0$	$\square_1$	$\square_2$	$\square_3$	$\square_4$
19. I have been able to resolve conflicts within myself	$\square_0$	$\square_1$	$\square_2$	$\square_3$	$\square_4$
20. I have felt it is all right to be the kind of person I am	$\square_0$	$\square_1$	$\square_2$	$\square_3$	$\square_4$

Simplified Personal Questionnaire Procedure (ver. 3; 6/07)

Reproduced with permission from Professor Robert Elliott. © **Simplified Personal Questionnaire Procedure** (ver. 3; 6/07) Robert Elliott, University of Strathclyde

The Personal Questionnaire (PQ) is an expanded target complaint measure that is individualized for each client. It is generated from the PQ Problem Description Form, completed by the client during the screening process. It is intended to be a list of problems that the client wishes to work on in therapy, stated in the client's own words.

Materials:

- 4" x 6" Index Cards
- Blank PQ Form (for writing in items)
- Problem Description Form (completed)

Procedure

1. Generating Items. The items generated for the PQ should be the most important in the client's view. However, an attempt should be made to include one or two problems from each of the following areas:

- Symptoms
- Specific performance/activity (e.g., work)
- Relationships
- Self-esteem
- Emotions and inner experiences

This means that if the client does not list a problem in a particular area, the interviewer should ask the client if s/he has any difficulties in that area that s/he wants to work on in therapy. If, however, the client does not wish to have an item for this area, the researcher does not insist on it.

This part of the procedure should be thought of as a brainstorming session, generating as many potential items as possible (around 15 is preferable). If the client has difficulty coming up with 10 problems, the interviewer can use other screening measures as sources of possible problems. For example, if the client has completed the SCL-90-R or CORE-Outcome Measure, the interviewer can ask the client about items with '3' or '4' ratings.

2. Refining the PQ items. Next, the interviewer helps the client to clarify his/her items and, if necessary, to rephrase the goals into problems. If necessary, the number of items is reduced to around 10.

2a. In this part of the procedure, the interviewer begins by writing each problem onto a separate index card, revising it in the process. Refining PQ items is not a mechanical procedure, but requires discussion with the client to make sure that the PQ reflects his/her chief concerns. It takes careful, patient communication to make sure that the PQ items truly reflect the client's experience of what is problematic.

PQ items should be present problems or difficulties, and should be worded 'I feel,' 'I am,' 'I can't,' 'My thinking,' and so on. It is useful to think of the list as things the client wants to change through therapy. A good PQ item has the following characteristics:

(i) It reflects an area of difficulty, rather than a goal (e.g., 'I am too shy' rather than 'I want to be more outgoing').
(ii) It is something that the client wants to work on in therapy.
(iii) It refers to a specific problem; that is, general, vague problems are to be specified and described explicitly where possible.

(iv) It refers to a single problem; that is, items referring to multiple problems (e.g., 'I'm uncomfortable around other people and have trouble talking about myself.') are divided up into multiple items.

(v) It is in the client's own words, not the interviewer's.

(vi) It is not redundant with another PQ item.

2b. After the interviewer writes down the items, s/he then asks the client if anything has been left out, adding further items as needed, until the client feels that the list is complete.

2c. The interviewer next reviews the items with the client, asking the client to revise or confirm them. If the client has generated more than 10 items, the interviewer asks the client to delete or combine repetitive items. If there are still more than 10 items, the interviewer asks the client if s/he wants to drop any. The interview should not force the client to generate exactly 10 items; but try to obtain 8–12 items where possible.

3. Prioritising the items. Next, the interviewer asks the client to sort the index cards into order, with the most important concern first, the next most important second, etc. The rank order of the item is written on the card.

4. Rating the PQ. After prioritising, the interviewer gives the client a blank PQ form and the rank-ordered index cards, and asks the client to use the blank form to rate how much each problem has bothered him/her during the past week. These ratings become the client's initial baseline score for the PQ.

5. Duration ratings. In addition, at this first administration of the PQ, the interviewer may want to find out how long each problem has bothered the client at roughly the same level or higher as it does now, using the Personal Questionnaire Duration Form. This can be useful for establishing a retrospective baseline for the PQ.

6. Prepare the PQ. Finally, the interviewer types or writes the PQ items onto a blank PQ form, making at least 10 copies for future use. In doing so, it is a good idea to leave two spaces blank for the client to add more items later, in case his/her problems shift over time.

7. Adding items. Clients may add items to their PQs, either on a temporary basis, by writing them in the space at the bottom on the form, or permanently, by requesting that the item be added to the printed form.

Your initials:___(Client ID:_)

Today's date:

Problem description form: Do this one first!

1. Please describe the main problems you are having right now that led you to seek treatment.

2. If you are seeking psychotherapy, please list the specific problems or difficulties that you would like assistance with. Please feel free to add to your list as you fill out other forms.

Personal questionnaire

Client ID: _____

Date: _____

Session: _____

Interviewer initials: _____

Instructions: Please complete before each session. Rate each of the following problems according to how much it has bothered you during the past seven days, including today.

	Not at all	Very little	Little	Moder- ately	Consider- ably	Very consider- ably	Maxi- mum possible
1.	1	2	3	4	5	6	7
2.	1	2	3	4	5	6	7
3.	1	2	3	4	5	6	7
4.	1	2	3	4	5	6	7
5.	1	2	3	4	5	6	7
6.	1	2	3	4	5	6	7
7.	1	2	3	4	5	6	7
8.	1	2	3	4	5	6	7
9.	1	2	3	4	5	6	7
10.	1	2	3	4	5	6	7
11.	1	2	3	4	5	6	7
12.	1	2	3	4	5	6	7
Additional Problems (optional) * Add to my printed form	1	2	3	4	5	6	7

References

American Psychological Association (APA) (2013). *Diagnostic and statistical manual of mental disorders* (5th edn) (DSM-5). New York: APA.

APPG (2019). *All party parliamentary* group for prescribed drug dependence. Available at http://prescribeddrug.org/ (accessed 18/01/19).

BACP (2004). BACP professional conduct hearing: finding, decision, sanction and appeal. *Counselling & Psychotherapy Journal, 15*(1), 58.

Baker, N. (2012). Experiential person-centred therapy. In P. Sanders (ed.), *The tribes of the person-centred nation: an introduction to the schools of therapy related to the person-centred approach* (2nd edition) (Ch. 4, pp. 67–94). Ross-on-Wye: PCCS Books.

Baldwin, S. A., Berkeljon, A., Atkins, D. C., Olsen, J. A., & Nielson, S. L. (2009). Rates of change in naturalistic psychotherapy: contrasting dose-effect and good enough level models of change. *Journal of Consulting and Clinical Psychology, 77*(2), 203–211.

Barkham, M., Connell, J., Stiles, W. B., Miles, J. N. V., Margison, F., Evans, C., & Mellor-Clark, J. (2006). Dose-effect relations and responsive regulation of treatment duration: the good enough level. *Journal of Consulting and Clinical Psychology, 74*, 160–167.

Barkham, M., Moller, N. P., & Pybis, J. (2017). How should we evaluate research on counselling and the treatment of depression? A case study on how the National Institute for Health and Care Excellence's draft 2018 guideline for depression considered what counts as best evidence. *Counselling and Psychotherapy Research, 17*(4), 253–268.

Barrett-Lennard, G. T. (1962). Dimensions of therapist response as causal factors in therapeutic change. *Psychological Monographs, 76*(43, Whole No. 562).

Barrett-Lennard, G. T. (2003). *Steps on a mindful journey: person-centred expressions*. Ross-on-Wye: PCCS Books.

Bayne, R., Horton, I., Merry, T., Noyes, E., & McMahon, G. (1999). *The Counsellor's Handbook* (2nd edn.). Cheltenham: Stanley Thornes.

Bedi, N., Chilvers, C., Churchill, R., Dewey, M., Duggan, C., Fielding, K., Gretton, V., Miller, P., Harrison, G., Lee, A., & Williams, I. (2000). Assessing effectiveness of treatment of depression in primary care. *British Journal of Psychiatry, 177*, 312–318.

Beitel, M., Bogus, S., Hutz, A., Green, D., Cecero, J. J., & Barry, D. T. (2013). Stillness and motion: an empirical investigation of mindfulness and self-actualization. *Person-Centered & Experiential Psychotherapies, 13*(3), 187–202.

Beitel, M., Wald, L. M., Midgett, A., Green, D., Cecero, J. J., Kishon, R., & Barry, D. T. (2014). Humanistic experience and psychodynamic understanding: empirical associations among facets of self-actualization and psychological mindedness. *Person-Centered & Experiential Psychotherapies, 14*(2), 137–148.

Beutler, L. E., Engle, D., Mohr, D., Daldrup, R. J., Bergan, J., Meredith, K., & Merry, W. (1991). Predictors of differential response to cognitive, experiential, and self-directed psychotherapeutic procedures. *Journal of Consulting and Clinical Psychology, 59*, 333–340.

Bohart, A. C. (2008). Response to Frankel & Sommerbeck. *Person-Centered Journal, 15*(1–2), 83–87.

Bohart, A. C. (2012). Can you be integrative and a person-centered therapist at the same time? *Person-Centered & Experiential Psychotherapies, 11*, 1–13.

Bohart, A. C., & Tallman, K. (1998). *How clients make therapy work: the process of active self-healing*. Washington, DC: American Psychological Association.

Bohart, A. C., & Tallman, K. (2010). Clients as active self-healers: implications for the person-centered approach. In M. Cooper, J. C. Watson and D. Hölldampf (eds.), *Person-centered and experiential psychotherapies work: a review of the research on counseling, psychotherapy and related practices* (pp. 91–131). Ross-on-Wye: PCCS Books.

Boss, M. (1988). Recent considerations in Daseinsanalysis. Psychotherapy for freedom: the Daseinsanalytic way in psychology and psychoanalysis. *The Humanistic Psychologist, 4*(1), 58–74.

Bozarth, J. D. (1984/2001). Beyond reflection: emergent modes of empathy. In R.F. Levant and J.M. Shlien (eds), *Client-centered therapy and the person-centered approach: new directions in theory, research and practice* (pp. 59–75). Westport, CT: Praeger. Reprinted in S. Haugh and T. Merry (eds) *Rogers' therapeutic conditions, Volume 2: Empathy* (pp. 131–54). Ross-on-Wye: PCCS Books.

Bozarth, J. D. (1998). *Person-centred therapy: a revolutionary paradigm*. Ross-on-Wye: PCCS Books.

Bozarth, J. D. (2008). Response-centered therapy: the good, bad and ugly. *Person-Centered Journal, 15*(1–2), 79–82.

Brettle, A., Hill, A., & Jenkins, P. (2008). Counselling in primary care: a systematic review of the evidence. *Counselling and Psychotherapy Research, 8*(4), 207–214.

British Association for Counselling and Psychotherapy (BACP) (2004). *Counselling & Psychotherapy Journal, 15*(1), 58.

British Association for Counselling and Psychotherapy (BACP) (2010). *Counselling for Depression (CfD) general information*. Available at: www.bacp.co.uk/learning/ Counselling%20for%20Depression/ (accessed 20/02/14).

Brodley, B. T., & Brody, A. F. (1996). Can one use techniques and still be client-centered? In R. Hutterer, P. F. Schmid, and R. Stipsits (Eds.), *Client-centered and experiential psychotherapy: a revolutionary paradigm in motion* (pp. 369–374). New York: Peter Lang.

Centre for Economic Performance Mental Health Policy Group (CEPMHPG) (2006). *The depression report: a new deal for depression and anxiety disorders*. London: London School of Economics and Political Science.

Chambless, D. L., & Hollon, S. D. (1998). Defining empirically supported therapies. *Journal of Consulting and Clinical Psychology, 66*, 7–18.

Cooper, M. (2008). *Essential research findings in counselling and psychotherapy*. London: Sage.

Cooper, P. J., Murray, L., Wilson, A., & Romaniuk, H. (2003). Controlled trial of the short- and long-term effect of psychological treatment of post-partum depression. *British Journal of Psychiatry, 182*, 412–419.

Craig, E. (2015). The lost language of being: ontology's perilous destiny in existential psychotherapy. *Philosophy, Psychiatry & Psychology, 2*(2), 79–92.

Cushman, P. (1995). *Constructing the self, constructing America*. Cambridge, MA: Da Capo Press.

Dagnan, D., Trower, P., & Chadwick, P. (2000). Psychometric properties of the Hospital Anxiety and Depression Scale with a population of members of a depression self-help group. *British Journal of Medical Psychology, 73*, 129–238.

Davies, J., & Read, J., (2018). A systematic review into the incidence, severity and duration of antidepressant withdrawal effects: are guidelines evidence-based? *Addictive Behaviors*, https://doi.org/10.1016/j.addbeh.2018.08.027.

Department of Health (2009). *New horizons: towards a shared vision for mental health consultation*. London: Department of Health.

Doshi, P., Dickersin, K., Healy, D., Vedula, S. S., & Jefferson, T. (2013). Restoring invisible and abandoned trials: a call for people to publish the findings. *British Medical Journal, 34*(f2865).

Drewitt, L., Pybis, J., Murphy, D., & Barkham, M. (2017). Practitioners' experiences of learning and implementing Counselling for Depression (CfD) in routine practice settings. *Counselling and Psychotherapy Research, 18*(1), 3–13.

Elliott, R. (2012). Emotion focused therapy. In P. Sanders (Ed.), *The tribes of the person-centred nation: an introduction to the schools of therapy related to the person-centred approach* (2nd edn.) (Ch. 5, pp. 103–130). Ross-on-Wye: PCCS Books.

Elliott, R., Bohart, A. C., Watson, J. C., & Murphy, D. (2018). Therapist empathy and client outcome: an updated meta-analysis. *Psychotherapy, 55*(4), 399–410.

Elliott, R., Wagner, J., Sales, C. M. D., Rodgers, B., Alves, P., & Café, M. J. (2016). Psychometrics of the personal questionnaire: a client-generated outcome measure. *Psychological Assessment, 28*(3), 263–278.

Elliott, R., Watson, J. C., Goldman, R. N., & Greenberg, L. S. (2004). *Learning emotion-focused therapy: the process-experiential approach to change*. Washington, DC: American Psychological Association.

Elliott, R., Watson, J. C., Greenberg, L. S., Timulak, L., & Freire, E. (2013). Research on humanistic-experiential psychotherapies. In M. J. Lambert (Ed.), *Bergin & Garfield's handbook of psychotherapy and behavior change* (6th edn.) (pp. 495–538). New York: Wiley.

Evans, C., Connell, J., Barkham, M., Margison, F., McGrath, G., Mellor-Clark, J., & Audin, K. (2002). Towards a standardised brief outcome measure: Psychometric properties and utility of the CORE-OM. *British Journal of Psychiatry, 180*, 51–60.

Flanagan, S., Patterson, T. G., & Joseph, S. (2015). A longitudinal investigation of the relationship between unconditional positive self-regard and posttraumatic growth. *Person-Centered & Experiential Psychotherapies, 14*(3), 191–200. DOI: 10.1080/14779757.2015.1047960.

Frankel, M., & Sommerbeck, L. (2008). Nondirectivity: Attitude or practice? *The Person-Centered Journal, 15*(1–2), 58–78.

Freire, E. (2007). *The Strathclyde Inventory: a psychotherapy outcome measure based on the person-centred theory of change*. Unpublished master's thesis, University of Strathclyde. Glasgow, UK.

Freire, E., Elliott, R., & Cooper, M. (2007). *The Strathclyde Inventory: validation of a person-centred outcome measure*. Paper presented at the 13th Annual BACP Counselling and Psychotherapy Research Conference, York, UK.

Freire, E., Elliott, R., & Westwell, G. (2014). Person-centred and experiential psychotherapy scale: development and reliability of an adherence/competence measure for person-centred and experiential psychotherapies. *Counselling and Psychotherapy Research, 14*(3), 220–226.

Gendlin, E. T. (1962). *Experiencing and the creation of meaning: a philosophical and psychological approach to the subjective*. New York: Free Press of Glencoe.

Gendlin, E. T. (1978/2003). *Focusing*. Revised and updated 25th anniversary edition. London: Rider.

Gendlin, E. T. (1998). *Focusing-oriented psychotherapy: a manual of the experiential method*. New York: Guilford Press.

Gibbard, I. (2004). Time-limited person-centred therapy. *Person-Centred Practice, 12*(1), 42–47.

Gibbard, I. (2007). 'In the world, but not of it': Person-centred counselling in primary care. In K. Tudor (Ed.), *Brief person-centred therapies*. London: Sage (pp. 113–23).

Glass, G. V., McGaw, B., & Smith, M. L. (1981). *Meta-analysis in social research*. Beverly Hills, CA: Sage.

Goldman, R. N., Greenberg, L. S., & Angus, L. (2006). The effects of adding emotion-focused interventions to the client-centred relationship conditions in the treatment of depression. *Psychotherapy Research, 16*, 537–49.

Golland, J. H. (1997). Not an endgame: termination in psychoanalysis. *Psychoanalytic Psychology, 14*(2), 259–270.

Gøtzsche, P. C. (2017). Antidepressants increase the risk of suicide, violence and homicide at all ages (Response). *British Medical Journal, 358*(j3697).

Grant, B. (1990). Principled and instrumental nondirectiveness in person-centered and client-centered therapy. *Person-Centered Review, 5*(1), 77–88.

Greenberg, L. S. (1984). A task analysis of intrapersonal conflict resolution. In L. N. Rice and L. S. Greenberg (Eds.), *Patterns of change: intensive analysis of psychotherapy process* (pp. 67–123). New York: Guilford Press.

Greenberg, L. S., & Safran, J. (1989). Emotion in psychotherapy. *American Psychologist, 44*(1), 19–29.

Greenberg, L. S., & Watson, J. C. (1998). Experiential therapy of depression: differential effects of client-centred relationship conditions and process experiential interventions. *Psychotherapy Research, 8*, 210–24.

Greenberg, L. S., Elliott, R., & Lietaer, G. (1994). Research on humanistic and experiential psychotherapies. In A. E. Bergin and S. L. Garfield (Eds), *Handbook of psychotherapy and behavior change* (4th edn.) (pp. 509–539). New York: Wiley.

Greenberg, L. S., Rice, L. N., & Elliot, R. (1993). *Facilitating emotional change: the moment-by-moment process*. New York: Guilford Press.

Guy, A. (2018). *An analysis of four current UK service models for prescribed medication withdrawal support*. Report to All Party Parliamentary Group PDD. Available at http://prescribeddrug.org/research/ (accessed 15/01/19).

Haddad, P. M. & Anderson, I. M. (2007). Recognising and managing antidepressant discontinuation symptoms. *Advances in Psychiatric Treatment, 13*, 447–457.

Harmon, C., Lambert, M. J., Smart, D. M., Hawkins, E., Nielsen, S. L., Slade, K., & Lutz, W. (2007). Enhancing outcome for potential treatment failures: therapist-client feedback and clinical support tools. *Psychotherapy Research, 17*(4), 379–392.

Hart, J. T. (1970). The development of client-centered therapy. In J. T. Hart and T. M. Tomlinson (Eds), *New directions in client-centered therapy*. Boston, MA: Houghton Mifflin.

Healy, D. (2005). *Psychiatric drugs explained* (4th edn). Oxford: Churchill Livingstone/Elsevier.

Higgins, E. T. (1987). Self-discrepancy: A theory relating self and affect. *Psychological Review, 94*, 319–340.

Hill, A. (2011). Curriculum for counselling for depression: continuing professional development for qualified therapists delivering high intensity interventions. London: National IAPT Programme Team. Available at https://webarchive.nationalarchives.gov.uk/20160302160209/www.iapt.nhs.uk/silo/files/curriculum-for-counselling-for-depression.pdf (accessed 23/01/19).

Holden, J. M., Sagovsky, R., & Cox, J. L. (1989). Counselling in a general practice setting: controlled study of health visitor intervention in treatment of postnatal depression. *British Medical Journal, 298*, 223–226.

House, R. (1996). General practice counselling: a plea for ideological engagement. *Counselling, 7*(1), 40–44.

Ivtzan, I., Gardner, H. E., Bernard, I., Sekhon, M., & Hart, R. (2013). Wellbeing through self-fulfilment: examining developmental aspects of self-actualization. *The Humanistic Psychologist, 41*(2), 119–132.

Jacobson, N. A., Follette, W., & Ravenstorf, D. (1984). Psychotherapy outcomes research: Methods for reporting variability and evaluating clinical significance. *Behaviour Therapy, 15,* 336–352.

Jacobson, N. S., & Truax, P. (1991). Clinical significance: A statistical approach to defining meaningful change in psychotherapy research. *Journal of Consulting and Clinical Psychology, 59*(1), 12–19.

Janoff-Bulman, R. (1992). *Shattered assumptions: towards a new psychology of trauma.* New York: Free Press.

Johnstone, L., & Boyle, M., with Cromby, J., Dillon, J., Harper, D., Kinderman, P., Longden, E., Pilgrim, D., & Read, J. (2018). *The power threat meaning framework: towards the identification of patterns in emotional distress, unusual experiences and troubled or troubling behaviour, as an alternative to functional psychiatric diagnosis.* Leicester: British Psychological Society.

Joseph, S. (2007). Is the CES-D a measure of happiness? *Psychotherapy and Psychosomatics, 76,* 60.

Joseph, S. (2015). *Positive therapy: building bridges between positive psychology and person-centred psychotherapy* (2nd edn). London: Sage.

Joseph, S., & Lewis, C. A. (1998). The depression–happiness scale: reliability and validity of a bipolar self-report scale. *Journal of Clinical Psychology, 54,* 537–544.

Joseph, S., & Wood, A. M. (2010). Assessment of positive functioning in clinical psychology: theoretical and practical issues. *Clinical Psychology Review, 30,* 830–838.

Joseph, S., Linley, A. P., Harwood, J., Lewis, C. A., & McCollam, P. (2004). Rapid assessment of well-being: Short Depression–Happiness Scale (SHDS). *Psychology and Psychotherapy: Theory, Research and Practice, 77,* 463–478.

Kadera, S. W., Lambert, M. J., & Andrews, A. A. (1996). *The Journal of Psychotherapy Practice and Research, 5,* 132–151.

Kirschenbaum, H. (2007). *The life and work of Carl Rogers.* Ross-on-Wye: PCCS Books.

Kirschenbaum, H. (2012). 'What is person-centered?' A posthumous conversation with Carl Rogers on the development of the person-centered approach. *Person-Centered & Experiential Psychotherapies, 11*(1), 14–30.

Kirschenbaum, H., & Henderson, V. L. (1990). *The Carl Rogers reader.* London: Constable.

Kohut, H. (1971). *The analysis of the self.* New York: International Universities Press.

Lambert, M. J. (2013a). Outcome in psychotherapy: the past and important advances. *Psychotherapy, 50*(1), 42–51.

Lambert, M. J. (2013b). The efficacy and effectiveness of psychotherapy. In M. J. Lambert (Ed.), *Bergin and Garfield's handbook of psychotherapy and behavior change* (Ch. 6, pp.169–257). Chichester: Wiley.

Leupold-Löwenthal, H. (1988). Notes on Sigmund Freud's "Analysis Terminable and Interminable." *The International Journal of Psychoanalysis, 69,* 261–272.

Lietaer, G. (1984). Unconditional positive regard: a controversial basic attitude in client-centered therapy. In R. F. Levant and J. M. Shlien (eds), *Client-centered therapy and the person-centered approach.* New York: Praeger.

Lietaer, G. (1990). The client-centered approach after the Wisconsin project: a personal view on its evolution. In G. Lietaer, J. Rombauts and R. Van Balen (Eds), *Client-centered and experiential psychotherapy in the nineties* (pp. 19–45). Leuven: Leuven University Press.

Lietaer, G. (2002). The client-centered/experiential paradigm in psychotherapy: development and identity. In J. C. Watson, R. N. Goldman and M. S. Warner (Eds), *Client-centered and experiential psychotherapy in the 21st century: advances in theory, research and practice.* Ross-on-Wye: PCCS Books.

Marzouk, P. K. (2019). Has IAPT eaten itself? *Mental Health Today*, January.

Maples, J. L., & Walker, R. L. (2014). Consolidation rather than termination: rethinking how psychologists label and conceptualize the final phase of psychological treatment. *Professional Psychology: Research and Practice, 45*(2), 104–110.

May, R. (Ed.) (1961). *Existential psychology*. New York: Random House.

Maynard, C. K. (1993). Comparison of effectiveness of group interventions for depression in women. *Archives of Psychiatric Nursing, 7*, 277–83.

Mearns, D. (1999). Person-centred therapy with configurations of the self. *Counselling, 10*(2), 125–130.

Mearns, D. (2003). *Developing person-centred counselling* (2nd edn). London: Sage.

Mearns, D., & Thorne, B. (2000). *Person-centred therapy today: new frontiers in theory and practice*. London: Sage.

Mearns, D. & Thorne, B. (2013). *Person-centred counselling in action* (4th edn). London: Sage.

Merry, T. (2002). *Learning and being in person-centred counselling* (2nd edn). Ross-on-Wye: PCCS Books.

Miller, S. D. (2010). Psychometrics of the ORS and SRS. Results from RCTs and meta-analyses of routine outcome monitoring and feedback: the available evidence. Available at www.scottdmiller.com/?q = blog/1&page = 2 (accessed 15/01/19).

Mohr, D. C., Boudewyn, A. C., Goodkin, D. E., Bostrom, A., & Epstein, L. (2001). Comparative outcomes for individual cognitive-behavior therapy, supportive-expressive group psychotherapy, and sertraline for the treatment of depression in multiple sclerosis. *Journal of Consulting and Clinical Psychology, 69*, 942–949.

Mohr, D. C., Hart, S. L., Julian, L., Catledge, C., Honos-Webb, L., Vella, L., & Tasch, E. T. (2005). Telephone-administered psychotherapy for depression. *Archives of General Psychiatry, 62*, 1007.

Morrell, C. J., Slade, P., Warner, R., Paley, G., Dixon, S., Walters, S. J., Brugha, T., Barkham, M., Parry, G., & Nicholl, J. (2009). Clinical effectiveness of health visitor training in psychologically informed approaches for depression in postnatal women: pragmatic cluster randomised trial in primary care. *British Medical Journal, 338* (a3045).

Murphy, D. (2017). Person-centred experiential counselling psychology. In D. Murphy (Ed.), *Counselling psychology: a textbook for study and practice* (pp. 72–87). Chichester: BPS-Wiley.

Murphy, D., Demetriou, E., & Joseph, S. (2015). A cross-sectional study to explore the mediating effect of intrinsic aspiration on the association between unconditional positive self-regard and posttraumatic growth. *Person-Centered & Experiential Psychotherapies, 14*(3), 201–213.

Murphy, D., Joseph, S., Demetriou, E., & Karimi-Mofrad, P. (2017). Unconditional positive self-regard, intrinsic aspirations and authenticity: pathways to psychological well-being. *Journal of Humanistic Psychology, 22*, 1–22.

Murphy, D., Slovák, P., Thieme, A., Jackson, D., Olivier, P., & Fitzpatrick, G. (2017). Developing technology to enhance learning interpersonal skills in counsellor education. *British Journal of Guidance & Counselling*, DOI: 10.1080/03069885.2017.1377337.

National Collaborating Centre for Mental Health (NCCMH) (2018). *The improving access to psychological therapies manual*. London: National Collaborating Centre for Mental Health.

NHS (2018). *Side effects*. Available at www.nhs.uk/conditions/antidepressants/side-effects/ (accessed 18/01/19).

NHS Digital (2017). Prescriptions dispensed in the community – statistics for England, 2006–2016. Available at https://digital.nhs.uk/data-and-information/publications/statistical/prescriptions-dispensed-in-the-community/prescriptions-dispensed-in-the-community-statistics-for-england-2006-2016-pas (accessed 18/01/19).

NICE (2009). Depression in adults: recognition and management. NICE clinical guide-line 90. Available at www.nice.org.uk/guidance/CG90 (accessed 22/11/19).

Nye, A., Connell, J., Haake, R., & Barkham, M. (2019). Person-centred experiential therapy (PCET) training within a UK NHS IAPS service: experiences of selected counsellors in the PRaCTICED trial. *British Journal of Guidance & Counselling*, DOI: 10.1080/03069885.2018.1544608.

Patterson, T. G. & Joseph, S. (2006). Development of a self-report measure of uncondi-tional positive self-regard. *Psychology and Psychotherapy: Theory, Research and Practice*, *79*, 557–570.

Pearce, P. (2014). Forty years on from Rogers' APA address, 'Some new challenges for the helping professions'. *Self & Society*, *41*(2), 38–44.

Pearce, P., Sewell, R., Hill, A., Coles, H., Pybis, J., Hunt, J., Robson, M., Lacock, L., & Hobman, P. (2012). Evaluating counselling for depression. *Therapy Today*, *23*(10).

Poston, J. M., & Hanson, W. E. (2010). Meta-analysis of psychological assessment as a therapeutic intervention. *Psychological Assessment*, *22*(2), 203–12.

Proctor, G., & Hayes, C. (2017). Counselling for depression: a response to counselling education in the twenty-first century. Ethical conflicts for a counselling approach operating within a medicalised bureaucratic health service. *British Journal of Guidance & Counselling*, DOI: 10.1080/03069885.2016.1274377.

Prouty, G. (1990). Pre-therapy: a theoretical evolution in the person-centered/experien-tial psychotherapy of schizophrenia and retardation. In G. Lietaer, J. Rombauts, and R. Van Balen (Eds), *Client-centred and experiential psychotherapy in the nineties* (pp. 645–658). Leuven: Leuven University Press.

PSNC (2019). NHS website. Available at https://psnc.org.uk/contract-it/pharmacy-it/nhs-website/ (accessed 18/01/10).

Purton, C. (2004). *Person-centred therapy: the focusing-oriented approach*. Basingstoke: Palgrave.

Pybis, J., Saxon, D., Hill, A., & Barkham, M. (2017). The comparative effectiveness and efficiency of cognitive-behaviour therapy and generic counselling in the treatment of depression: evidence from the 2nd UK National Audit of psychological therapies. *BMC Psychiatry*, *17*(215).

Read, J., Gee, A., Diggle, J., & Butler, H. (2019). Staying on, coming off, antidepres-sants: the experiences of 752 UK adults. *Addictive Behaviors*, *88*(Jan.), 82–85.

Rennie, D. L. (1998). *Person-centred counselling: An experiential approach*. London: Sage.

Rogers, C. R. (1951). *Client-centered therapy: its current practice, implication and theory*. Boston, MA: Houghton Mifflin.

Rogers, C. R. (1957a). A note on the nature of man. *Journal of Consulting Psychology*, *4*(3), 199–203.

Rogers, C. R. (1957b). The necessary and sufficient conditions of therapeutic personal-ity change. *Journal of Consulting Psychology*, *21*(2), 95–103.

Rogers, C. R. (1959). A theory of therapy, personality, and interpersonal relationships as developed in the client-centered framework. In S. Koch (Ed.), *Psychology: a study of a science. Vol. 3: Formulations of the person and the social context* (pp. 184–256). New York: McGraw-Hill.

Rogers, C. R. (1961). *On becoming a person: a therapist's view of psychotherapy*. London: Constable.

Rogers, C. R. (1964). Toward a modern approach to values: the valuing process in the mature person. *Journal of Abnormal and Social Psychology*, *68*(2), 160–167.

Rogers, C. R. (1966). Client-centered therapy. In S. Arieti (Ed.), *American handbook of psychiatry*, Volume 3 (pp. 183–200). New York: Basic Books.

Rogers, C. R. (1970). Empathic: an unappreciated way of being. *The Counselling Psychologist*, *5*, 2–10.

Rogers, C. R. (1980). *A way of being*. London: Constable.

Roth, A. D. and Pilling, S. (2009). *A competence framework for the supervision of psychological therapies*. London: University College, London. Available at www.researchgate.net/publication/26587280_A_competence_framework_for_the_supervision_of_psychological_therapies/download (accessed 09/04/19).

Russell, J. A., & Feldman Barrett, L. (1999). Core affect, prototypical emotional episodes, and other things called emotion: dissecting the elephant. *Journal of Personality and Social Psychology, 76*, 805–819.

Sanders, P. (2006). *The person-centred counselling primer*. Ross-on-Wye: PCCS Books.

Sanders, P. (2011). *The tribes of the person-centred nation: an introduction to the schools of therapy related to the person-centred approach* (2nd edn). Ross-on-Wye: PCCS Books.

Sanders, P. (2017). Principled and strategic opposition to the medicalization of distress and all its apparatus. In S. Joseph (ed), *The handbook of person-centred therapy and mental health, theory, research and practice (Person-centred psychopathology)*. Ross-on-Wye: PCCS Books.

Sanders, P., & Hill, A. (2014). *Counselling for depression: a person-centred and experiential approach to practice*. London: BACP/Sage.

Sanders, P., & Wilkins, P. (2010). *First steps in practitioner research: a guide to understanding and doing research in counselling and health and social care*. Ross-on-Wye: PCCS Books.

Saxon, D., Ashley, K., Bishop-Edwards, L., Connell, J., Harrison, P., Ohlsen, S., Hardy, G. E., Kellett, S., Mukuria, C., Mank, T., Bower, P., Bradburn, M., Brazier, J., Elliott, R., Gabriel, L., King, M., Piling, S., Shaw, S., Waller, G., & Barkham, M. (2017). A pragmatic randomized controlled trial assessing the non-inferiority of counselling for depression versus cognitive-behaviour therapy for patients in primary care meeting a diagnosis of moderate or severe depression (PRaCTICED): study protocol for a randomized controlled trial. *Trials, 18*(93). Available at https://trialsjournal.biomedcentral.com/articles/10.1186/s13063-017-1834-6 (accessed 17.11.18).

Schmid, P. F. (2001). Comprehension: the art of not knowing. Dialogical and ethics perspectives on empathy as dialogue in personal and person-centred relationships. In S. Haugh and T. Merry (Eds), *Empathy*. Series, G. Wyatt (Ed.), Rogers's therapeutic conditions: evolution, theory and practice. Ross-on-Wye: PCCS Books.

Schmid, P. F. (2013). The anthropological, relational and ethical foundations of person-centred therapy. In M. Cooper, M. O'Hara, P. F. Schmid and A. C. Bohart (Eds), *The handbook of person-centred psychotherapy and counselling* (2nd edn). Basingstoke: Palgrave MacMillan.

Seeman, J. (1983). *Personality integration: studies and reflections*. New York: Human Sciences Press.

Shafran, R., Cooper, Z., & Fairburn, C. G. (2002). Clinical perfectionism: a cognitive-behavioural analysis. *Behaviour Research and Therapy, 40*, 773–91.

Shapiro, M. B. (1961). A method of measuring psychological changes specific to the individual psychiatric patient. *British Journal of Medical Psychology, 34*, 151–155.

Sharbanee, J. M., Elliott, R., & Bergman J. (2015). *A meta-analysis of the effectiveness of humanistic and experiential therapies for depression*. Paper presented at the Society for Psychotherapy Research 46th International Annual Meeting, Philadelphia, USA.

Sharma, T., Guski, L. S., Freund, N., & Gøtzsche, P. C. (2016). Suicidality and aggression during antidepressant treatment: systematic review and meta-analysis based on clinical study reports. *British Medical Journal, 352*(i65).

Sheldon, K. M., Arndt, J., & Houser-Marko, L. (2003). In search of the organismic valuing process: the human tendency to move towards beneficial goal choices. *Journal of Personality, 71*(5), 835–869.

Siddaway, A. P., Wood, A. M., & Taylor, J. P. (2017). The Centre for Epidemiological Studies-Depression (CES-D) scale measures a continuum from well-being to depression: testing two key predictions of positive clinical psychology. *Journal of Affective Disorders, 213,* 180–186.

Simpson, S., Corney, R., Fitzgerald, P., & Beecham, J. (2003). A randomised controlled trial to evaluate the effectiveness and cost-effectiveness of psychodynamic counselling for general practice patients with chronic depression. *Psychological Medicine, 33,* 229–239.

Slovák, P., Thieme, A., Murphy, D., Tennent, P., Olivier, P., & Fitzpatrick, G. (2015). On becoming a counsellor: challenges and opportunities to support interpersonal skills training. *CSCW,* March, 1336–1347.

Spitzer, R. L., Williams, J. B. W., Kroenke, K., Linzer, M., deGruy, F. V. 3rd, Hahn, S. R., Brody, D., & Johnson, J.G (1994). Utility of a new procedure for diagnosing mental disorders in primary-care: The PRIME-MD 1000 Study. *Journal of the American Medical Association, 272,* 1749–1756.

Standal, S. W. (1954). *The need for positive regard: A contribution to client-centered theory.* Doctoral Thesis. The University of Chicago.

Stice, E., Rohde, P., Gau, J. M., & Wade, E. (2010). Efficacy trial of a brief cognitive-behavioral depression prevention program for high-risk adolescents: effects at 1- and 2-year follow-up. *Journal of Consulting and Clinical Psychology, 78,* 856–67.

Stiles, W. B., Barkham, M., Connell, J., & Mellor-Clark, J. (2008). Responsive regulation of treatment duration in routine practice in United Kingdom primary care settings: replication in a larger sample. *Journal of Consulting and Clinical Psychology, 76*(2), 280–305.

Stiles, W. B., Meshot, C. M., Anderson, T. M., & Sloan, W. W., Jr. (1992). Assimilation of problematic experiences: the case of John Jones. *Psychotherapy Research, 2,* 81–101.

Tillich, P. (1952). *The courage to be.* New Haven, CT: Yale University Press.

Totton, N. (1997). Inputs and outcomes: the medical model and professionalisation. In R. House and N. Totton (Eds), *Implausible professions: arguments for pluralism and autonomy ion psychotherapy and counselling.* Ross-on-Wye: PCCS Books.

Traynor, W., Elliott, R., & Cooper, M. (2011). Helpful factors and outcomes in person-centered therapy with clients who experience psychotic processes: therapists' perspectives. *Person-Centered & Experiential Psychotherapies, 10*(2), 109–104.

Truax, C. B., & Carkhuff, R. (1967). *Toward effective counselling and psychotherapy: training and practice.* Chicago: Aldine.

Truijens, F., Zülke-van-Hulzen, L., & Vanheule, S. (2018). To manualize, or not to manualize: is that still the question? A systematic review of empirical evidence for manual superiority in psychological treatment. *Journal of Clinical Psychology.* Available at https://doi.org/10.1002/jclp.22712 (accessed 15/01/19).

Tudor, K. (Ed.) (2008). *Brief person-centred therapies.* London: Sage.

Tudor, K., & Merry, T. (2002/2006). *Dictionary of person-centred psychology.* London: Whurr. Re-published in 2006 by PCCS Books, Ross-on-Wye.

Tudor, K., & Worrall, M. (Eds) (2004). *Freedom to practise: person-centred approaches to supervision.* Ross-on-Wye: PCCS Books.

Tudor, K., & Worrall, M. (2006). *Person-centred therapy: a clinical philosophy.* Hove: Routledge.

Tyson, G. M., & Range, L. M. (1987). Gestalt dialogues as a treatment for mild depression: time works just as well. *Journal of Clinical Psychology, 43,* 227–231.

Ward, E., King, M., Lloyd, M., Bower, P., Sibbald, B., Farrelly, S., Gabbay, M., Tarrier, N., & Addington-Hall, J. (2000). Randomised controlled trial of non-directive counselling, cognitive-behaviour therapy, and usual general practitioner care for patients with depression. *British Medical Journal, 321,* 1383–1388.

Warner, M. S. (1997). Does empathy cure? A theoretical consideration of empathy, processing and personal narrative. In A. C. Bohart and L. S. Greenberg (Eds). *Empathy Reconsidered* (pp. 124–40). Washington, DC: American Psychological Association.

Warner, M. S. (2005). A person-centered view of human nature, wellness and psychopathology. In S. Joseph and R. Worsley (Eds), *Person-centred psychopathology: a positive psychology of mental health* (pp. 91–109). Ross-on-Wye: PCCS Books.

Watson, D., Wiese, D., Vaidya, J., & Tellegen, A. (1999). The two general activation systems of affect: structural findings, evolutionary considerations, and psychobiological evidence. *Journal of Personality and Social Psychology, 76,* 820–838.

Watson, J. C., Gordon, L. B., Stermac, L., Kalogerakos, F., & Steckley, P. (2003). Comparing the effectiveness of process-experiential with cognitive-behavioral psychotherapy in the treatment of depression. *Journal of Consulting and Clinical Psychology, 71,* 773–781.

Watson, N., Bryan, B. C., & Thrash, T. M. (2010). Self-discrepancy: comparisons of the psychometric properties of three instruments. *Psychological Assessment, 22* (4), 878–892. Available at http://psycnet.apa.org/record/2010-24850-005 (accessed 15/01/19).

Westwell, G. (2018). *Articulating person-centred experiential practice: the development of the PCEPS-10. A competence/adherence measure for PCE therapy.* Paper presented at PCE 2018, Conference of the World Association for the Person-Centered and Experiential Psychotherapies and Counselling, Vienna, July.

Whelton, W. & Greenberg, L. S. (2002). Psychological contact as dialectical construction. In G. Wyatt and P. Sanders (Eds), *Rogers' therapeutic conditions: evolution, theory and practice, Volume 4: Contact and perception* (pp. 96–114). Ross-on-Wye: PCCS Books.

Wickberg, B., & Hwang, C. P. (1996). Counselling of postnatal depression: a controlled study on a population based Swedish sample. *Journal of Affective Disorders, 39,* 209–216.

Wood, A. M., Linley, P. A., Maltby, J., Baliousis, M., & Joseph, S. (2008). The authentic personality: a theoretical and empirical conceptualization and the development of the authenticity scale. *Journal of Counseling Psychology, 55*(3), 385–399.

Wood, A. M., Linley, P. A., Maltby, J., Baliousis, M., & Joseph, S. (2008). The authentic personality: A theoretical and empirical conceptualization and the development of the Authenticity Scale. *Journal of Counseling Psychology, 55,* 385–399.

Wood, A. M., Taylor, P. J., & Joseph, S. (2010). Does the CES-D measure a continuum from depression to happiness? Comparing substantive and artifactual models. *Psychiatry Research, 177,* 120–123.

Wyatt, G. (Ed.) (2001). *Rogers' therapeutic conditions: evolution, theory and practice, Volume 1: Congruence.* Ross-on-Wye: PCCS Books.

Yik, M. S. M., Russell, J. A., & Feldman Barrett, L. (1999). Structure of self reported current affect: integration and beyond. *Journal of Personality and Social Psychology, 77,* 600–619.

Zech, E., Brison, C., Elliott, R., Rodgers, B., & Cornelius-White, J. H. D. (2018). Measuring Rogers' conception of personality development: validation of the Strathclyde Inventory – French version. *Person-Centered & Experiential Psychotherapies, 17*(2), 160–184.

Zimring, F. (2000/2001). Empathic understanding grows the person .... *Person-Centered Journal, 7*(2), 101–13. Reprinted in S. Haugh and T. Merry (Eds), (2001) *Rogers' therapeutic conditions, Volume 2: Empathy* (pp. 86–98). Ross-on-Wye: PCCS Books.

Index